BERNHARD KNOLLENBERG

George Washington

The Virginia Period,

1732-1775

DUKE UNIVERSITY PRESS

DURHAM, NORTH CAROLINA

1 9 6 4

© 1964, Duke University Press
Library of Congress Catalogue Card number 64-24989
Printed in the United States of America
by the Seeman Printery, Durham, N. C.

FOREWORD

Another book on Washington? Hasn't his story been exhausted by the numerous biographies published in the past twenty years, not to mention the scores of earlier ones? A writer who offers a new work on Washington must be prepared to answer this question.

Previous biographers, faced with the dearth of contemporary evidence concerning Washington's early life, have filled the gap with so many dubious reminiscences and conjectures that readers of a scholarly bent who wish for an account based solely on contemporary evidence do not know where to turn. My first object is to supply this need.

A second need is for a biography based on the same critical approach to Washington's own statements as to other evidence. Stephenson and Dunn, for example, declare that for Washington "To dissemble was . . . an impossibility," and a similar tacit assumption is evident throughout the works of nearly all of Washington's other biographers. In my study I have examined Washington's own statements as critically as those of anyone else, and, if the weight of evidence indicates that he lied or was mistaken, I follow the weight of evidence.

A third need is to refrain from undue glorification of Washington, not only to avoid a distorted picture of him, but because his glorification has often been at the expense of injustice to the reputation of others.

Another need is to bring together topically the scattered evidence on important aspects of Washington's life before the Revolution which are obscured by a strictly chronological arrangement. Among these are Washington's frustrated desire during the French and Indian War for a royal commission in the regular army as distinguished from a commission in the provincial service issued by the Governor of Virginia; his relations with his wife, step-children, and friends; his career as a planter and businessman; and his services as a member of the Virginia House of Burgesses, vestryman of Truro parish, and justice of the Fairfax county court.

The recent coming to light of the original of the love letter of Washington to Sally Fairfax, which created so much controversy when published from a dubious copy by Rupert Hughes some years ago, leads me to devote a brief chapter to the reconsideration of this famous letter, the authenticity of which is now beyond question.

The chapter which probably throws the most new light on Washington's life and character before the Revolution is the one dealing with the acquisition of his great land holdings in the Ohio Valley. Here the reader will find not only striking evidence of his remarkable tenacity, which later contributed so much to the winning of the war for independence, but of some less admirable aspects of his character.

In the chapters dealing with Washington's opposition to British measures encroaching on colonial rights and privileges, I quote at length from his letters denouncing these measures to bring out a point not, I think, heretofore sufficiently developed. Washington, though known, and justly so, as primarily a man of action, was also one of the great penmen of the Revolution. No one, whether it be James Otis, Benjamin Franklin, John Dickinson, Thomas Jefferson, Samuel Adams, John Adams, or Thomas Paine, wrote with more vividness and force than he when he was thoroughly aroused. Nothing short of his own living words can make this clear.

In the concluding chapter concerning Washington's services as a member of the Second Continental Congress and his election as Commander-in-Chief of the Continental Army, I deal with the statement in John Adams' autobiography, written many years after the event, that, until he spoke up for Washington on the floor of Congress, a majority of the members favored other candidates. I believe Adams' widely accepted account is fanciful, and am convinced from the contemporary evidence that, as soon as the question of the chief command arose, Washington was favored for the post by the great majority of his fellow members.

CONTENTS

George Washington: The Virginia Period

CHAPTER ONE

Early Life and Influences

As everyone knows, Washington was born February 22, 1732 (February 11, 1731, Old Style), in Westmoreland county, Virginia, to Augustine Washington and his second wife, Mary Ball Washington.[1] Augustine was then about thirty-eight and Mary about twenty-five.[2]

Augustine's paternal grandfather, an Englishman, settled in Virginia in 1656 or 1657, where he and his son Lawrence, Augustine's father, prospered as planters.[3] Augustine, too, was a planter,[4] but his chief occupation was manager of the locally famous Principio Company's iron mine and furnace at Accokeek Creek, about eight miles northeast of Fredericksburg, Virginia.[5]   He was a vestryman and justice of the peace;[6] but the statement sometimes made that he was a member of the Virginia House of Burgesses is not true.[7]

When George was three, his parents moved from Westmoreland county farther up the Potomac to a plantation, later called Mount Vernon,[8] at Little Hunting Creek in present Fairfax county, Virginia. A few years later, perhaps to be nearer Augustine's business, the family moved again, this time to a plantation, later called the Ferry Farm, in present Stafford county, on the left bank of the Rappahanock across from Fredericksburg.[9]   And there in April, 1743,[10] when George was only eleven, Augustine died, leaving seven children—two sons, Lawrence and Augustine, Jr., who were much older than George, by a first marriage, and by the second, four sons—George, the oldest, Samuel, John Augustine (Jack), and Charles—and a daughter, Betty.[11] Augustine's widow did not remarry, and continued to live for many years at the Ferry Farm.[12]

Accounts of Washington's father's kindness, great strength, and probable influence on him are based on extremely dubious evidence.[13] George himself in his more than twenty thousand surviving letters, memoranda, and diary entries mentions his father on only three occasions and then briefly and non-comittally. In a letter written in 1784, he spoke of being "early deprived of a father"; in a series of remarks for David Humphreys, written probably about 1786, he spoke of his father's having "died when I was only 10 years old"; and in a statement of "lineage" written in 1792 he listed the names of his father's parents, wives, and children and gave the date of his death, his age at death, and his place of burial—[14] but nothing more.

As to Washington's mother, the little authentic evidence neither bears out the high praise of her by some of his earlier biographers[15] nor supports the bitter disparagement of her by Samuel Eliot Morison[16] and other of Washington's later biographers.[17] We know that George lived with her at Ferry Farm (though with long absences on surveying trips and in the army) until he moved to Mount Vernon in 1755,[18] that she successfully opposed a plan of his older half brother Lawrence to send him to sea;[19] that she was later alarmed at his serving as an aide to General Braddock[20] and uneasy over his intention to re-enter the service after Braddock's disastrous defeat;[21] and that (unlike a great many Virginia women of her day)[22] she was able to write and did so, though lamely.[23] In later life she became a trial to George, but, so far as we know, during his youth she had and deserved his love and esteem.[24]

The conventional accounts of Washington's schooling[25] are based on as highly dubious evidence as that concerning his father's strength and kindness. We know from George's early exercise books, including some sample land surveys and a copy made by him of a set of "Rules of Civility and Decent Behaviour," that before his teens he wrote an excellent hand, spelled reasonably well, was a neat draftsman, and had spent more or less time in studying arithmetic, geography, astronomy, composition, deportment, simple geometry, and surveying.[26] A remark in a letter to Washington in 1756, apparently overlooked by Washington's previous biographers, that a boy named Piper had been a "school fellow" of his,[27] indicates that George's schooling was not limited to family tutoring, but beyond these limited facts nothing certain has come to light concerning his formal education.

The first real glimpse of George is at the age of fourteen when, as previously noted, his brother Lawrence, who was about fourteen years his senior,[28] wished to send him to sea. This appears from contemporary letters, the first commenting on Mary's opposition to Lawrence's "advise in putting Him [George] to Sea with good Recommendation,"[29] the other, to Mary from her brother Joseph Ball, in London, stating:

> I recd yrs of the 13th of December last by Mr. James Dun. . . . I understand you are advised, and have some thought of sending your son George to sea. I think he had better be put aprentice to a tinker; for a common sailor before the mast has by no means the common liberty of the Subject; for they [the Royal Navy] will press him from a [merchant] ship where he has 50 shillings a month and make him take three and twenty; and cut him and staple him and use him like a Negro, or rather, like a dog. And as for any considerable preferment in the Navy, it is not to be expected, there are always too many grasping for it here, who have interest and he has none.

And if he should get to be master of a Virginia ship (which will be very difficult to do) a planter that has three or four hundred acres of land and three or four slaves, if he be industrious, may live more comfortably, and leave his family in better Bread, than such a master of a ship can.[30]

Though Lawrence was overruled in this matter, his influence on George's career was so important that he deserves particular notice. Sent to school at Appleby, Westmoreland county, England,[31] Lawrence returned to Virginia some time before the summer of 1740, when he was commissioned a captain in a British regular army regiment,[32] recruited in America to participate in a British expedition against Cartagena and other Spanish possessions in America.[33] On his return from this unsuccessful expedition in or before January, 1743,[34] he lived on his father's plantation at Little Hunting Creek,[35] which he named Mount Vernon,[36] doubtless in honor of Admiral Edward Vernon, with whom he had recently served.[37] And on his father's death the following April, he inherited this plantation and much other property.[38]

The year which followed was one of great importance to Lawrence. He was appointed Adjutant General of the Virginia militia[39] and a justice of the peace for Fairfax county, was elected one of the county's representatives in the Virginia House of Burgesses,[40] and married Ann Fairfax, daughter of William Fairfax of neighboring Belvoir.[41] As a member of the Governor's Council and the agent in Virginia for Lord Fairfax, by far the largest holder of land in the colony, Lawrence's father-in-law was in a position to help George,[42] and that he did so is known from a letter from George to his brother Jack in May, 1755, stating, "I shou'd be glad to hear you live in Harmony with the family at Belvoir, as it is in their power to be very serviceable upon many occassion's to us, as young beginer's . . .; to that Family I am under many obligations, particularly to the Old Gentleman [William Fairfax]."[43]

Lawrence was also closely connected with Robert Dinwiddie, Governor of Virginia from 1751 to 1758,[44] who, as we shall see in later chapters, contributed greatly to George's early advancement. Lawrence, from its beginning, was one of the leading partners in the famous Ohio Company, formed in 1747 to engage in the Indian trade and to acquire and settle 500,000 acres of land in the Ohio Valley.[45] In 1750 Dinwiddie became one of the partners in the company,[46] and, through this association, was in correspondence with Lawrence even before he came to Virginia as governor.[47]

To return to George, we find that he began to do some surveying, perhaps only for practice, as early as August, 1747,[48] and in the following spring assisted in making many surveys on a trip to the Valley of Virginia with William Fairfax's son, George William Fairfax, and a party of surveyors headed by James Genn, County Surveyor of Prince William county.[49]

Washington kept a diary of this trip, from which we know that he had by this time attained a pretty good command of English and had become familiar at this early date with the region beyond the Blue Ridge mountains which he later came to know so well. Furthermore, one of the descriptions in the diary, of an Indian war dance, is of interest not only because Washington wrote it, but as one of the most illuminating descriptions of such a dance that has come down to us:

> March 23 [1748]. Rain'd till about two oClock and Clear'd when we were agreeably surpis'd at y. [the] sight of thirty odd Indians coming from War with only one Scalp. We had some Liquor with us of which we gave

them Part; it elevating their Spirits put them in y. Humour of Dauncing of whom we had a War Daunce; their manner of Dauncing is as follows Viz They clear a Large Circle and made a Great Fire in y. middle, then seats themselves around it; y. Speaker makes a grand speech telling them in what Manner they are to Daunce after he had finished; y. best Dauncer jumps up as one awaked out of a Sleep and runs and jumps about y. Ring in a most comical Manner; he is followed by y. Rest; then begins there Musicians to Play; ye. Musick is a Pot half of Water with a Deerskin Stretched over it as tight as it can and a goard with some Shott in it to Rattle and a Piece of an horses Tail tied to it to make it look fine; y. one keeps Rattling and y. other Drumming all y. while y. others is Dauncing.[50]

Some time within the next year, if not before, George must have decided to make surveying his vocation, for, on July 20, 1749, he was sworn in as official surveyor for the newly established county of Culpeper on the upper Rappahannock.[51] Two days later, his account book reveals the receipt of £2.3.0 for surveying a four-hundred-acre tract for Richard Barnes in Culpeper county,[52] and during the next two years he was engaged in surveying for Lord Fairfax, the Ohio Company, and many others on the northwestern Virginia frontier.[53] His pay was extremely good, as we know from a letter to an unidentified friend stating that, when the weather permitted his going out, he was making from a doubloon to six pistoles (well over a pound) per day.[54]

In September, 1751, Washington's surveying was interrupted by a trip to Barbados with Lawrence, who was very ill,[55] probably with tuberculosis. Little is known of this journey beyond the facts, stated in Washington's diary of the trip, that the brothers were warmly welcomed by Gedney Clarke, a brother of Lawrence's mother-in-law, and that George was "strongly attacked with the small Pox,"[56] which confined him for nearly a month. On his way home, he stopped in Williamsburg to deliver some letters to Governor Dinwiddie, who received him graciously and invited him to dinner.[57] So far as is known this was George's first meeting with the man who was so important a factor in his remarkable early career.

Soon after his return from Barbados, George did some further surveying in the Valley of Virginia,[58] and also, while there, bought 552 acres of land on the South Fork of Bullskin Creek in the northern part of the Valley. But by May he was again at home, as appears from a letter dated May 20, 1752, to William Fauntleroy, a leading resident of Richmond county, whose home was on the Rappahannock about forty miles south of the Ferry Farm, concerning his daughter Betsy. Explaining that on his return from Frederick county (across the Blue Ridge) he had been laid "very low" by "a violent pleurisie," George stated that, as soon as he recovered his strength, he intended "to wait on Miss Betsy, in hopes of a revocation of the former cruel sentence, and see if I can meet with any alteration in my favor."[59] But Betsy did not relent; she married Bowler Cocke, of a distinguished Virginia family,[60] and George remained a bachelor for over six years longer.

Lawrence's trip to Barbados (and from there to Bermuda) proving of no benefit to his health, he returned to Mount Vernon, and died there in July, 1752.[61] During Lawrence's absence George evidently learned that the Virginia Adjutancy was to be divided into several districts, and on June 10, 1752, he applied to Governor Dinwiddie for appointment as one of the district adjutants.[62] The Adjutancy was in fact divided, and on December 13, 1752, George, not yet twenty-one, was appointed Adjutant of the

Southern District, with the rank of major and a salary of £100 a year.[63]

In view of Washington's long, though apparently not very devoted membership in the Masonic brotherhood,[64] it is interesting to note that his affiliation began at this early date. A few weeks before his appointment as adjutant he was initiated into the Masonic lodge of his then home town, Fredericksburg, Virginia.[65]

CHAPTER TWO

Mission to Fort Le Boeuf

In June, 1753, Governor Dinwiddie wrote the Board of Trade reporting French advances in the upper Ohio valley and proposing to build forts on the Ohio to hold the valley for Great Britain.[1] Two months later, George II replied, approving construction of the forts and ordering the Governor, if either Indians or Europeans should presume to hinder building these forts, to require them "peaceably to depart" and, if they paid no heed to this message, to "drive them off by force of arms."[2] These instructions were enclosed in a letter of August 28, to Dinwiddie from Lord Holderness, Secretary of State for the Southern Department, the Department dealing with colonial affairs,[3] and on October 22, Dinwiddie presented them at a meeting of the Virginia Council.

Just how Washington, not yet twenty-one, happened to be offered the mission of bearing the summons to the French—a mission obviously involving hardship and danger, but also offering an exceptional opportunity for public distinction—is not known. But we know from the Council's records that the meeting was attended by Washington's friend and patron William Fairfax, and, presumably, he promptly notified Washington of the opportunity. In any event, at the next meeting of the Council, five days later, an offer from Washington to deliver the required message to the French was presented, and immediately accepted.[4] A committee headed by Fairfax was appointed to prepare the message and a commission, instructions, and passport for Washington, all of which were delivered to him on October 31.[5]

Under his instructions Washington was to act not only as a messenger, but as an intelligence officer. He was "to inquire into the numbers and force of the French on the Ohio, and the adjacent country; how they are likely to be assisted from Canada . . . and to be truly informed what forts the French have erected, and where; how they are garrisoned, and appointed; and what is their distance from each other . . ."[6] facts obviously of much military importance if the jockeying between the French and British for control of the Ohio Valley should terminate in war.

The journey to deliver Dinwiddie's summons is described by Washington in a journal prepared the day after his return from rough minutes jotted down during the trip[7] and also in a diary kept by his guide, Christopher Gist.[8]

On November 15, accompanied by a French-English interpreter, Jacob Van Braam, Gist, four other white men, and a train of pack horses, Washington set out on horseback from the frontier outpost near the mouth of Will's Creek, later Fort Cumberland, on the Maryland side of the Potomac. Their first destination was Logstown, an Indian village and trading post on the north bank of the Ohio near present Ambridge, Pennsylvania, which they reached in ten days. There they found some deserters from the French garrison at Kaskaskia in the Illinois country from whom Washington obtained considerable information.[9]

According to the Frenchmen's account the fort at Kaskaskia mounted six cannon and was garrisoned by at least three companies of forty men each. There were, they said, four forts between the Illinois country and New

Orleans, with thirty or forty men and a few cannon in each, and New Orleans itself had a stronger fort mounting eight guns and having a garrison of thirty-five companies of forty men each. Washington also learned at Logstown from the Half-King, a friendly Indian chief, of the nearest French fort—Fort Le Boeuf at present Waterford, Pennsylvania, on French Creek.[10]

On November 30 Washington and his party, accompanied by the Half-King and three other Indians, left for Fort Le Boeuf by way of Venango at the junction of French Creek and the Allegheny. There they found Captain Philippe Joincare, "Interpreter in Chief . . . in the Army," and two other French officers. They invited Washington and some of his party to dinner, where, having "dosed themselves pretty plentifully" with wine, they began to talk freely. From their conversation, Washington learned that the military route from Venango to Montreal was about 675 miles, that this route was covered by seven forts of which the first (Fort Le Boeuf) was sixty miles up French Creek from Venango, the next, fifteen miles farther north on Lake Erie (at present Erie, Pennsylvania), the third at Niagara Falls, and the fourth twenty miles eastward on Lake Ontario; and that these four nearest forts were at this time garrisoned by about 150 men each.[11]

Leaving Venango on December 7, Washington and his party had four days of heavy going before reaching Fort Le Boeuf. On December 12 Washington presented his credentials and Dinwiddie's letter to the commander of the fort, Captain le Gardeur de St. Pierre,[12] who, after conferring with his officers the next day, replied, as was to be expected, that he refused to withdraw.[13]

While the officers were in conference Washington seized the opportunity "of taking the Dimensions of the Fort, and making what Observations I could." These

observations were not only of immediate military importance but, thanks to Washington's experience as a surveyor, give us one of the most detailed and presumably
accurate descriptions of a French frontier fort of the
period that has come down to us:

> It is situated . . . near the Water; and is almost surrounded
> by the Creek, and a small Branch of it which forms a
> Kind of Island. Four Houses compose the Sides. The
> Bastions are made of Piles driven into the Ground, stand-
> ing more than 12 Feet above it, and sharp at Top: With
> Port-Holes cut for Cannon, and Loop-Holes for the small
> Arms to fire through. There are eight 6 *lb*. Pieces
> mounted, in each Bastion; and one Piece of four Pound
> before the Gate. In the Bastions are a Guard-House,
> Chapel, Doctor's Lodging, and the Commander's private
> Store: Round which are laid Plat-Forms for the Cannon
> and Men to stand on. There are several Barracks without
> the Fort, for the Soldiers Dwelling; covered, some with
> Bark and some with Boards, made chiefly of Loggs. There
> are also several other Houses, such as Stables, Smiths
> Shops &c.

Washington could not ascertain the precise number
of men at the fort (he estimated it at about a hundred),
but some of his party were able to make an exact count of
the canoes, and found that there were 170 of them made of
pine, 50 of birch bark, and many others "blocked-out, in
Readiness to make."[14]

Plentifully supplied by the commander's orders with
"Liquor, Provision, etc.," and also with a canoe, Washington left the fort on December 16 and, after "a tedious and
very fatiguing Passage down the Creek," reached Venango
on December 22.[15]

At Venango the whole party resumed their return
journey by land on the west side of the Allegheny River;
but after three days slow going, Washington, in order to

make better time, left the pack train in charge of Van Braam and set off on foot with Gist as his sole companion. The next day they had a close call when shot at by an Indian who, though "not 15 steps off," luckily hit neither of them.[16] They had another misadventure the following day when Washington, in poling the crude raft on which they were crossing to the east bank of the Allegheny headed for Shannapins Town a few miles above Pittsburgh, fell into the icy water and barely saved himself from being swept downstream.[17]

The two men pushed forward the next morning (December 29) and by evening reached the post of John Frazier, an Indian trader, at the mouth of Turtle Creek on the Monongahela. By the eleventh of January, 1754, Washington was at Belvoir, William Fairfax's place on the Potomac, and on the sixteenth reported to Dinwiddie at Williamsburg.[18]

The mission had been a great success, for Washington not only delivered the summons and gained important military intelligence concerning the French forts and garrisons, but brought back notes from which he prepared an admirable map of the upper Ohio region,[19] and also valuable information covering a site for a fort on the Ohio that the Ohio Company proposed to build. En route to Logstown, he had inspected not only the site below the Forks of the Ohio River which the Company had in mind, but also the terrain at the Forks (present Pittsburgh), where the Monongahela and Allegheny join to form the Ohio, and reported that the site at the Forks was much the superior[20]—a report which presumably influenced the Company's decision to build there.

Dinwiddie sent copies of Washington's journal to the Secretary of State for the Southern Department, to the Board of Trade, and to British colonial governors throughout North America.[21]   The journal also was published as a pamphlet, *The Journal of Major George Washington,* in Virginia and in England and was reprinted in full in the *Maryland Gazette* and the *Boston Gazette* and in large part in the *London Magazine* for June, 1754.[22]   Thus, when he was only twenty-two, Washington's name was widely and favorably known on both sides of the Atlantic.

CHAPTER THREE

Washington's First Engagement with the French

Washington's able execution of his mission to Fort Le Boeuf soon was rewarded. In the latter part of January, 1754, Dinwiddie commissioned him and William Trent, an employee of the Ohio Company, captains in the service of Virginia.[1] Each was to raise a company of a hundred men to protect the workmen engaged in building a fort for the Ohio Company at the site recommended by Washington at the Forks of the Ohio. Washington's instructions were "to finish and compleat in the best Manner and as soon as You possibly can, the Fort which I expect is there already begun by the Ohio Company. You are to act on the Defensive, but in Case any Attempts are made to obstruct the works or interrupt our Settlements by any Persons whatsoever You are to restrain all such Offenders; and in Case of resistance to make Prisoners of or kill and destroy them."[2]

Soon afterwards, the Virginia legislature voted £10,000 currency for the defense of British settlers in the Ohio valley, and Dinwiddie took steps to organize a regiment of three hundred men for this purpose, with Joshua Fry, a prominent member of the Virginia House of Burgesses, as colonel.[3] Washington, who promptly applied for the commission, was appointed lieutenant-colonel.[4]

Learning that a French force was about to descend the river, Dinwiddie ordered Washington to march immediately to reinforce Trent, who had already left for the Ohio,[5] and on April 2, Washington set out from Alexandria with a detachment of about a hundred and forty officers and men.[6] "Six feet high and proportionately made; if any thing rather slender than thick with pretty long Arms and thighs," (according to Washington's description of himself to his London tailor),[7] a horseman since boyhood, and dressed in gay regimentals,[8] he must have been a striking figure as he rode forth at the head of his troops.

In the meanwhile, the French were bestirring themselves, too. On April 17 Captain Claude Pecaudy de Contrecoeur with over a thousand men and eighteen cannon arrived at the Forks of the Ohio, where Ensign Edward Ward of Trent's company and forty-odd men were building the proposed fort. Since Great Britain and France were formally at peace and engaged in trying to reach a peaceful settlement of their conflicting claims to the upper Ohio Valley and other territory, Contrecoeur, though ordering the Virginians to withdraw, treated them courteously and allowed them to carry away all their belongings, including their arms and tools.[9]

News of this development reached Washington, when, some days later, he encountered Ward and his men on their way back from the Forks.[10] Abandoning his march to the Ohio, Washington began building a wagon road to a storehouse established by the Ohio Company at the mouth of the Redstone Creek on the Monongahela (near present Brownsville, Pennsylvania), about thirty-seven miles south of the Forks. There he planned to establish a base and await reinforcements.[11]

Learning of the movements of the Virginia troops from some Indians, Contrecoeur, on May 23, sent out Ensign

(Second Lieutenant) Joseph Coulon Sieur de Jumonville, with an interpreter and thirty-three officers and men to ascend the Monongahela by water as far as the mouth of Redstone Creek and then proceed by land as far as the road the English were reported to be building, reconnoitering the country through which he passed. If Jumonville found any English troops in this region he was to deliver a message from Contrecoeur to the English commander summoning him to withdraw, and if the answer was unfavorable and English forces remained on the Ohio side of the mountains, he was to meet force with force— "repousser la force par la force."[12]

On May 24, Washington received a message from the Half-King, the Indian chief who had accompanied him to Fort Le Boeuf, stating that a French army was on its way to meet Washington and intended to strike the first English they saw; and three days later Christopher Gist, Washington's former guide to Fort Le Boeuf, reported that a party of fifty French were somewhere in the neighborhood.[13] On the same evening the Half-King sent news that he had discovered the French camp near his own.[14]

Taking forty of his officers and men, Washington set out for the Indian camp, which he reached about sunrise on the morning of May 28. After talking with the Half-King, Washington "got his assent to go hand in hand and strike the French," and soon marched off with him, Monacatoocha (another Indian chief), and a few other Indians for the attack, which took place near present Farmington, Pennsylvania, on the morning of May 29.

We "form'd a disposition to attack them on all sides," wrote Washington to Dinwiddie the next day, "which we accordingly did, and, after an Engagement of ab't 15 Minutes, we killed 10, wounded one, and took 21 Prisoners. Amongst those that were killed was Monsieur Jumonville, the Commander. . . . In this Engagement we had only one man kill'd, and two or three wounded. . . ."[15] French accounts of the attack add nothing material except an allegation that Jumonville's interpreter tried to read the summons mentioned above, before the French returned Washington's fire.[16]

In describing the attack on Jumonville in his brilliant biographical sketch of Washington in the first volume of *The American Revolution,* Trevelyan wrote, "at twenty-two he fought his first battle, . . . and won a victory, on its own small scale, as complete as that of [Wolfe at] Quebec," and Freeman, in a chapter entitled "First Military Success," boasts of Washington's having "achieved the ideal of the soldier, the destruction of the adversary as a fighting force."[17] Perhaps the killing of Jumonville and his men may be condoned on the ground of Washington's youth and inexperience, but for a biographer or historian to glorify the affair as comparable to Wolfe's brilliant victory at Quebec or as achieving a soldier's ideal, is preposterous.

The prisoners taken by Washington, sent under guard to Winchester and thence to Alexandria,[18] were shipped, the next spring, to England.[19] What happened to them then is not known, but, since Great Britain was still formally at peace with France, they presumably were sent to France or Canada.

CHAPTER FOUR

Capitulation at Fort Necessity and Washington's Resignation

While Washington was on his way to the Forks of the Ohio, Dinwiddie had enlarged his military plans for 1754 to include the expected arrival of a regiment from North Carolina under the command of Colonel James Innes, a former captain holding a royal commission in the expedition against Cartagena mentioned in Chapter 1, two independent (non-regimented) companies of regular troops from New York, and an independent company of regular troops from South Carolina.[1] The entire force, including the Virginia regiment, was placed under Innes' command,[2] which Dinwiddie hoped would obviate disputes over command that might arise when the provincial and regular units served together in the field[3] if an officer holding only a provincial commission claimed the right to command an officer of lower rank holding a royal commission.

Colonel Joshua Fry, commander of the Virginia regiment, died on May 31, and Washington was promptly appointed by Dinwiddie to succeed him.[4] "Believe me," wrote Washington to Dinwiddie, "when I assure you my Breast is warm'd with every generous sentiment that your goodness can inspire; I want nothing but opportunity to testifie my sincere regard for your Person, to whom I stand indebted for so many unmerited favours."[5]

If Innes had joined the advance party of Virginians under Washington before any regular troops reached them, all might have been well. But the South Carolina company of regulars, under Captain James Mackay, joined the Virginians about June 15, while Innes was still in the rear, and a dispute arose over Washington's claim of right, as a provincial colonel, of "giving the parole and countersign" to Mackay's troops as well as to his own.[6] Mackay, who not only held a commission as captain directly from the King but was much Washington's senior in age and length of service (having been commissioned a regular officer a few years after Washington was born),[7] did not claim any kind of command over the Virginia troops; he simply maintained that Washington had no right to exercise any over his.[8] Dinwiddie, puzzled as to his authority to decide the question, avoided giving a decision,[9] and the dispute was still unresolved when the parties to it jointly surrendered to the French at Fort Necessity.

Following his attack on Jumonville, Washington had built a small fort, later called Fort Necessity, at the Great Meadows, near where he had set out for the attack.[10] Here Mackay and his company remained, while Washington, reinforced by the arrival of the remaining men of his regiment,[11] pushed forward thirteen miles to Gist's plantation.[12]

In the meanwhile the French had been active, too. When informed of the killing of Jumonville and his men, the French government, of course, protested to the British Ambassador to France, but, apparently hopeful of preserving the uneasy peace between Great Britain and France, instructed the Governor of Canada, the Marquis Du Quesne, not to make reprisals.[13] Nevertheless, long before this instruction could reach Du Quesne, the commander at Fort Duquesne, as the fort at the Forks of the

Ohio was now called, had taken steps to avenge the death of Jumonville by sending out a detachment of about four hundred French troops and an unstated number of allied Indians under Jumonville's brother, Captain Louis Coulon de Villiers.[14]

On receipt of a report from a friendly Indian chief of the proposed French expedition, described with considerable exaggeration as consisting of eight hundred French and four hundred Indians, Washington held a council of war with his own officers and Mackay, at which it was decided that the Virginians should fall back to the fort at the Great Meadows.[15] There the combined British forces, numbering between three and four hundred whites[16] (all Washington's Indian allies had decamped)[17] would make a stand.

The French and allied Indians reached the Great Meadows at noon on July 3, immediately attacked, and by evening had inflicted such heavy losses on the defenders[18] that Washington and Mackay surrendered under Articles of Capitulation in French reciting that the object of Villiers' expedition was solely to avenge "l'assassin" of a French officer and stipulating that the persons taken prisoners "dans l'assassinat" of Jumonville would be released.[19] Since "l'assassinat" then as now meant "murder," Washington, in signing the Articles, virtually admitted that he and his party had murdered Jumonville.

When later criticized for having made so damaging an admission,[20] Washington explained that he had signed the Articles under a misunderstanding of the meaning of the word "l'assassinat"; that the interpreter, "a Dutchman little acquainted with the English tongue," had mistranslated the Articles as referring merely to "the death, or the loss, of the Sieur Jumonville."[21] But the truth of this explanation is open to question.[22] The interpreter was Jacob

Van Braam, who, as we have seen, was Washington's French interpreter on his mission to Fort Le Boeuf, and had apparently given satisfaction, for Washington made no complaint concerning him and, some months later, recommended him to Dinwiddie for a captaincy in the Virginia regiment—[23] a place for which he would hardly be fitted if he was "little acquainted with the English tongue." Furthermore, soon after Washington and Mackay reached Williamsburg following the capitulation, Dinwiddie wrote a long letter to the British Board of Trade, in which, though evidently trying to put the best possible face on Washington and Mackay's conduct, he said nothing of the officers' having been misled by their interpreter.[24]

Thanks to the capitulation, Washington's regiment was still in being, but its situation was deplorable. By September 6, the regiment had been reduced by sickness, death, wounds, and desertion to 150 men, and the supporting North Carolina troops had been disbanded for lack of funds.[25]

Having brought his men to Winchester and the Articles of Capitulation to Williamsburg in the middle of July, Washington went to Alexandria to drum up recruits for his depleted regiment.[26] So far as is known, he was still there in early October when Governor Arthur Dobbs of North Carolina arrived in Williamsburg from England bringing a military fund of £10,000 sterling for Dinwiddie.[27] Dobbs also brought a royal commission as lieutenant-colonel for Governor Horatio Sharpe of Maryland, a retired British officer, with orders to take "Command of the Combined Forces that shall be assembled in America to oppose the Hostile Attempts Committed by the French in Different parts of his Majesty's Dominions. . . ."[28]

At a conference in Williamsburg from October 19 to 25, Dinwiddie, Sharpe, and Dobbs decided to try to raise

700 provincial troops to co-operate with three companies of British regulars for an attack on Fort Duquesne before winter.[29] Presumably the conferees considered, among other things, the ticklish question of the right to command raised by Washington in his dispute with Mackay, for, not long after the conference, Dinwiddie issued an order dissolving the regimental organization of the Virginia troops, leaving only independent companies, with captain as the highest rank.[30]

When informed of this action, Washington threatened to resign rather than submit to the reduction in rank.[31] An effort was made to induce him to change his mind by permitting him to retain his colonel's commission, but with only the pay and right of command attaching to a captain's commission. He would have none of this. He wrote his friend William Fitzhugh of Maryland, thanking him for the "kind assurances of his Excellency Governour Sharpe's good wishes toward me," but declaring that the suggested arrangement "has filled me with surprise; for if you think me capable of holding a commission that has neither rank nor emolument annexed to it, you must entertain a very contemptible opinion of my weakness, and believe me more empty than the Commission itself." Besides, he added in disgust, "every Captain, bearing the King's Commission, every half-pay Officer, or other, appearing with such a commission would rank before me. . . ."[32]

The date of Washington's resignation has not been found. But on November 16 Dinwiddie wrote Sir Thomas Robinson that Washington had resigned,[33] and on December 12 the former lieutenant-colonel of the regiment, Adam Stephen,[34] now senior captain of the Virginia companies, was designated by Dinwiddie "to Command the Virginia Forces."[35]

CHAPTER FIVE

The Ownership of Mount Vernon

Shortly after he left the army, Washington took up residence at Lawrence's old home, Mount Vernon,[1] where, except when on duty in the army or as President, he lived for the rest of his life.

Mount Vernon played so important a part in Washington's life, and there has been so much misunderstanding as to the nature of his ownership that it seems worthwhile to present in complete sequence the facts of the matter, even though this carries us far beyond 1775.

George's father, Augustine, who died in 1743, devised the property, comprising about two thousand acres, to Lawrence, with the proviso that if he should "dye without heir of his body Lawfully begotten" the property should go to George when he was twenty-one.[2] Lawrence begot a lawful daughter, Sarah, who was living when he died,[3] so George acquired no interest in Mount Vernon under his father's will. His limited ownership, as we shall see, was derived from Lawrence's will.

On his death in 1752 Lawrence devised Mount Vernon to his wife, Ann Fairfax Washington, during her life and, after her death, to Sarah; with, however, the proviso that if Sarah died without issue, the property should go to George and his heirs but if he died "without lawful issue" then to Lawrence's brother Augustine.[4] Thus, if George survived Ann and Sarah and the latter died without issue, George would be entitled to the property during his life but he could not sell it or leave it to anyone by will. If he had lawful issue at his death it would descend to them according to the established rules of descent in Virginia. If he had no issue the property would descend to Augustine or those holding under him.

Sarah died without issue not long after Lawrence,[5] and on December 10, 1754, her mother Ann, who had married George Lee, joined with her second husband in leasing Mount Vernon to George for the entire period of her life. (The annual rent for the property and eighteen accompanying slaves was 15,000 lbs. of tobacco or, at George's option, cash at the rate of a penny and a half Virginia currency for each pound of tobacco. This came to about £80 Virginia currency, normally worth about £64 sterling.)[6]

Ann died in 1761,[7] whereupon Washington became entitled to Mount Vernon for the rest of his life. However, under the terms of Lawrence's will, he had, as we have seen, no power to sell or will the property, and was so advised by his lawyer, Edmund Pendleton, in 1769.[8]

Washington died December 14, 1799, without ever having had lawful issue. Consequently, under the will of Lawrence Washington, Mount Vernon became legally the property of those holding under Augustine Washington, who had died in 1762.[9] But, presumably forgetful of the limited nature of his ownership of the original Mount Vernon property, to which he had added hundreds of acres that he owned outright, Washington willed the entire estate to Martha Washington for her life and after her death to Bushrod Washington, a Justice of the United States Supreme Court and son of George's favorite brother, Jack.[10]

In his *George Washington and Mount Vernon*, Moncure D. Conway stated, "on good authority," that, after Washington's death, Augustine's son and heir, William Augustine Washington, wrote Martha "although a wrong had been done he would not oppose the will."[11] I have not been able to find this supposed letter or any like it, but in any event William Augustine did not claim the property.

Why he made this decision is anybody's guess. Eugene E. Prussing in his valuable *The Estate of George Washington, Deceased,* points out that, under the common law rule as to inheritance, then in force in Virginia, an heir could not claim both under and against a will, and suggests that, since Augustine's heirs were willed four twenty-thirds of their uncle George's large residuary estate, they may well have found that the value of their bequest, which they would have to relinquish if they laid claim to the original Mount Vernon property, would equal or exceed the value of that property.[12]

But this hypothesis is based on the assumption that Augustine's remainder interest in Mount Vernon descended to all of his heirs, whereas, in fact, his son William Augustine was the sole heir of his real estate.[13] Under his uncle George's will William Augustine was entitled only to a one twenty-third interest in the residuary estate and to three lots and a sword. Probably these were worth less than the original Mount Vernon property. If so, esteem for his uncle's wishes and memory rather than a pecuniary reason was probably the chief motive for William Augustine's decision not to contest the will.

CHAPTER SIX

Washington in Braddock's Expedition against Fort Duquesne

On receiving news of the capitulation at Fort Necessity, General Lord Albemarle, British Ambassador to France, wrote the Duke of Newcastle, September 11, 1754, "*Washington* & many *Such,* may have courage & resolution, but they have no Knowledge or Experience in our Profession; consequently there can be no dependence on them! Officers, & good ones must be sent to Discipline the Militia, & to Lead them on. . . ."[1] The Ministry went a step further than Albemarle suggested, by sending to Virginia not only experienced officers but two regiments of British regulars under the command of Major General Edward Braddock,[2] who arrived at Hampton, Virginia, on February 19, 1755.[3]

Braddock's secret instructions from the King directed him to drive the French from their posts on the Ohio; build a strong fort at the most suitable place on that river; garrison the fort strongly with the three companies of regular troops already in Virginia and such additional provincial troops as should be found necessary; and then drive the French from points on the Great Lakes, on Lake Champlain, and in Nova Scotia where they had established themselves on land claimed by Great Britain. The expedition was to be based on the post at Will's Creek (later called Fort Cumberland) on the Maryland side of the Potomac, established the preceding year, which was to be strengthened and well supplied by the Deputy Quartermaster General, Colonel Sir John St. Clair.[4]

The force assembled by Braddock for his first objective, the reduction of Fort Duquesne, included nine companies of Virginia troops.[5] But Washington, though participating in the expedition, was not their commander; he went only in the capacity of a volunteer aide to the General.[6]

Washington wrote John Robinson, Speaker of the Virginia House of Burgesses, that Braddock had "importuned" him to come and that his "sole motive" in going was "the laudable desire of serving my country. . . ."[7] But the truth seems to be that he needed no importunity to induce him to accept Braddock's invitation and that there were motives in addition to patriotism for his acceptance.

Braddock's correspondence with Washington, conducted through the General's aide, Captain Robert Orme, discloses that Washington took the initiative in getting in touch with Braddock by writing him "a congratulatory letter upon his arrival etc."[8] and that, from this letter or otherwise, Braddock understood Washington as wishing "to make the Campaigne" with him, which he invited him to do.[9]

As to motives, Washington wrote Orme, "I must be ingenuous enough to confess that, in addition to a desire to serve King and Country, I am not a little biass'd by selfish and private views. To be plain, Sir, I wish for nothing more earnestly than to attain a small degree of knowledge in the Military Art; and believing a more favourable opportunity cannot be wished than serving under a Gentleman of his Excellencys known ability and experience, it will, you must reasonably imagine, not a little contribute to influence me in my choice."[10] Furthermore, in a letter to his brother John Augustine (Jack), Washington said, "I have now a good oppertunity, and shall not neglect it, of forming an acquaintance, which may be serviceable hereafter, if I can find it worthwhile pushing my Fortune in the Military way."[11]

Leaving Mount Vernon in charge of Jack,[12] Washington joined Braddock at Frederick, Maryland, on or about May 1, 1755,[13] and proceeded with him to Fort Cumberland, where they arrived on May 10.[14] Soon afterwards he was sent to Williamsburg to bring needed funds for the army, and did not return until May 30.[15]

On his return he got into a dispute with Braddock over the latter's criticism of colonial lethargy, as appears from a letter from Washington to William Fairfax of June 7, stating:

> The General, by frequent breaches of Contracts, has lost all degree of patience; and . . . instead of blaming the Individuals as he ought, he charges all his Disappointments to a publick Supineness . . . ; we have frequent disputes on this head, which are maintained with warmth on both sides, especially on his, who is incapable of Arguing without; or giving up any point he asserts, let it be ever so incompatible with Reason.[16]

But apparently Braddock held no grudge against Washington for his brashness, since later letters indicate that he and the General were on excellent terms.[17]

By early June, Braddock had collected 1,760 regular troops fit for duty, consisting of two regiments, the 44th and 48th, three independent (unregimented) companies and a detachment of royal artillery, and 463 provincials, consisting of eight companies of Virginia provincials and a company each from Maryland and North Carolina.[18]   In addition he was loaned thirty British sailors to handle some big guns taken for the expedition from the British warships which had convoyed the British regiments to Virginia.[19]

The first contingent of six hundred men under St. Clair left Fort Cumberland on May 28, 1755, to bridge a creek about ten miles up the road towards Fort Duquesne.[20]   Ten days later the rest of the army began to move forward—the 44th regiment under Colonel Sir Peter Halkett on June 7; the regular and provincial independent companies under Lieutenant Colonel Ralph Burton on the eighth; and the 48th regiment under Colonel Thomas Dunbar, with Braddock and doubtless his aides, on the tenth.[21]

On June 14 Washington fell seriously ill with "Fevers and Pains," but was still with Braddock several days later when the latter consulted him as to what should be done to speed up the extremely slow advance of the expedition. "I urg'd it in the warmest terms I was Master off," wrote Washington, "to push on, if we even did it with a chosen Detacht. for that purpose, with the Artillery and such other things as were absolutely necessary; leav'g the baggage and other Convoys with the Remainder of the Army, to follow by slow regular Marches. . . ." "This was a Scheme that took," said Washington, "and it was det'd [determined] that the Genl. with 1,200 chosen Men and Officers of all the differ't Corps . . . with such a certain number of Waggons as the Train [of artillery] w'd absolutely require, shou'd March. . . ."[22]

This picked division, led by Braddock, started ahead on June 19, and though Washington was soon too ill to proceed, he exacted a promise from the General to see that he got to the front before the advanced division reached

Fort Duquesne.[23]   Consequently, though still very weak, he was brought to the front by wagon on July 8,[24] and was with Braddock the next day when he was attacked and disastrously defeated on the banks of the Monongahela only seven miles from the fort.

Following the defeat, Washington returned to Fort Cumberland, from where he wrote the following vivid account of the battle to his mother.

Honour'd Mad'm: As I doubt not but you have heard of our defeat, and perhaps have it represented in a worse light (if possible) than it deserves; I have taken this earliest oppertunity to give you some acct. of the Engagement, as it happen'd within 7 miles of the French Fort, on Wednesday the 9th. Inst.

We March'd on to that place with't any considerable loss, having only now and then a stragler pick'd up by the French Scoutg. Ind'ns. When we came there, we were attack'd by a Body of French and Indns. whose number, (I am certain) did not exceed 300 Men;[25] our's consisted of abt. 1,300 well arm'd Troops; chiefly of the English Soldiers, who were struck with such a panick, that they behav'd with more cowardice than it is possible to conceive; The Officers behav'd Gallantly in order to encourage their Men, for which they suffer'd greatly; there being near 60 kill'd and wounded; a large proportion out of the number we had! The Virginia Troops shew'd a good deal of Bravery, and were near all kill'd; for I believe out of 3 Companys that were there, there is scarce 30 Men left alive; Capt. Peyrouny and all his Officers down to a Corporal was kill'd; Capt. Polson shar'd near as hard a Fate; for only one of his was left: In short the dastardly behaviour of those they call regular's expos'd all others that were inclin'd to do their duty to almost certain death; and at last, in dispight of all the efforts of the Officer's to the Contrary, they broke and run as Sheep pursued by dogs; and it was impossible to rally them.

The Genl. was wounded; of w'ch he died 3 Days after; . . . I luckily escap'd with't a wound, tho' I had four

Bullets through my Coat, and two Horses shot under me; Captns. Orme and Morris two of the Genls. Aids de Camp, were wounded early in the Engagem't. which render'd the duty hard upon me, as I was the only person then left to distribute the Genl's. Orders which I was scarcely able to do, as I was not half recover'd from a violent illness. . . . I fear I shall not be able to stir till towards Sept., so that I shall not have the pleasure of seeing you till then, unless it be in Fairfax; please to give my love to Mr. Lewis and my Sister, and Compts. to Mr. Jackson and all other Fds. that enquire after me. I am, Hon'd Madam Yr. most dutiful Son.[26]

As brought out in Pargellis *Braddock's Defeat* and other discussions of the battle, Braddock and some of the British officers were more at fault than one would gather from Washington's letter; but, on the whole, it is well corroborated by other contemporary evidence and seems to be as trustworthy an account of the battle as any that has come down to us.[27]

This is questionable, however, with respect to Washington's much later statement that early in the attack he had offered "to head the Provincials and engage the enemy in their own way . . . but the propriety of it was not seen until it was too late for execution."[28] This statement, uncorroborated by Washington's own letters or other contemporary evidence,[29] might well be ignored but for the possible implication of obstinacy on Braddock's part in not adopting Washington's suggestion, which, coupled with his letter to William Fairfax, quoted earlier in the chapter, is probably in large measure responsible for the passages in many American histories as to Braddock's extreme obstinacy.[30]

This is a pity, for Braddock seems in fact to have welcomed advice and, if favorably impressed, to have acted on it. Orme, who knew him well, wrote in August, 1755, "It is very hard . . . that he [Braddock] who would hear Opinions more freely than any Man should be accused of Obstinacy,"[31] and his acceptance of Washington's advice to divide his force in order to speed his advance tends to support Orme's view.

But to return to Washington's career, whatever may have been said of others, his part in the battle seems to have been universally applauded. Orme reported that Washington had behaved throughout the battle "with the greatest courage and resolution," his friend Charles Lewis wrote him "of the good Opinion the Governor, Assembly etc. entertain of you; . . . [indeed] scarce anything else is talked of . . .," and his influential neighbor, William Fairfax, assured him that his "safe Return gives an uncommon Joy to Us and will no doubt be sympathiz'd by all true Lovers of Heroic Virtue."[32] It is therefore not surprising that when Governor Dinwiddie and the Virginia legislature re-established the Virginia regiment,[33] Washington was offered the colonelcy—which he accepted on or shortly before September 3, 1755.[34]

CHAPTER SEVEN

Defense of the Virginia Frontier: 1755-1756

Following Braddock's defeat and death, the surviving senior British line officer, Colonel Thomas Dunbar, withdrew all the British troops except the invalids to Philadelphia,[1] leaving Virginia to fend for itself.

Faced with the menace to Fort Cumberland and the Virginia frontier settlements extending over three hundred and fifty miles,[2] the Virginia legislature took measures for defense at a special session convened by Governor Dinwiddie in August, 1755.[3] Forty thousand pounds were voted for the maintenance of twelve hundred men[4]—a regiment of a thousand, and four independent (unregimented) companies of rangers—[5] all under Washington's command.[6] Adam Stephen was commissioned lieutenant colonel and Andrew Lewis, major, and Washington appointed Captain George Mercer his aide.[7] The troops for the regiment were to rendezvous at Fredericksburg on the Rappahannock, at Alexandria on the Potomac, and at the frontier village of Winchester, Washington's future headquarters, across the Blue Ridge in the Valley of Virginia.[8]

Washington's first concern was to prepare for receiving the expected recruits and to look over the situation at Fort Cumberland, where remnants of the Virginia com-

panies that had served under Braddock were stationed.[9]
Setting out from Williamsburg about September 3,[10]
he visited each of the reception centers, and then proceeded to Fort Cumberland, where he arrived about the
middle of September.[11]   Having issued instructions for
strengthening the fort and stationing two companies there
under Stephen,[12] he inspected the northwestern frontier of
Virginia from Fort Cumberland to Fort Dinwiddie, a
fort about a hundred and twenty miles southwest of Cumberland commanded by Captain Peter Hogg.[13]

From Fort Dinwiddie Washington turned back to
Williamsburg, presumably to confer with the Governor;
but, nearing the capital, was overtaken (October 7 or 8)
by a message from Stephen that bands of Indians were
ravaging the frontier.[14]   Rushing to Winchester,[15] he
worked feverishly to hasten recruiting and to reassure
frightened settlers who were flocking there for protection.[16]   Within a few days after he reached Winchester,
he got word that the enemy Indians had left,[17] and, at
Governor Dinwiddie's request,[18] again headed for Williamsburg, where he arrived November 3.[19]

Though he wrote nothing as to his mode of travel,
Washington presumably covered on horseback all of the
many hundreds of miles that he had traversed since leaving
Williamsburg in September.   In any case, it had been a
hard, though an exciting and important, two months for
him in his new command.

After about two weeks in the capital, Washington spent
a few days in Fredericksburg[20] and then proceeded to
Alexandria (near Mount Vernon), where he stayed most
of the time until early in February,[21] when he set out on
the trip to Boston described in the next chapter.

Soon after Washington got back to Willamsburg from
his Boston trip (about March 30, 1756),[22] he received

word that the Indians were again on the rampage[23] and left immediately for Winchester, where he arrived on April 6.[24]

He wrote letter after letter to Dinwiddie concerning the terror of the frontier people and the imperative necessity of providing more men and military supplies for their protection, and finally on April 24, sent one of his officers with a frantic letter to Dinwiddie saying, "Not an hour, nay scarcely a minute passes, that does not produce fresh alarms and melancholy accounts. So that I am distracted what to do! . . . But as it is not in my power to give your Honor a full account of every thing, I have sent Captain [William] Peachey to wait upon you, who can be more ample and satisfactory on every point, that requires your Honor's notice."[25]

Obviously something must be done to protect the frontier settlements from a repetition of the disaster that had befallen them, but what to do was not clear. Dinwiddie and Washington were agreed that the surest protection would be afforded by driving the French and their Indian allies from Fort Duquesne,[26] their base of operations. But, as Washington observed in a letter of April 24 to his friend John Robinson, Speaker of the House of Burgesses and member of a committee appointed by the House to control the funds voted for defense,[27] such an expedition was practicable only with outside help[28] and the prospect of such help was small.[29] Virginia itself, Washington pointed out, did not have "stores or provisions, arms or ammunition, wagons or horses in any degree proportioned to the service, and to undertake an offence, where we are sure to fall through, would be productive of the worst consequences and another defeat would entirely lose us the interest of every Indian."

The day after reaching Winchester, Washington had

written Dinwiddie of his disapproval of the reported intention of the House of Burgesses to defend the frontier by a chain of frontier forts, because of the "inconceivable number of men"[30] required to implement this plan. But by the time he wrote Robinson on April 24, he had come to the conclusion that, since there was no immediate prospect of taking the offensive with success, "there is no way to protect the people, or save ourselves but by a chain of forts. . . ." These forts, he continued, should be not more than "fifteen and eighteen miles, or a days march, asunder," and should be garrisoned by not less than "eighty or an hundred men each." Furthermore, a strong fort should be built at Winchester "for a general receptacle of all the stores etc., and a place of residence for the commanding officer."[31] Washington wished that the legislature had provided for two thousand men instead of fifteen hundred, as had recently been voted,[32] but the difference proved to be immaterial since not even a thousand were obtained.[33]

The Virginia House of Burgesses had already passed a bill for a chain of forts, such as Washington had in mind,[34] and, on learning of his recommendation for a strong fort at Winchester in addition to the chain of small forts, the House immediately passed a resolution that "a strong Fort" be erected there.[35]

A large body of "Gentlemen Associators" or "Gentlemen Volunteers," headed by Peyton Randolph, Attorney-General of Virginia and a member of the House of Burgesses, was to march along the border, and, after advising with Washington, determine where the forts were to be built.[36] But in the end the location of the forts was left to the decision of a council of officers, presided over by Washington.[37] The council itself fixed the location of the northern tier of forts, but delegated the location of those south of Fort Dinwiddie to Captain Hogg, with a general instruction to build the forts "about twenty or thirty miles distance as the situation of the Country requires, or Ground will permit, And to have particular regard to the body of inhabitants to be defended and the passes most frequented by the Enemy. . . ."[38]

Fortunately for Virginia, during the summer of 1756 the French concentrated their forces, including their Indian allies, on capturing Fort Oswego, a highly important British post on Lake Ontario,[39] with the result that Virginia suffered only one heavy French and Indian raid during the summer and fall of 1756.[40] Hence, despite the deficiency of recruits for the Virginia regiment and the unreliability and insubordination of the Virginia militia who were to help build the forts,[41] the work made much progress, as Washington found in a three weeks'[42] tour of the forts from Fort Dinwiddie to the North Carolina line which he made in September and October, 1756.[43]

Shortly before leaving on his tour of inspection Washington had written Dinwiddie recommending abandonment of the plan for a chain of small frontier forts in favor of four strong forts;[44] but his letter did not reach the Governor until after the legislature had risen, and hence there was nothing to do but proceed along the lines previously approved.[45] Having found in the course of his tour that fifteen of the proposed forts were already built, Washington now (November 9) recommended that these be retained and four more be added to complete the chain, and that the inefficient and costly militia and companies of rangers guarding the frontier be replaced by "a regular force."[46] Dinwiddie replied that this would be "very agreeable" to him, but asked "where are the men to be gotten when You have not been able in a twelve Month to compleat Your Regiment,"[47] a pertinent question to which Washington made no response.

In addition to the perplexing question of the best method of defense, Washington was faced throughout 1756 with many difficult problems of pay, supply, and discipline of his regiment.[48]   But the statement sometimes made that Dinwiddie largely contributed to these difficulties[49] is unjust.   As the correspondence between him and Washington and other evidence amply shows, the Governor was in fact highly co-operative[50] except on one point—his refusal to accept Washington's recommendation to withdraw the Virginia troops from Fort Cumberland, the fort established by Braddock on the Maryland side of the Potomac.

A Maryland act, voting a small number of troops for the defense of that colony, did not permit their use to garrison Fort Cumberland,[51] so that withdrawal of the Virginia troops would mean abandonment of this fort, which foreseeably would again become of great importance whenever a renewed effort was made to drive the French from Fort Duquesne.

However, pointing out that the troops and stores at Fort Cumberland could be used to greater advantage in the defense of the Virginia frontier if brought into Virginia than if left at Fort Cumberland, and that the withdrawal of the Virginia troops would eliminate a lingering dispute over command of the fort between Washington and Stephen on the one hand and Captain John Dagworthy, a protégé of Sharpe, on the other, Washington repeatedly proposed to Dinwiddie that Fort Cumberland be evacuated.[52] Dinwiddie, though unsure of his authority to abandon the fort without authority from the Commander-in-Chief of the British forces in North America, and fearful that its evacuation would give encouragement to the enemy,[53] at last (September 30) authorized Washington to call a council of officers, and, if the council advised this, to withdraw the Virginia troops.[54] The officers' council (Washington not present) agreed unanimously that the question was too important for it to decide,[55] and when Dinwiddie submitted the question to the Virginia Council, the latter not only advised against withdrawal but voted that the fort be strengthened with a hundred men from the garrison at Winchester.[56]

On Washington's alarmed reply that this would strip the fort (now called Fort Loudoun) at Winchester,[57] the Governor and Council voted to obtain the proposed additional men by evacuating some of the small frontier forts,[58] and, on December 19, Washington reported that he had issued the required orders for this.[59] Here the matter stood until the Maryland legislature finally (May, 1757) provided for Maryland troops which could be, and promptly were, used to replace the Virginia garrison at Fort Cumberland.[60]

Even more upsetting to Washington than his difference with Dinwiddie over the evacuation of Fort Cumberland was his receipt in April, 1756, of word from several correspondents that he and some of his officers were being severely criticized. His friend William Fairfax wrote him that his "Appointment of an Aide-de-Camp & Secretary is thought extraordinary" and feared "the Committee will not allow pay for [them]."[61] Another of his friends, Speaker John Robinson, wrote of the "terrible reports" concerning the conduct of some of the officers, and Dinwiddie reported the House of Burgesses as "greatly inflamed, being told that the greatest Immoralities & Drunkenness have been much countenanced and proper Discipline neglected."

Washington was so much disturbed that, though defending himself by pointing out he had issued orders discountenancing drinking, gambling, and other irregularities among his officers,[62] he seems to have thought seriously of resigning. This appears from a letter of his to Dinwiddie indicating that he was thinking of quitting and from letters of friends in the House of Burgesses urging him not to.[63]

The matter blew over at this time, only to be revived later in the year by an article in the *Virginia Gazette* of September 3, 1756, signed "The Virginia-Centinel," exclaiming, ". . . when the common Soldiers are abused, in a fit of Humour or Passion, or through an Ostentation of Authority; . . . when the Militia Men are brow-beat . . .; when the Officers give their Men an example of all Manner of Debauchory, Vice and Idleness; when they lie sculking in Forts, . . . instead of searching out the Enemy . . .— When this is the Case, how wretchedly helpless must a Nation be?"[64]

This time Washington unquestionably considered resigning, as we know from a letter of his half brother Augustine, in reply to a letter, now missing, assuring him that he was still held in high esteem by nearly everyone, pointing out the harm his resignation would do to the country and warning him for his own sake not to resign, since he would "be blamed by your Country more for that than every other action of Your life."[65] Washington apparently took this sound advice to heart, for, as we shall see, he did not resign until much later.

CHAPTER EIGHT

Futile Efforts to Obtain a King's Commission

One of the most admirable features of Washington's later life was his utter devotion to duty as Commander-in-Chief of the Continental Army during the Revolution. Throughout the eight weary years of the war he never once left his troops except for about ten days spent at Mount Vernon on the march to and from Yorktown in the latter part of 1781.

The same cannot be said of his conduct as senior officer of the Virginia troops in the French and Indian War. As we have seen, he resigned in a huff and was out of the army for many months in 1754-1755, and in December, 1758, again resigned, this time permanently, nearly two years before the war in North America was over. Furthermore, while in the service he was on sick leave for the entire winter of 1757-1758 and obtained two long leaves of absence from Governor Dinwiddie to try to obtain a King's commission.[1]

Just how high a commission in the regular army Washington sought is not clear. However, a letter from him to William Byrd in 1755 concerning a possible commission in the regular army from Braddock, stating "I . . . am pretty well assur'd it is not in Genl. Braddock's [power] to give such a one as I would accept off, as I am told a

Company [i.e., a captaincy] is the highest Commission that is now vested in his gift,"[2] and the fact that, as we shall see, one of the reasons for his desire for a King's commission was to give him indisputable seniority to captains in the regular army, shows he was aiming at higher than a captaincy. And in view of his youth, his relatively short period of service, and his lack of political influence in Great Britain, he can hardly have hoped to obtain so high a commission as lieutenant-colonel. Hence it seems likely that he was seeking a majority.

It is also not clear whether Washington was prepared to pay the large going price for a King's commission,[3] or whether he expected to obtain the commission as a gift. "Gift" as used by Washington in his letter to Byrd may have meant merely appointment, but the absence in his repeated applications for a King's commission of any expression of willingness to pay for the commission indicates that he expected to obtain it without cost.

Washington's intense desire for a King's commission as major or higher is readily understandable. A King's commission usually carried with it half pay for life if the officer was retired for disability or on the reduction of his regiment after the war. Furthermore, such a commission would give him indisputable seniority over regular officers of lower rank than major. Then, too, his chance for making a career of arms (as, for a time at least, he wished to do)[4] would be slight unless he obtained a commission in the regular army, since, after the war, the Virginia government presumably would disband its little army of enlisted men and again rely exclusively on the militia. And a desire to emulate his brother Lawrence, who, as stated in Chapter 1, had a King's commission in 1740-1742 during the war against Spain, may also have been a significant influence.

But whatever the reasons, Washington's desire for and efforts to obtain a King's commission played an important part in his life for some years, and the frustration of these efforts may well have contributed to his extreme irritation reflected in many of his letters and even to his frequent illnesses during this period.[5]

The earliest mention in Washington's surviving correspondence of the advantage of having a commission from the King was in a letter to Governor Dinwiddie in May, 1754, complaining that his pay as a provincial lieutenant-colonel in the Virginia regiment was only 12/6 a day, and that even this would continue only so long as he was in service, while the pay of a lieutenant-colonel holding a King's commission was 22/ a day and would be continued "for ever,"[6] i.e., for life.

An additional reason for desiring a King's commission was acutely brought home to Washington by the dispute with Captain James Mackay, discussed in Chapter 4, and by a similar dispute which arose soon after the Virginia regiment was re-established in the summer of 1755 and Washington was restored to his provincial colonelcy.

This latter dispute arose on the arrival of a detachment from the Virginia regiment sent by Dinwiddie to help garrison Fort Cumberland in Maryland. There, Captain John Dagworthy, who held or had held a King's commission but now had command only of a company of Maryland provincial troops,[7] insisted on commanding the Virginia troops stationed at the fort. He based his claim apparently not on the fort's being in Maryland and he the senior Maryland officer present, but on the strength of his King's commission.[8] Washington disputed his asserted right of command, but Governor Sharpe of Maryland ordered Dagworthy not to yield.[9]

On November 4, 1755, Dinwiddie wrote General Wil-

liam Shirley, who had succeeded Braddock as Commander-in-Chief in North America, asking him to resolve the
dispute by issuing brevet commissions in the King's name
to Washington and the other two field officers of the Virginia regiment, giving them rank corresponding to their
provincial rank but with no pay other than their pay from
Virginia.[10] Shirley replied on December 4, in a letter now
missing, apparently declining to grant the requested brevet commissions but stating he had instructed Sharpe "to
write Captain Dagworthy to remove the Difficulties now
subsisting between Washington and him in respect of
Rank."[11]

On January 4, 1756, Sharpe wrote Dinwiddie that he
had ordered Dagworthy not "to assume any Authority
over the Virginians" posted at Fort Cumberland.[12] But
this did not satisfy Washington, who wrote Dinwiddie
threatening to resign his commission unless the Governor
granted him leave of absence to present a petition to
Shirley on behalf of himself and other officers of the Virginia regiment for King's commissions.[13]

Dinwiddie consented, and, on February 4, 1756, Washington set out for Shirley's headquarters in Boston, travel-
ing in considerable state with his aide-de-camp, Captain
George Mercer, and two servants.[14]

One of the interesting sidelights of this trip is our
earliest[15] description of Washington. Captain David Kennedy, a regular officer, who accompanied him on one leg
of the journey, described him some months later as "about
6 foot high of a Black Complection, Black hair which he
then wore in a Bag, looks like a Forrener, a Strong Man.
. . . his uniform . . . Bleau faced with Red and Laced."[16]

The trip, which consumed nearly two months,[17] was
successful to the extent of Washington's obtaining an
order from Shirley that "in case it shall happen that Col.

Washington and Capt. Dagworthy should join at Fort Cumberland, it is my Order that Colonel Washington should take the Command."[18] But he failed to obtain the desired King's commission, and again considered resigning.[19]

However, on reaching Williamsburg he decided to remain in the service, for a time at least, and soon was again in pursuit of a royal commission, this time from Sharpe, whom Shirley had appointed to command a new expedition against Fort Duquesne with troops from Pennsylvania, Maryland, Virginia, and South Carolina.[20] On learning of this expedition Washington asked Sharpe for a commission, presumably as major, and appointment as his second in command.[21] Sharpe apparently was not empowered to grant Washington's requests without authority from Shirley, for instead of granting them, he wrote Shirley on April 10, 1756, "As Mr. Washington is much esteemed in Virginia & really seems a Gentleman of Merit I should be exceedingly glad to learn that your Excellency is not averse to favouring his Application and Request."[22]

Shirley replied on May 16, saying nothing about giving Washington a commission, but stating that he would be highly pleased to appoint him second in command unless expected orders from the King interfered. He added, "I know no Provincial officer upon this Continent to whom I should so readily give it as to himself . . .";[23] but by the time he penned these gracious words, Shirley knew that he had been superseded, and that whatever might be done for Washington would have to be by his successor.

In May, 1756, Great Britain had finally declared war,[24] and the King, anticipating that America would be a major theater of the impending struggle, appointed Lord Loudoun, a distinguished British general, to succeed Shirley, with General James Abercromby as second in command.[25]

Even before Loudoun arrived in America, Washington asked Dinwiddie to recommend him to Loudoun for a commission. Dinwiddie replied that he would be glad to do so, but since General Abercromby was a particular friend of his and influential with Loudoun, he thought it best to write Abercromby.[26] This he promptly did in a letter stating:

> As we are told the Earl of Loudoun is to raise 3 Regiments on this Continent, on the british Establishment . . . give me leave to pray your Interest with his Lordship in favor of Collo. George Washington, who, I will venture to say, is a very deserving Gentleman, and has from the beginning commanded the Forces of this Dominion. Gen'l Braddock had so high an Esteem for his Merit that he made him one of his Aid-de-Camps, and if he had surviv'd I believe he would have provided handsomely for him in the Regulars. He is a person much beloved here and has gone through many hardships in the Service, and I really think he has great Merit, and believe he can raise more Men here than any one present that I know. If his Lordship will be so kind as to promote him in the British Establishment I think he will answer my recommendation.[27]

So far as is known, Abercromby did not reply concerning Dinwiddie's recommendation, but a direct appeal to Loudoun, who had been appointed Governor of Virginia[28] as well as Commander-in-Chief in North America, might still yield success. In January, 1757, Washington obtained leave of absence from Dinwiddie to confer with Loudoun, who was expected in Philadelphia,[29] and, soon afterwards, sent the General a long letter, enclosed in a covering letter to his aide-de-camp, Captain James Cunningham. After describing the extreme difficulties of his Virginia command, Washington added:

> Altho' I had not the honor to be known to your Lordship, your Lordship's name was familiar to my ear, on

account of the important services performed to his Majesty in other parts of the world. Do not think, my Lord, that I am going to flatter; notwithstanding I have exalted sentiments of your Lordship's character and respect your rank, it is not my intention to adulate. My nature is open and honest and free from guile![30]

We have, my Lord, ever since our defeat at the Meadows, and, behaviour under his Excellency General Braddock, been tantalized, nay, bid to expect most sanguinely a better establishment, and have waited in tedious expectation of seeing this accomplished. . . . With regard to myself, I cannot forbear adding, that, had his Excellency General Braddock survived his unfortunate defeat, I should have met with preferment agreeable to my wishes.[31] I had his promise to that purpose, and I believe that gentleman was too sincere and generous to make unmeaning offers, where no favors were asked. General Shirley was not unkind in his promises, but he has gone to England. I do not know, my Lord, in what light this short and disinterested relation may be received by your Lordship; but with the utmost candor and submission it is offered. . . .[32]

Washington set out for Philadelphia about February 14,[33] but because of a long delay by Loudoun in reaching the city,[34] did not get to see him until March 20. There is nothing in Washington's or Loudoun's papers concerning the interview except a brief entry in the latter's diary for March 20, stating, "Called in Col. Washington and made a new disposition of Va troops."[35] Whether anything was said about a King's commission for Washington is unknown, but, in any event, none was forthcoming. Thus, after another six weeks or more away from his troops,[36] Washington again returned empty-handed.

What a field for speculation as to the difference it might have made in the history of the British Empire if Loudoun had gratified Washington's ambition!

CHAPTER NINE

Defense of the Virginia Frontier, 1757, and the Break with Dinwiddie

As the year 1757 opened, the prospects for Virginia and for Washington seemed brighter than a year earlier. The numerous frontier forts, though imperfectly garrisoned, should afford considerable protection to the frontier inhabitants; the Indian auxiliaries, greatly desired by Washington,[1] were beginning to come in;[2] and Loudoun, the new Commander-in-Chief, not only was a more experienced soldier than Shirley[3] but as Governor of Virginia, presumably would be especially interested in its troops and the defense of its frontier.

But, in the event, the year 1757 proved to be as unhappy as the year before. As we have seen, Washington's hope for a royal commission again proved illusory;[4] and Loudoun's campaign in the north was a failure; the Indian auxiliaries, chiefly Cherokees and Catawbas, though useful,[5] created extremely vexing problems of discipline and supply;[6] and French and Indian raids continued to harass the Virginia frontier.[7] Moreover, the regiment could not be brought to full strength.[8] In spite of floggings and threatened sentence of death,[9] the soldiers, both draftees and enlisted men, deserted in shoals.[10] Some of the latter maintained that they had been induced to enlist by the misrepresentation of one of the captains as to the term of service—which gave Washington concern not so much over the deception or the soldiers' plight as over the fact that a commissioned officer rather than a sergeant was responsible. "Captain Gist," he wrote, "declares on his honor, that he never mentioned limiting their time of service in any other than this, that they should be discharged at the conclusion of the War or Expedition, which might possibly be ended in 6 or 8 months: which could be deemed nothing more than one of those little subterfuges, which, from the disagreeable nature of the Recruiting Service, has, at some junctures been considered necessary: Though I must still think [it] would come with a better grace, from a Sergeant, than a commissioned Officer."[11]

Even the one pleasing development, replacement of the Virginia troops garrisoning Fort Cumberland with troops from Maryland, referred to in Chapter 7, proved to have its drawbacks. When a party of Indians sent out by Washington stopped off at Fort Cumberland with the scalp of a French officer and the orders found on his body, Washington's old bête noire, Captain John Dagworthy, now in command of the fort, kept the orders without even sending Washington a copy.[12]

Furthermore, the old charge of misconduct in the Virginia regiment cropped up again, and this time in a form particularly galling to Washington because directly involving him.

News of this came in a letter from Captain William Peachy in August, 1757, saying that Charles Carter of Shirley had recently questioned him as to the truth of a report concerning him and Washington. According to Carter, Peachy had been quoted as saying that Washington's purpose in sending him to Williamsburg in the spring of 1756 had been to further a "Scheme"[13] of Washington to induce the House of Burgesses to make large levies of men and money for frontier defense when there was not an Indian in the neighborhood, and that this report had injured Washington in the esteem of the Governor and some other leading men. Peachy wished Washington to know that he had in fact truly stated his mission, which was to warn the country of the frontier's imminent danger from the French and Indians.[14]

Washington replied that the report was, of course, absurd[15]—and would have done well to drop the matter there. But having noticed a change in the Governor's attitude towards him, seeming to confirm Carter's statement, he sent Peachy's letter to Dinwiddie with a letter saying:

> It is evident, from a variety of circumstances, and especially from the change in your Honor's conduct towards me,[16] that some person, as well inclined to detract, but better skilled in the art of detraction, than the author of the above stupid scandal, has made free with my character. For I cannot suppose, that malice so absurd, so barefaced, so diametrically opposite to truth, to common policy, and, in short, to every thing but villainy, as the above is, could impress you with so ill an opinion of my honor and honesty.[17]

Dinwiddie replied on September 24, 1757, that he had not heard nor would have believed the report concerning Washington, but added, in response to Washington's opening remark, "My Conduct to You from the Beginning was always friendly, but You know I had reason to suspect You of Ingratitude, which I'm convinced your own Conscience and reflection must allow."[18]

Washington replied "my actions and their motives have been maliciously aggravated," that he knew of nothing to justify Dinwiddie's suspicion of ingratitude and that if he had been given instances of his ungrateful behavior he would have answered to them.[19] Dinwiddie made no reply concerning these remarks,[20] so that just what he referred to by his reproach is unknown. But what he had in mind may well have been a letter from Washington to Robinson of August 5, 1756, relating to the proposed abandonment of Fort Cumberland,[21] concerning which, as we saw in Chapter 7, Dinwiddie and Washington had sharply disagreed.

In his letter to Robinson, Washinton had written:

> When I was down [in Williamsburg], I applied to the Governor for his particular and positive direction in this affair. The following is an exact copy of his answer. "Fort Cumberland is a King's fort, and built chiefly at the charge of the colony, therefore properly under our direction, until a governor is appointed." Now whether I am to understand this ay or no, to the plain, simple question asked, vizt. "Is the fort to be continued or removed?" I know not. But in all important matters I am directed in this ambiguous and uncertain way.[22]

If the passage quoted from Dinwiddie's letter—a letter of June 12, 1756—had been the whole of his answer, the letter might, indeed, have been ambiguous and uncertain. But this passage was not the whole. In the very next sentence, omitted by Washington, Dinwiddie added, "It's absolutely necessary to detain a sufficient quantity of Stores now at Fort Cumberland which You may do by my Command and Orders,"[23] thus plainly implying the fort was not to be abandoned—an implication, moreover, which, judging from later letters from him to Dinwiddie, Washington clearly understood.[24]

Washington's statement to Robinson that "in all matters" Dinwiddie's directives were "ambiguous and uncertain" also was untrue. Though he often gave Washington broad discretion in matters as to which he thought the latter, at the front, was in a better position to decide than himself, Dinwiddie was in general clear and definite in his letters to Washington, as their correspondence, long in print, reveals.[25]

Dinwiddie's reproachful letter of September 24 must have been particularly distressing to Washington because it arrived at the peak of his difficulties and frustrations in defense of the frontier mentioned earlier in this chapter. Of the last batch of draftees, nearly half had deserted;[26] a recent Indian raid had resulted in further deaths, destruction, and terror;[27] parties sent in pursuit of the raiders had returned empty-handed.[28] Furthermore, several parties of Cherokees recently arrived at Winchester were worse than useless because Atkin, the Indian Superintendent, who alone was empowered to deal with them, was absent himself and had taken with him the only interpreter able to communicate with them.[29] Added to this, Washington was now seriously ill, suffering from a severe form of dysentery.[30]

He carried on as best he could for some time, but by November he had become too ill to hold out any longer. On November 9, Captain Robert Stewart, his second in command at Fort Loudoun,[31] wrote Dinwiddie that

> For upwards of three Months past Colonel Washington has labour'd under a Bloody Flux; about a week ago his Disorder greatly increas'd attended with bad Fevers; the day before yesterday he was seiz'd with Stitches & violent Pleuretick Pains upon which the Doctor Bled him and yesterday he twice repeated the same operation. This complication of Disorders greatly perplexes the Doctor as what is good for him in one respect hurts him in another; the Doctor has strongly recommended his immediately changing his air and going some place where he can be kept quiet (a thing impossible here) being the

best chance that now remains for his Recovery; the Colonel objected to following this Advice before he could procure Your Honor's Liberty but the Doctor gave him such reasons as convinc'd him it might then be too late and he has at length with reluctance agreed to it; therefore has Directed me to acquaint Your Honor (as he is not in condition to write himself) of his resolution of leaving this immediately and of his reasons for doing it which I have now the honor to do.[32]

A week later Washington arrived at Mount Vernon,[33] where he remained until the following April.[34]

CHAPTER TEN

The Disputed Love Letter to Sally Fairfax

On Washington's arrival, desperately ill, at Mount Vernon in November, 1757, his local doctor, the Reverend Charles Green of Alexandria, immediately ordered him to give up meat and eat only "jellies and such kinds of food."[1] Jack Washington's wife, Hannah Bushrod Washington, who resided with her husband at Mount Vernon during Washington's service in the army, was away.[2] So, needing a woman's help to prepare the prescribed diet, Washington turned to Sally Fairfax, wife of his old friend and neighbor, George William Fairfax.[3] The latter's father, William Fairfax, had recently died,[4] and the son, temporarily away on a business trip to England,[5] was now master of Belvoir.

Sally presumably gave Washington the requested help, and, during his long period of convalescence, he evidently fell in love with her if the following letter, the authenticity of which has been questioned, is genuine.

Camp at Fort Cumberland, 12th. Septr. 1758.—
Dear Madam,
Yesterday I was honourd with your short, but very agreable favour of the first Instt. .—how joyfully I catch at the happy occasion of renewing a Corrispondance which I feard was dis-relishd on your part, I leave to time, that never failing Expositor of all things—and to a Monitor equally as faithful in my own Breast, to testifie.—In silence

I now express my Joy—Silence which in some cases—I
wish the present—speaks more Intelligably than the sweet-
est Eloquence.—

If you allow that any honour can be derivd from my
opposition to Our present System of management, you
destroy the merit of it entirely in me by attributing my
anxiety to the annimating prospect of possessing Mrs.
Custis.[6]——When——I need not name it.—guess yourself.—
Shoud not my own Honour and Country's welfare be the
excitement? 'Tis true, I profess myself a Votary to Love.
I acknowledge that a Lady is in the Case—and further I
confess, that this Lady is known to you.—Yes Madam, as
well as she is to one who is too sensible of her Charms
to deny the Power, whose Influence he feels and must
ever Submit to. I feel the force of her amiable beauties
in the recollection of a thousand tender passages that I
coud wish to obliterate, till I am bid to revive them.—but
experience, alas! sadly reminds me how Impossible this
is.—and evinces an Opinion which I have long entertaind,
that there is a Destiny, which has the Sovereign controul
of our Actions—not to be resisted by the strongest efforts
of Human Nature.—

You have drawn me my dear Madam, or rather have I
drawn myself, into an honest confession of a Simple Fact—
misconstrue not my meaning—'tis obvious—doubt in [it]
not, nor expose it,—the World has no business to know the
object of my Love,—declard in this manner to—you, when
I want to conceal it——One thing, above all things in this
World I wish to know, and only one person of your Acquaintance can solve me that, or guess my meaning.—but
adieu to this, till happier times, if I ever shall see them.—
the hours at present are melancholy dull.—neither the
rugged Toils of War, nor the gentler conflict of A——B——s
is in my choice.[7]—I dare believe you are as happy as you
say—I wish I was happy also. Mirth, good Humour, ease
of Mind and.—what else? cannot fail to render you so,
and consummate your Wishes.—

If one agreeable Lady coud almost wish herself a fine
Gentleman for the sake of another; I apprehend, that
many fine Gentlemen will wish themselves finer, e'er Mrs.
Spotswood[8] is possest.—She has already become a reigning

Toast in this Camp; and many there are in it, who intend— (fortune favouring) —to make honourable Scar's speak the fulness of their Merit, and be a messenger of their Love to Her.

I cannot easily forgive the unseasonable haste of my last Express, if he deprivd me thereby of a single word you intended to add.—the time of the present messenger is, as the last might have been, entirely at your disposal.— I cant expect to hear from my Friends more than this once, before the Fate of the Expedition will, some how or other be determind, I therefore beg to know when you set out for Hampton, & when you expect to Return to Belvoir again—and I shoud be glad to hear also of your speedy departure, as I shall thereby hope for your Return before I get down; the disappointment of seeing your Family woud give me much concern.—From any thing I can yet see 'tis hardly possible to say when we shall finish. I don't think there is a probability of it till the middle of November.—Your letter to Captn. Gist[9] I forwarded by a safe hand the moment it came to me.—his answer shall be carefully transmitted.

Colo. Mercer[10] to whom I deliverd your message and Compliments, joins me very heartily in wishing you and the Ladies of Belvoir the perfect enjoyment of every Happiness this World affords. Be assurd that I am D Madam with the most unfeignd regard,

Yr. Most Obedient
& Most Obligd Hble Servt
Go Washington

N.B.—

Many Accidents happening (to use a vulgar saying) between the Cup and the Lip, I choose to make the Exchange of Carpets myself—since I find you will not do me the honour to accept of Mine[11]

The letter was printed in the New York *Herald* of March 30, 1877, sold at auction that same day, and then disappeared.[12]

If the letter had been dated a year earlier and had been addressed to an unmarried woman, it probably would have been hailed with delight by Washington's worshipful biographers as demonstrating that he was not the cold fish many suppose. But it was addressed to a married woman, wife of a friend and neighbor, and was written at a time when he reputedly was engaged to Martha Custis.[13] Hence, many of Washington's biographers passed over the letter in silence, interpreted it as merely bantering, or, as there was reason for doing, questioned its authenticity.[14]

Rupert Hughes, however, followed a different course. In his *George Washington: The Human Being and the Hero, 1732-1762,* published in 1926, he not only accepted the letter as unquestionably genuine but devoted a long chapter to its text and implications.[15]

Taking issue with Hughes, and questioning the authenticity of the letter, Professor Nathaniel Wright Stephenson wrote in "The Romantics and George Washington," published in the January, 1934, issue of the *American Historical Review:*

> If it still exists, its owner is keeping it carefully hidden. No writer on Washington has ever seen it—or, at least, will not say that he has. None of them has subjected it to the tests which any careful student insists on having made by experts in the matter of a doubtful manuscript—tests of paper, ink, handwriting. Up to date, so far as historians are aware, the Sally Fairfax myth has for its foundation a newspaper article and nothing else. . . . Scattered letters to Mrs. Fairfax known to have been written by Washington can be juggled any way you want . . . but without the crucial missing letter they prove nothing. The Romantics are zealously holding in air an arch without a keystone.[16]

The letter was included by John C. Fitzpatrick in the Bicentennial Edition of Washington's writings, but with an editorial note calling attention to its "unsettled status."[17]

If authentic, the letter was so interesting from a number of angles that I spent much time in trying to locate it and determine its authenticity. I found a letter to a "Miss" Fairfax in Volume VI of the *Catalogue of the Collection of Autograph Letters and Historical Documents* of the famous English collector, Alfred Morrison of Fonthill, published in 1892, which was apparently the missing letter. But it had been sold in 1918 at an auction of the Morrison collection at Sotheby's in London,[18] to the well-known house of Maggs Brothers of London,[19] and I could not find what happened to it thereafter.

I recently learned that a letter, said to be the missing letter to Sally, had been given to the Harvard College Library by the daughter of a famous American collector. After examining it carefully, I have no question of its authenticity,[20] and, since there are a few (though not important) differences between the actual letter and the letter as previously published, I have, with the kind permission of the Library, quoted it as written rather than as previously published.

Sally's reply to the famous letter has not been found, but she evidently did reply because on September 25, Washington wrote her "Dear Madam: Do we still misunderstand the true meaning of each other's Letters? I think it must appear so, tho' I would feign hope the contrary as I cannot speak plainer without,—But I'll say no more, and leave you to guess the rest. . . ."[21]

In the following January Washington married Martha Custis, and the Washingtons and the Fairfaxes were apparently close friends as well as neighbors until the latter moved to England in 1773.[22] But so far as is known Washington did not write Sally again until May 16, 1798, when, long after her husband's death[23] and about a year and a half before his own, he penned a letter to her recalling how much she had once meant to him. "So many important events have occurred," he wrote, "and such changes in men and things have taken place, as the compass of a letter would give you but an inadequate idea of. None of which events, however, nor all of them together, have been able to eradicate from my mind, the recollection of those happy moments, the happiest in my life, which I have enjoyed in your company. . . ."[24]

CHAPTER ELEVEN

Taking of Fort Duquesne and Washington's Retirement from Service

By the time Washington returned to duty in April, 1758,[1] the ground had been laid for the long hoped-for offensive against Fort Duquesne.

On December 30, 1757, Secretary of State William Pitt sent a circular letter to the governors of Pennsylvania, Maryland, Virginia, North Carolina, and South Carolina requesting them "to furnish a body of several Thousand Men, to join the King's forces in those parts, for some offensive Operations against the Enemy. . . ." The British Government would furnish arms, ammunition, provisions, tents, artillery, and artillerymen, and Parliament would be asked to reimburse part of the colonies' expenses in recruiting, paying, and clothing their troops.[2] Furthermore, previous orders as to rank were modified favorably to colonial field officers by an order of the King giving them seniority over all regular officers of lower rank,[3] so that Washington, for example, as a provincial colonel, would now clearly outrank not only regular company officers such as Captains Mackay and Dagworthy, but also lieutenant-colonels and majors.

The regular troops for the expedition were to land at

Philadelphia rather than at Hampton or Alexandria in Virginia, as Braddock's had done,[4] and the advance base was established not at Fort Cumberland but at Raystown (present Bedford), Pennsylvania.[5] The commander of the expedition was Brigadier General John Forbes, an able and experienced officer of over twenty years' service in the British regular army,[6] whose regulars consisted of about sixteen hundred infantry and a small force of artillery.[7]

The Virginia legislature responded to Pitt's letter by continuing Washington's regiment and providing for a second, commanded by Colonel William Byrd, having a combined strength of about fifteen hundred officers and men,[8] while Pennsylvania went Virginia one better by voting funds for three regiments of nine hundred officers and men each.[9]   Maryland, North Carolina, and Delaware together furnished about fifteen hundred troops.[10]

On rejoining his regiment, Washington hastened to write General John Stanwix, with whom he had corresponded the preceding summer:

> I must . . . beg, that you will . . . mention me in favorable terms to General Forbes (if you are acquainted with that gentleman) not as a person who would depend upon him for further recommendation to military performent, for I have long conquered all such expectancies . . . but as a person, who would gladly be distinguished in some measure from the *common run* of provincial officers, as I understand there will be a motley herd of us.[11]

It was to be many months before he met Forbes, and then, as we shall see, not under the happiest of circumstances.

In May several companies of Washington's regiment were detached, under Lieutenant-Colonel Adam Stephen, for service with Colonel Henry Bouquet, the senior regular army colonel under Forbes;[12] but until the latter part of September, Washington himself, with part of his own and Byrd's troops, was stationed first at Fort Loudoun and later at Fort Cumberland.[13]   There, while impatiently awaiting Forbes' command to move forward, Washington wrote his famous letter to Sally Fairfax, discussed in the previous chapter.

Forbes' most puzzling problem was the route to follow beyond Raystown. He preferred to build and follow a road almost due west direct to Fort Duquesne.[14] This would be at least forty miles shorter than the alternative route from Raystown southwestward to Fort Cumberland and thence along the old Braddock road northwestward to Fort Duquesne.[15]   The road preferred by Forbes would have the additional advantage of avoiding the crossing of the Youghiogheny River,[16] which, in case of fall floods, it was feared, might seriously hold up the expedition.[17] But Bouquet, who was leading the advance, got conflicting reports as to the practicability of the proposed new road, largely, he thought, because of rivalry between the Pennsylvanians and the Virginians.[18]   Opening a road directly from Raystown to Fort Duquesne would tend to give protection to the frontier settlements of Pennsylvania and to channel the lucrative Indian trade through Pennsylvania, whereas reopening and completing the old Braddock road would tend to give these advantages to Maryland and Virginia.[19]

One of the strongest opponents of building a new, direct road instead of following the old round-about route by way of Fort Cumberland was Washington,[20] who maintained that the Cumberland route would be only nineteen miles longer than the other and would have various advantages more than offsetting this relatively small addition of mileage.   He protested that he did not have "any Private interest" and was thinking only of "the General Good" in

advocating the Fort Cumberland route.²¹   But it is understandable that Bouquet and Forbes should have taken
these protestations with a grain of salt, for, though they
may not have known that Washington had a large plantation—his Bullskin plantation—not far off the road from
Winchester to Fort Cumberland, which gave him an immediate interest in preferring the Fort Cumberland route,
some of his arguments were so weak as to cast doubt on his
disinterestedness.

In the first place, his argument as to the road he favored
being only nineteen miles longer than the other was based
on taking a route that widely by-passed Raystown, which,
having long been established as the advanced base of
the expedition, could not be by-passed.   Furthermore,
Washington's assertion that even in case of heavy rains
the difficulties of crossing the Youghiogheny would be
"so trivial that they are really not worth mentioning,"²²
was incredible.   And the same was true of his assertion
that a road fit even for pack horses could not be built
from Raystown to Fort Duquesne.²³

It is therefore not surprising that Forbes decided to
build a road direct from Raystown to Fort Duquesne, in
spite of Washington's advice to clear and follow the old
Braddock road, and orders for this were issued on August
2.²⁴

The new road advanced so slowly that by the first of
September Washington was convinced the expedition
would not reach Fort Duquesne before winter closed in.
He wrote his friend Speaker Robinson:

> We seem then, to act under an evil Geni, the conduct of
> our Leaders (if not actuated by superior Orders) is tem-
> per'd with something, I don't care to give a name to,
> indeed I will go further, and say they are d——ps, or some-
> thing worse to P—s—v—n Artifice, to whose selfish views

I attribute the miscarriage of this Expedition, for nothing now but a Miracle can bring this Campaigne to a happy Issue. . . . See therefore how our time has been mispent; behold the golden opportunity lost; and perhaps never regain'd. How is it to be accounted for? can G——l F——s have Orders for this? Impossible: Will then our Injur'd Country pass by such abuses? I hope not. Rather let a full Representation of the matter go to His Majesty. Let him know how grossly his Hon'r and the Publick money have been prostituted.[25]

Washington wrote in similar vein to several other correspondents in Virginia, denouncing Forbes' choice of routes and predicting the failure of the expedition—[26] letters not only highly defeatist in tendency but very unfair to Forbes, whose correspondence clearly shows that, while underestimating the difficulties of constructing the direct road, he had no bias in favor of Pennsylvania.[27]

Forbes, who had been extremely ill,[28] finally reached Raystown on September 15, and the following day Washington came up from Fort Cumberland for an interview with him.[29] No account of this meeting has been found, but it could hardly have been a comfortable one for Washington, since Forbes was aware of his attitude concerning the choice of roads. On August 9 he wrote Bouquet, "By a very unguarded letter of Col. Washington that Accidentally fell into my hands, I am now at the bottom of their [the Virginians'] Scheme against this new road, a scheme that I think was a shame for any officer to be concerned in,"[30] and he later wrote Bouquet that, while he was to consult Washington about whether to march the army forward by divisions or as a unit, he must be cautious in weighing the Virginian's advice, since "his Behaviour about the roads was no ways like a Soldier."[31]

Following his interview with Washington, Forbes ordered him to bring his men to Raystown. Shortly before

their arrival on September 21,[32] news had been received of
the recent defeat of an advance force under one of Forbes'
regular officers, Major James Grant, in which many of the
Virginians in Stephen's detachment were killed and
wounded[33]—news which naturally heightened Washington's pessimism. Washington and his men remained at
Raystown, apparently inactive,[34] until the middle of October when Forbes ordered them forward to Bouquet's
advanced post on the Loyalhanna River at present Ligonier, Pennsylvania, about fifty miles southeast of Fort
Duquesne.[35] They arrived there on October 19, and were
joined two weeks later by Forbes.[36]

In the meanwhile the Virginia legislature, because of
"the long delay of the March of the Forces, . . . the par-
tiality they imagined shewn to Pennsylvania . . . and not
thinking any attempt would be made on Fort Duquesne
so late in the Year," passed an act to stop the pay of the
Virginia troops on December 1, unless they were sent back
to guard the Virginia frontiers on or before that date.[37]
The act was accompanied by an address from the Virginia
House of Burgesses to Dinwiddie's successor, Governor
Francis Fauquier, requesting Forbes' return of the Virginia troops immediately after December 1.[38]

How far Washington's suspicious and discouraging
letters influenced this decision is unknown, but since he
was the senior Virginia officer on the expedition, their
influence presumably was great.

The bad news from Virginia and other unfavorable
circumstances were considered at a council of war on
November 11, attended by Washington and seven other
colonels, at which it was decided that "prudence dictates"
making no further advance.[39] How Washington voted on
the question does not appear.

Luckily for Forbes he was spared the hard decision of

whether or not to adopt this recommendation by the capture, the very next day in a foray led by Washington, of
three prisoners, who stated that Fort Duquesne was very
weakly defended.[40]   Apparently convinced of the credi-
bility of this intelligence,[41] Forbes divided his force into
three brigades (of which Washington, as third in seniority
among the colonels present, was assigned one) and pushed
forward immediately.[42]   Many years later Washington
wrote that he commanded the "leading" brigade,[43] but
the contemporary evidence indicates that the advance was
led by Colonel John Armstrong of Pennsylvania (famous
for his successful expedition against the Indian village of
Kittaning in 1756) of Bouquet's brigade.[44]

The French, who were in fact very weak, decamped as
the British drew near, setting fire to the fort, the ruins of
which were occupied by Forbes November 25, 1758.[45]

Ordering Colonel Hugh Mercer of Pennsylvania to
take command of what was left of the fort, now renamed
Fort Pitt,[46] Forbes left shortly for Philadelphia, where,
worn by illness and fatigue, he died the following March.[47]
An indomitable and successful leader, he has generally
received less credit than he deserves, largely, I think, because of Washington's unfavorable letters concerning him.

Washington, too, stayed only a little while at Fort Pitt.
He was back at the post on the Loyalhanna on December
2, reached Winchester, Virginia, on the eighth, spent a
few days at Mount Vernon and was in Williamsburg by
the thirtieth.[48]

Then or perhaps a little earlier, plagued, as he later
wrote, "by an inveterate disorder in his Bowels,"[49] Washington resigned his command[50]—to the great regret of
officers of his regiment, testified by an affectionate address
signed by nearly all of them, begging him to reconsider.[51]
But, though war continued with the French in New York

and Canada until the French surrender at Montreal in
September, 1760,[52] and with the French-inspired Cherokees in the South for a year longer,[53] his retirement was
permanent.　His letters from 1759 to 1761 contain frequent references to the fighting still in progress, but in a
tone of detachment.[54]　Having done his bit in trying to
protect the Virginia frontier and in helping to drive the
French from Fort Duquesne, he apparently threw himself
with complete absorption into the new life of peaceful
pursuits to which we now turn.

CHAPTER TWELVE

Marriage, Family, and Friends

In deciding to resign his commission, Washington presumably was influenced not only by ill health but by his impending marriage to Martha Dandridge Custis, wealthy widow of Daniel Parke Custis and the mother of two young children, Jack and Patcy Custis, which took place January 6, 1759.[1]

Nothing is more frustrating to a student of Washington's life than the disappearance of nearly all his correspondence with his wife. We know from several sources that they wrote many letters to each other,[2] but all but two or (if a letter of doubtful authenticity is counted) three of his letters to her and all but one of hers to him have disappeared[3]—destroyed, it is said, by Martha after his death.[4] Hence, any description of the nature of their relationship must be largely guesswork.

The sole surviving missive of Martha to Washington, an affectionate postscript to a letter from Lund Washington to him, dated March 30, 1767, when Washington was in Williamsburg attending the Virginia legislature, comments on the weather, expresses her regret that he will not be home as soon as she had expected, and mentions her hopes that her sister will defer a projected visit to Mount Vernon until May.[5]

The impression of a simple, affectionate nature given by this letter is confirmed by letters from Martha to others,

of which the following to her sister, Nancy Dandridge
Bassett, wife of Burwell Bassett, written in 1762, is typical.

> My dear Nancy,—I had the pleasure to receive your
> kind letter of the 25 of July just as I was setting out on
> a visit to Mr. Washington in Westmoreland whare I spent
> a weak very agreabley I carred my little patt with me
> and left Jackey at home for a trial to see how well I
> coud stay without him though we ware gon but won
> fortnight I was quite impatiant to get home. If I at aney
> time heard the doggs barke or a noise out, I thought
> thair was a person sent for me. . . .
> Please to give my love to Miss Judy [the Bassett's young
> daughter] and your little babys and make my best compli-
> ments to Mr. Bassett and Mrs. Dawson.[6]

I have found no comments on Martha before 1776, but
in that year Mercy Warren wrote of her sweetness of manner,[7] and Mrs. John Adams, not given to gushing, wrote,
soon after meeting her in 1789, of Martha's "great ease and
politeness," her "modest and unassuming" manners, and
the pleasantness of her expression.[8]

The stories of Washington's alleged scandalous sex
life circulated by the enemy during the Revolution and
later by anti-Federalists were discredited by Fitzpatrick in
The George Washington Scandals (1929),[9] and I concur in
Fitzpatrick's findings that they are entirely unsupported.
Indeed, though the marriage may initially have been one of
convenience, it seems to have turned out to be an excep-
tionally happy one on both sides.[10]

The personal relationship of Washington in the period
before the Revolution, as to which we have the most evidence, was with his stepson and ward Jacky (John Parke)
Custis. There are many entries in Washington's diary
concerning Jacky, several letters between them, and a great
many letters to and from Washington concerning Jacky
and his affairs. Some of these bear only on the manage-

ment of Jacky's plantations; but many others, including an almost complete sequence of letters from June, 1768, to April, 1773, between Washington and Jacky's schoolmaster, the Reverend Jonathan Boucher, a Church of England clergyman, are chiefly of a personal nature.

Jacky was four years old at the time of his mother's second marriage.[11]   When he was not quite seven, Washington engaged a tutor, Walter Magowan, who lived as a member of the family at Mount Vernon until the boy was thirteen.[12]   Shortly after Magowan's arrival, Washington sent an order to England for books, the list of which is highly interesting to any student of the education of the sons of well-to-do Virginians in the eighteenth century. The books were exclusively for the study of Latin: *Rudiments of Latin,* Phaedrus' *Fables,* Eutropius, Sallust, Horace, Terence, Ruddiman's *Latin Grammar,* Cornelius Nepos, a volume of *Grammatical Exercises* (probably in Latin), Main's *Erasmus* and Littleton's and Aynsworth's Latin-English dictionaries.[13]   Later Jacky evidently acquired other textbooks, for, in May, 1768, Washington wrote of his ward's having been reading for over two years in Virgil and of having just begun to read the New Testament in Greek.[14]

In the spring of 1768 Magowan left for Great Britain to take holy orders in the Church of England,[15] whereupon Washington placed Jacky in a school conducted by Boucher, first in Caroline county, Virginia, and later at Annapolis, Maryland.[16]

Washington's opening letter, in his long correspondence with Boucher concerning Jacky, described him as "a boy of good genius, . . . untainted in his morals, and of innocent [simple] manners,"[17] and at first Boucher wrote of "Jack" or "Master Custis" (as Jacky was now usually called) in similarly favorable terms.[18]   But by July, 1769, he was complaining to Washington of Jack's laziness, and in December, 1770, he wrote that he had never known a youth "so exceedingly indolent, or so surprisingly voluptuous." Indeed, "one would suppose," wrote Boucher, that "Nature had intended him for some Asiatic Prince." What the voluptuousness chiefly consisted of is perhaps explained by a later passage in Boucher's worried letter stating that "Jack has a Propensity to the [other] Sex, which I am at a loss how to judge of, much more how to describe."[19]

In writing Boucher, two weeks later, Washington said nothing of the schoolmaster's criticism of Jack, but he did express concern at the narrowness of his ward's studies. He remarked that, though he left the decision wholly to Boucher's judgment, a knowledge of French, arithmetic and other mathematics, and "moral and natural philosophy" (i.e., what we would call philosophy and the natural sciences) might be more useful to Jack than the proposed resumption of the study of Greek.[20] Though Latin was apparently Jack's principal study, other subjects were evidently not wholly neglected; for, in July, 1769, Washington sent to England for over a hundred books to be charged to Jack's account. Chiefly in English, they included books on religion, Milton's complete works, Thomson's poems, Hume's and Mrs. Macauley's histories of England, Hooke's *Roman History*, Robertson's *History of Scotland*, Beccaria's famous *Essay on Crimes and Punishments*, and a number of books on composition.[21]

Washington took Jack to task in August, 1771, for his poor spelling and composition. Jack penitently confessed that he had written in too great haste and promised to do better in the future, but nevertheless maintained that when he took pains he could "write as good English & spell as well as most people"—a claim borne out by his letters.[22]

Boucher was eager to have Washington send Jack and him on a tour of England and the Continent, and Washington gave a great deal of consideration to the project.[23] But in the end he decided instead to send Jack to college.[24] Boucher was in favor of William and Mary,[25] but Washington, having heard unfavorable reports of conditions there,[26] favored New Jersey College (Princeton) or the College of Philadelphia (later to become the University of Pennsylvania).[27]   After careful investigation of the alleged "Mismanagement" at William and Mary, Washington convinced Boucher that it was not the place for Jack; but the schoolmaster urged that another college under the aegis of the Church of England, King's College (present Columbia University), should be given the preference, and, as we shall see, that is where Jack finally went.

In the meanwhile Jack had become engaged to Nelly (Eleanor) Calvert,[29] daughter of Benedict Calvert, an illegitimate though acknowledged son of the fifth Lord Baltimore.[30]   Calvert was a leading citizen of Maryland,[31] and Nelly was a fine girl;[32] but Washington, in true eighteenth-century fashion, tried to make as good a financial bargain as possible for his ward.   To this end he wrote Nelly's father that since Jack's estate consisted of fifteen thousand acres of land, most of it near Williamsburg, several lots in that city, between two and three hundred slaves, and eight or ten thousand pounds in notes or money, he, as Jack's guardian, would expect Calvert to "be willing to do something genteel by your Daughter" by way of marriage settlement.[33]

Calvert replied that, having ten children, he could not provide any great fortune for Nelly, but, to promote so pleasing a union, he would assure her of receiving at least as large a share of his personal estate as any other of his children,[34] and, so far as is known, Washington was satisfied with this.

It was decided, presumably with Jack's approval, that the engagement should not interfere with his contemplated college career, and, on May 10, 1773, Washington and he set out from the Calvert's home, "Mount Airy," for New York. Their journey was a stately one. They spent two days in Annapolis at the mansion of Governor Robert Eden, whose wife, a legitimate daughter of the fifth Lord Baltimore, was the half sister of Nelly's father; a week in Philadelphia, where they dined several times with Governor Richard Penn; and a couple of days with Lord Sterling at Basking Ridge, New Jersey. On May 26 they finally reached New York, where Washington dined with General Thomas Gage, whom he had served with under Braddock and who was now Commander-in-Chief of the British army in North America. As soon as he had entered Jack at college, Washington made a quick trip home.[35]

Jack, who had a horse, a boy, Joe, for valet and groom, and a suite of three rooms, must have cut quite a figure in the little college of less than fifty students.[36] His courses were mathematics, "Languages" (not further identified), and moral and experimental philosophy, and he complacently assured his parents that his professors were not "the least remiss in their Duty" towards him and that there was "as much Distinction made between me, & the other Students as can be expected."[37]

Washington was delighted to have reports of Jack's excellent progress;[38] but when he came home for vacation in September, he persuaded his mother to let him give up college and marry Nelly, and Washington, with great reluctance, consented.[39] The marriage took place at the Calvert home in February, 1774.[40]

We know much less of Martha's younger child, Patcy (Eleanor Parke) Custis, who was probably only two years old when she became Washington's stepdaughter,[41] than of Jacky. There are no known letters to or from her and only scattered references to her. Though we get glimpses from Washington's diary of her visits with him and Martha to friends and neighbors, and from other sources, of the kinds of clothes and toys purchased for her, we know nothing of what she was like or of her stepfather's feelings for her.

In June, 1768, when she was about twelve years old, there is an ominous entry in Washington's diary: "Sent for Doctr. Rumney to Patcy Custis who was seized with fitts,"[42] and from then on there are successive entries indicating that she was suffering from epilepsy. All kinds of remedies were tried, including various sorts of medicines, the application of an expensive "iron ring," and a trip to the then famous Warm Springs, present Berkeley Springs, West Virginia.[43] But none of these availed. In June, 1773, Washington had the sad office of breaking the news to Martha's sister that Patcy had died in one of her attacks, leaving her mother "almost reduced to the lowest ebb of misery."[44]

The entries in Washington's surviving diaries between the time of his marriage and the Revolution record visits from dozens of acquaintances,[45] but he never added any comments that might give us a clue as to who were his particular friends at this period. For this we must turn to his surviving correspondence, which points to three persons: Robert Stewart, George William Fairfax, and Burwell Bassett.[46]

Stewart, a Scot or Englishman by birth,[47] who served as a captain in the First Virginia regiment under Washington,[48] remained in the service when Washington retired.[49] He returned to Great Britain after the war,[50] moved to Jamaica in 1768 as Comptroller of Customs there, [51] and was back in England by 1774. His letters to Washington express the utmost affection for him, and the latter's replies, though more restrained, indicate a strong feeling of friendship for Stewart—friendship evidenced in a practical way in 1763 by Washington's lending Stewart £300 sterling without security and free of interest.[52] In arranging for repayment of the loan, five years later, Stewart thanked Washington warmly for his kindness,[53] but, so far as we know, they had no further correspondence until after the Revolution, when it was briefly renewed on Stewart's request and Washington's refusal to help him get a government post in the United States.[54]

As we saw in earlier chapters, Fairfax and Washington had known each other well since at least as early as 1748, when they were companions on a surveying trip in the Shenandoah valley. They also were relations by marriage, Washington's brother Lawrence having married Fairfax's sister Ann. Their letters, mainly about business affairs, are cordial but less intimate than those between Washington and Stewart. Whether Fairfax had any inkling of Washington's being in love with his wife, we do not know; there is nothing to indicate he did, and there certainly was no rift between the two men. Washington took great pains in looking after Fairfax's affairs when he (permanently as it turned out) left for England in 1773,[55] and Fairfax named Washington one of the executors of his estate in Virginia.[56]

The most engaging correspondence is that between Washington and Bassett. In general, Washington's letters are rather stiff, but those to Bassett are consistently easy and sometimes contain flashes of humor not often found in his other letters, as illustrated in the following to Bassett of August 28, 1762:

> I was favoured with your Epistle wrote on a certain 25th of July when you ought to have been at Church, praying as becomes every good Christian Man who has as much to answer for as you have; strange it is that you will be so blind to truth that the enlightning sounds of the Gospel cannot reach your Ear, nor no Examples awaken you to a sense of Goodness; could you but behold with what religious zeal I hye me to Church on every Lords day, it would do your heart good, and fill it I hope with equal fervency.
>
> But hark'ee; I am told you have lately introduced into your Family, a certain production which you are lost in admiration of, and spend so much time in contemplating the just proportion of its parts, the ease, and conveniences with which it abounds, that it is thought you will have little time to animadvert upon the prospect of your crops &c; pray how will this be reconciled to that anxious care and vigilance, which is so escencially necessary at a time when our growing Property, meaning the Tobacco, is assailed by every villainous worm that has had an existence since the days of Noah (how unkind it was of Noah now I have mentioned his name to suffer such a brood of vermin to get a birth in the Ark) but perhaps you may be as well of[57] as we are; that is, have no Tobacco for them to eat and there I think we nicked the Dogs, as I think to do you if you expect any more; but not without a full assurance of being with a very sincere regard etc.
>
> P.S. don't forget to make my Compls. to Mrs. Bassett, Miss Dudy, and the little ones, for Miss Dudy cannot be classed with small people without offering her great Injustice. I shall see you I expect about the first of November.[58]

Most of the surviving correspondence between Washington and Bassett deals with exchanges of visits between Eltham, the Bassetts' home in New Kent county, and Mount Vernon, and details of family or business affairs;

but Washington's last letter to Bassett in our period, reporting his election as Commander-in-Chief, is the one containing the famous passage:

> May God grant . . . that my acceptance of it, may be attended with some good to the common cause, and without Injury (from want of knowledge) to my reputation. I can answer but for three things, a firm belief of the justice of our Cause, close attention in the prosecution of it, and the strictest Integrity. If these cannot supply the place of Ability and Experience, the cause will suffer and more than probable my character along with it . . . but it will be remembered, I hope, that no desire or insinuation of mine, placed me in this situation.[59]

CHAPTER THIRTEEN

Planter and Businessman

A satisfactory study of Washington's career as a planter and businessman cannot be made without the letters to Washington from his principal British correspondent, Robert Cary & Co. of London, almost all of which are missing.[1] But there is enough evidence from other sources to come to some tentative conclusions in this important field.

At the time of his marriage in 1759, Washington, as we have seen in Chapter 5, was leasing from his sister-in-law the Mount Vernon property of 2,126 acres which, on her death in 1761, became his for life.[2] He also had bought an adjoining farm of five hundred acres, the Dogue Run Farm, from Sampson Darrell, and owned considerable other tracts elsewhere.[3] Of these the Ferry Farm inherited from his father, where his mother was still living, and a farm on Bullskin Creek, west of the Blue Ridge mountains, were probably the most valuable.

By his marriage to Martha, Washington greatly increased his holdings, because, under the old common law rule still prevailing in Virginia as well as in England, marriage gave the husband outright ownership of his wife's property.[4] If she was rich, he became not the husband of a rich wife as he would today, but rich in his own right. A husband's certificate of marriage had much the same effect as a valid will has for an heir today—a fact brought out in a letter from Washington to Robert Cary & Co. not long after his marriage.

"Gentln.," he wrote, "The Inclos'd is the Ministers Certificate of my Marriage with Mrs. Martha Custis, properly as I am told, Authenticated. You will therefore for the future please to address all your Letters which related to the Affairs of the late Danl. Parke Custis Esqr. to me, as by Marriage I am entitled to a third part of that Estate. . . ."[5]

Through his marriage, Washington acquired the use, during the period of marriage, of about six thousand acres of improved plantation land and a hundred slaves (the so-called "dower" land and slaves) and the outright title to cash and other personal property amounting to about £5,500 sterling in value.[6] Furthermore, on the death of Martha's daughter, Patcy, in 1773, Martha inherited over £8,000 which likewise, because of his marriage to Martha, became Washington's own property.[7] These accessions enabled him to buy and develop several farms adjoining Mount Vernon having a total of somewhat more than double the acreage of the original estate.[8]

At first, tobacco seems to have been the principal cash crop on all Washington's plantations, but by 1766 wheat had apparently replaced tobacco as the chief cash crop at Mount Vernon.[9] In 1771 Washington built or rebuilt a flour mill there at which he milled his own wheat and also that of others. The mill was described by a young Englishman, Nicholas Creswell, in 1774, as "a very complete one. Dressing and Bolting Mills the same as in England with a pair of Cologne and a pair of French stones, and makes as good flour as I ever saw."[10]

In July, 1772, Washington sought an outlet for part of his flour in the British West Indies, making a shipment of 273 barrels to Barbados with the recommendation to his agent Daniel Jenifer Adams, that the flour be "lumped off, rather than sold in small parcels for tryal, as it was ground out of indifferent Wheat; and will, I fear, look better to the eye than it will proove agreeable to the taste, being a little Musty." But the venture turned out badly when the agent sold the musty flour but pocketed the proceeds.[11] (Washington finally recovered part, perhaps all of the proceeds, but not until after prolonged anxiety and litigation.) Three years later, he made another West Indian venture, shipping a hundred barrels of flour on consignment to a merchant in Jamaica. But this, too, proved disappointing, and Washington seems to have abandoned further efforts to build up a direct West Indian trade.[12]

In addition to growing cash crops of tobacco and wheat, Washington conducted at Mount Vernon an extensive herring (ale-wives) fishery on a commercial scale. He also raised or processed for home consumption a wide range of other produce, including corn, timber, flour, cattle, milk, butter, cider, horses, sheep, poultry, many kinds of fruits, vegetables, hay, and flax. Corn (Indian corn) was probably the most important of these because the grain, prepared in various forms, was the slaves' staple food and the stalks were used for fodder.[13]

Mount Vernon was also the center of a number of business activities besides farming and fishing. Carpenters, bricklayers, shoemakers, and blacksmiths, free and slave, were constantly employed; many of the female slaves were engaged in spinning and weaving;[14] and, as previously mentioned, Washington had his own flour mill at Mount Vernon. After the war, distilling became an important business,[15] but no record has been found of Washington's having any commercial still during the period here considered.

Washington also carried on extensive experiments in various kinds of seeds and fertilizers, in the grafting of fruit trees, and with new types of farm implements. Lack of sufficient fertilizer seems to have been a particularly difficult problem. Considering the large number of slaves, night soil might have gone far to supply the deficiency; but no evidence has been found of this having been used by Washington or other plantation owners.

Mount Vernon was divided into three large farms, managed by overseers,[16] and into many small farms rented to tenant farmers on a crop-sharing basis. Washington acted as his own general manager, at first alone, later with the assistance of a second cousin, Lund Washington, who continued to manage the estate throughout Washington's long absence during the American Revolution.[17]

The Bullskin Creek farm was managed by successive overseers[18] under the occasional inspection of Washington or Lund. The Custis lands, on which tobacco was apparently the chief cash crop, were managed on behalf of Washington and Jacky Custis jointly by a steward (first Joseph Valentine, later James Hill) with an overseer over each of the several farms into which the property was divided. Part of the tobacco from all the plantations was shipped on consignment to Robert Cary & Co. of London and other merchants in England, part was sold to dealers in Virginia.

Another of Washington's occupations, and a highly important one, was purchasing supplies for the household, his mill, and his and Jacky's plantations. This meant, not driving to the nearest local stores to pick up what was needed at the moment, but planning months in advance for orders to England covering a wide range of items— clothing, cloth, needles and thread, furniture, carpets, cooking utensils, candles, tableware, tea, snuff, a great range of groceries, medicine, mill equipment, hardware of all kinds, steel, seed, and farm implements. His opening order to Robert Cary & Co., for example, covers six printed pages,[19] and, though some of the items were for permanent use, most were evidently for current consumption and would have to be reconsidered from year to year.

In letter after letter he complained to Robert Cary & Co., his chief factor in England, as to the low prices obtained by the company for his tobacco and as to the high prices, poor quality, defects, and slipshod packing of the goods bought through the company for him.[20] But, since the company's replies are missing, it is impossible to judge to what extent the complaints were reasonable.[21]

At first, judging from his diary entries from January to May, 1760, Washington stuck very closely to his farm work, with little time off for pleasure. But after securing the services of Lund Washington in 1764, he probably began to take things easier. In any event, by 1768, when regular diary entries begin again, he was spending a considerable part of his time, except in the three months of June, July, and August when farm work was at its peak, in foxhunting, shooting, fishing, and visiting. Comparison of the diary entries for 1760 and 1768, many of them interesting and revealing, are brought together in an appendix to this chapter.

One of the inevitable questions relating to Washington as a tobacco planter and farmer is whether or not his extensive planting and farming operations paid. Prussing, who is in general one of the most careful and dependable of Washington's biographers, states categorically in his *Estate of George Washington* (p. 403) that Washington's agriculture "never became a source of profit." But he gives no evidence to support this statement, and, in this instance, there is reason to question his conclusion.

In considering profit and loss on Washington's farming operations, it must, of course, be borne in mind that excess of cash disbursements over cash receipts does not necessarily mean the farming was unprofitable. For, to get a true picture of profit, there must be added to the cash receipts the value of farm products consumed by the Washington family, their numerous house servants and guests and the horses and dogs kept for pleasure, and so must the value of the natural increase in domestic animals and slaves retained on the plantations, and of farm improvements such as new hedges, fences, ditches, roads, and outbuildings. The available evidence concerning these items is too meager to justify an assured conclusion; but, once Washington abandoned his unsuccessful efforts to grow high-grade tobacco at Mount Vernon and turned to wheat as his chief cash crop, there seems to be no reason to conclude that his farming operations were not profitable.

An important break in Washington's life as a planter was his trip, of which he kept a detailed diary, to inspect the bounty land in the Ohio valley discussed in the next chapter. Accompanied by two servants and Dr. James Craik, an officer of his old regiment, Washington left Mount Vernon on October 5, 1770, and soon afterwards was joined by a surveyor, William Crawford, who was an important member of the party. On the eleventh they struck the old Braddock Road, at a point about ten miles west of Fort Cumberland, and followed this route, most of it familiar to Washington, to Pittsburgh, a flourishing village which had grown up near Fort Pitt, where they arrived on the seventeenth.[22]

After looking over land in the vicinity of Pittsburgh and dining at the fort with the officers of its small British garrison, the whole party, accompanied by an interpreter and two Indians, set off in canoes down the Ohio for the Great Kanawha, which they reached on October 31.

Paddling up that river for about fifteen miles, Washington found the flanking hills "rather steep and poor," but the bottom lands "in many places very rich" and "upon the whole exceeding valuable."[23]

Washington's diary of the trip on the rivers describes an encounter with a party of Indians headed by Kiashuta, who had accompained him to Fort Le Boeuf in 1753, and has occasional entertaining observations on the variety and abundance of wild life, including many buffalo of which they killed five. But in general the entries merely note distances traveled, the points at which the party camped for the night, the streams passed, and the character of the land, and are interesting chiefly for their evidence of Washington's extensive knowledge of trees and the relationship between them and the quality of the soil on which they grew.[24] Setting off for home on November 5, the party reached Pittsburgh in sixteen days, and by December 1 Washington was back at Mount Vernon after an absence of nearly two months.[25]

In addition to managing his farms and tobacco plantations, Washington embarked on several outside ventures from 1763 to 1773.

The first was participation in a company, formed on or before May 25, 1763, consisting of himself, his brother-in-law Fielding Lewis, William Nelson, Thomas Nelson, Robert Burwell, Robert Tucker, Thomas Walker, William Waters, John Syme, and Samuel Gist, to secure rights in 148,000 acres of Crown land in the Great Dismal Swamp region of southeastern Virginia.[26] Since the granting of Crown land in Virginia was at this time in the hands of the Governor and the provincial Council,[27] and three of the syndicate members, the Nelsons and Burwell, were members of the Council,[28] the syndicate was in a good position to secure favorable action.

In May and again in November the members of the syndicate petitioned the Governor and Council for an exclusive option for seven years[29] to take up 148,000 acres of land in the Dismal Swamp region not already entered by others.[30] The requested option was granted in November, 1763, and renewed for another seven years in November, 1769.[31]

From the very beginning, Washington was one of the most active participants in the project, which involved the draining of the Swamp and converting it into farm land. He invested at least £157 cash and the labor of an unstated number of his slaves in the company,[32] and from May, 1763, to October, 1768, he visited the Swamp at least seven times.[33] Work on the project was halted by the Revolution and apparently never resumed;[34] but the venture proved profitable in the end because of valuable timber in the Swamp.[35]

In June, 1763, Washington embarked on an even vaster land project when he and eighteen other residents of Virginia or Maryland signed Articles of Agreement for the organization of the Mississippi Company[36] to secure the grant of a huge tract of Crown land east of the Mississippi river, to which the French had relinquished all claim in the recent Treaty of Paris.[37] The nineteen founding members included Washington's brother John Augustine, Presley Thornton, a member of the Virginia Council, and four of the famous Lee brotherhood, Richard Henry, Francis Lightfoot, William, and Thomas Ludwell Lee. The Articles of Agreement provided for the framework of the company and mode of procedure, including the holdings of meetings for the assessment of required funds and the election of a secretary-treasurer and an executive committee to conduct the affairs of the company between meetings.[38]

At the opening meeting in the following September, the members present, including Washington, adopted a petition to the King for a twelve years' option on 2,500,000 acres of Crown land to be selected in an area, north and south of the Ohio River, extending from the Mississippi eastward to a point in the western part of the present state of Ohio, embracing much of the richest land in the present states of Illinois, Indiana, Ohio, Kentucky, and Tennessee, to be exempt from quitrents and taxes for at least twelve years after the selected land was surveyed. In return for the option and requested exemption, the petitioners were "to seat the said lands with two hundred Families, at least, if not interrupted by the Savages or any foreign enemy," failing which the grant was to be forfeited.[39]

At this opening meeting, the shareholders also elected William Lee secretary-treasurer and an executive committee, including John Augustine Washington, and provided for the appointment of Thomas Cumming of London as the company's agent in England. He was to try to secure the desired option and to procure up to nine additional members for the company, presumably in Great Britain, "of such influence and fortune as may be likely to promote its success" for which he was to be offered a share in the company and a hundred guineas "as an earnest of . . . present and future good Will."[40]

Later in the month the executive committee met at Westmoreland Court House and adopted a letter to Cumming along the lines resolved upon at the recent shareholders' meeting;[41] but before he could have received this letter, the Royal Proclamation of October 7, 1763, temporarily reserving the land west of the Alleghenies for the Indians, was issued,[42] thus destroying any hope of present favorable action.

Various efforts were made to revive the project in later years,[43] but by the end of 1771 Washington apparently considered the project hopeless, for on January 1, 1772, he charged off his modest investment in the company (£27.13.5) as a total loss.[44]

In 1773 Washington formed a partnership with one of his former tenants, Gilbert Simpson, to build and run a flour mill on land in southwestern Pennsylvania acquired by Washington some years earlier. But because of Simpson's carelessness and mismanagement the venture proved to be a source of great vexation and an eventual loss to Washington, who, when the partnership was wound up after the Revolution, received only a small sum from an investment of about £1,200.[45]

However, Washington's losses in the Mississippi Company and the Pennsylvania mill venture were far more than offset by the value of the bounty lands, one of the principal assets in his estate at the time of his death,[46] which he acquired under circumstances described in the next chapter.

Washington's years as owner and manager of his estate are important not only as the chief interest and occupation of his life from 1759 to 1774 but because of their bearing on his career as Commander-in-Chief of the American army. Probably neither his military experience in the French and Indian War nor his long service in the Virginia House of Burgesses, described in Chapter 15, important as these were in his successful leadership in the American Revolution, contributed so much to this as his many years of managing a large plantation.

CHAPTER FOURTEEN

Washington's Bounty Land

In 1754 Governor Dinwiddie issued a proclamation encouraging enlistment in the Virginia regiment, of which Washington was then lieutenant colonel, by offering 200,000 acres of Crown land on the south and east side of the Ohio River, free of the customary fees for issuing Crown grants, and exempt for fifteen years from the annual quitrent payable to the Crown.[1]

The title of the proclamation, "A Proclamation for Encouraging Men to enlist in his Majesty's Service for the Defense and Security of this Colony," indicates that its object was to encourage soldiers to enlist, not to encourage officers to accept commissions. The intention to embrace the soldiers alone is further indicated by the provision in the body of the proclamation that the land was to be "granted to such Persons who by their voluntary Engagement and good Behaviour in the said Service shall deserve the same . . . in a Proportion due to their respective Merit, as shall be represented to me by their Officers . . . ," implying that the officers themselves were not to share the bounty land.[2] And Washington seems to have so understood the Proclamation at this time, since, in arguing with Dinwiddie as to the inadequacy of the officers' pay, he apparently took no account of their sharing any part of the 200,000 acres of land offered in the Proclamation.[3]

Many years passed before Dinwiddie's proclamation could be fulfilled. In the beginning, no allotment could be made because of the French and Indian War and later because of the Royal Proclamation of October 7, 1763, reserving, "for the present," land west of the Alleghenies to the Indians and forbidding any white settlement or grants of land there. Not until after the Indian treaties of Fort Stanwix and Hard Labour in 1768,[4] was the land in the region covered by Dinwiddie's proclamation of 1754 reopened for grant and settlement.[5]

In May, 1769, Washington mentioned "in a cursory manner" to Dinwiddie's successor, Governor Lord Botetourt, "the claim of Sundry Officers of the first Troops raisd in this Colony in behalf of themselves, and the Soldiery of that day, to certain Lands westward of the Aligany Mountains."[6] And, in December he presented a petition to the Governor and Council "in behalf of himself and the Officers and Soldiers who first Imbarked in the Service of this Colony," asking that the 200,000 acres promised in Dinwiddie's proclamation be allotted to them "in one or more surveys . . . on the Monongahela its Waters from the long Narrows up to . . . Nicholas Knobs; on the New River or Great Canhawa from the Great Falls therein to the Mouth thereof; and on Sandy Creek . . . from the Mouth to the Mountains. . . ."[7] The petition included a request for permission to employ a special surveyor because employment of an official county surveyor would entail delay and an "Expence much beyond what a poor Soldier is able to bear."

The petition was favorably acted upon in an order issued December 15, 1769, authorizing "the Petitioners" to take up the 200,000 acres in the areas described in their petition, with the privileges and immunities mentioned in Dinwiddie's proclamation. Since Washington's petition was stated to be on behalf of the officers as well as the soldiers of his old regiment, this order in effect held that the officers were to share in the allotment, though to what extent was not indicated. The order directed Washington to publish notice to all claimants to file their claims with him; and to apply to the President and Masters of William and Mary College, who controlled the appointment of official surveyors, to appoint a qualified person to survey the land as soon as possible.[8]

Washington promptly carried out the order of December 15, 1769, by publishing the required notice. He also petitioned the President and Masters of William and Mary College to appoint a special surveyor for the proclamation land,[9] recommending William Crawford,[10] with whom he was on a particularly confidential footing, as we know from a letter from him to Crawford in 1767, stating:

> It is possible that Pennsylvania Customs will not permit so large a quantity of Land as I require to be entered together; if so this may possibly be evaded by making several entries to the same amount if the expense of doing which is not too heavy. . . . The other matter . . . is attempting to secure some of the most valuable Lands in the King's part which I think may be accomplished after a while notwithstanding the Proclamation of 1763 that restrains at present. . . . I woud recommend it to you to keep this matter a profound Secret . . . by a Silent management . . . , snugly carried on by you under the pretense of hunting other Game which you may I presume effectually do at the same time you are in pursuit of the Land. . . . I will have the Lands immediately surveyed to keep others off and leave the rest to time and my own Assiduity to Accomplish.[11]

In the fall of 1770, as brought out in the preceding chapter, Crawford, Washington, and his friend and neighbor Dr. James Craik took a trip to inspect the land on the Great Kanawha included in the Governor and Council's order of December, 1769. And in the following March Washington held a meeting with some of the former officers of the old regiment in Winchester, at which resolutions were adopted authorizing him to employ Crawford to make surveys of the land for all concerned, the cost to be borne as follows: field officers, £11-5/ each; captains, £6-15/ each; subalterns, £4-10/ each; and the soldiers, 9 shillings each.[12]

In November, 1771, having considered a "Memorial" (now missing) presented by Washington, the Governor and Council ordered distribution of the proclamation land as follows:

3 field officers (including Washington)	15,000 acres each		45,000 acres	
5 captains	9,000	"	"	45,000	"
8 subalterns	6,000	"	"	48,000	"
2 cadets	2,500	"	"	5,000	"
7 sergeants	600	"	"	4,200	"
4 corporals	500	"	"	2,000	"
52 privates who had filed claims	400	"	"	20,800	"
	Total immediate allotment		170,000	"

The residue of 30,000 acres was to be held for soldiers who had not yet filed claims. Any remainder after all claims were filed was to be divided among the claimants who contributed to the cost of surveys and other incidental expenses in proportion to the amount of their contributions,[13] (Washington eventually got 3,500 of the 30,000 acres thus reserved).[14]

By the fall of 1772 Crawford had surveyed thirteen tracts in the proclamation area totaling about 128,000 acres.[15] He spent from October 24 to 30, 1772, at Mount Vernon going over his surveys with Washington,[16] who soon afterwards presented a plan to Botetourt's successor, Governor Lord Dunmore, and Council ("the Board," as they collectively were called) for allotment of the surveyed tracts, which was approved November 6, 1772.[17]

The Board's order included the allotment to Washington himself of four tracts totaling 20,147 acres—15,000 on account of his own claim and 5,147 on account of claims purchased by him from others in the regiment[18]—with the proviso that, if within a reasonable period there was any complaint concerning Washington's allotment, which the Board found to be just, he was to "give up all his interest under his Patent, and submit to such regulations as the Board may think fit."[19] At a subsequent meeting (December 9, 1772) the Board ordered that any complaints against the allotment to Washington must be filed by "the End of the Oyer and Terminer Week in June next" and that Washington publish notice of the several allotments made in the Board's order of November 6[20]—which he did in a letter of December 23, 1772, published in *The Virginia Gazette* (Rind's) of January 14, 1773.[21]

Soon after these orders were issued Washington took steps to secure patents for the tracts to which he was provisionally entitled under the order of November 6, and these were issued to him December 15, 1772.[22]

So far as is known, the soldiers were not dissatisfied with the quality of the land surveyed for them. But when, after the specified time for filing complaints had expired, some of the officers looked over their land they seemed, wrote Crawford to Washington in November, 1773, to be "a good deal shagereened . . . as there front on the River was not over a Mile and a half, the most of them, and Run back almost five mile and you in Cheif of your Survays have all bottom as also Dr. Crages Land; none in that Country is so good as your Land and his Land."[23] As Washington himself later said, he had got "the cream of the Country."[24]

So far as is known, Washington did not reply to Crawford's letter concerning the officers' complaint, but a letter

in January, 1774, to Major George Muse suggests that he
was in an ugly mood:

> Your impertinent Letter of the 24th ulto., was delivered
> to me yesterday by Mr. Smith. As I am not accustomed
> to receive such from any Man, nor would have taken the
> same language from you personally, without letting you
> feel some marks of my resentment; I would advise you
> to be cautious in writing me a second of the same tenour;
> for though I understand you were drunk when you did
> it, yet give me leave to tell you, that drunkness is no
> excuse for rudeness; and that, but for your stupidity and
> sottishness you might have known, by attending to the
> public Gazettes . . . that you had your full quantity of ten
> thousand acres of Land allowed you; . . . all my concern
> is, that I ever engag'd in behalf of so ungrateful and
> dirty a fellow as you are.[25]

Though the period for possible dissatisfied claimants
to attack the allotment to Washington had expired, the
patents issued to him on the basis of the allotment were
open to attack on a wholly different ground—Crawford's
failure to take the oaths of office[26] required of official surveyors of Crown land.[27] Freeman states that Washington
did not know of Crawford's having failed to take the required oaths,[28] but he gives no evidence in support of
this statement, and apparently none exists. In any event,
in the spring of 1775 Washington heard that Crawford's
surveys had been declared void, and he immediately
(April 3, 1775) wrote Governor Dunmore, telling him of
this report, dilating on the hardship to himself and the
other grantees who shared in the proclamation land if
their patents were declared void, and asking Dunmore
what steps the grantees should now take.[29]

The implication in this letter that Washington and the
other grantees all stood to suffer alike if Crawford's surveys were held void and new surveys were required, was

not correct. On the contrary, the officers, other than Washington himself and Dr. Craik, stood to benefit if new surveys were required since they would then be in a position to insist on receiving a proportionate share of the valuable bottom lands granted to Washington and Craik on the basis of Crawford's surveys.

Furthermore, Washington had another interest, not shared by the other officers, in having the outstanding patents remain undisturbed. In including only rich bottom land in his surveys for Washington, Crawford had infringed a Virginia law requiring that grants of Crown land be in tracts not more than three times as long as they were broad.[30] The length of the tracts surveyed by him for Washington were much more than three times their breadth.[31] If new surveys were made by a surveyor who had taken the oaths of office, he presumably would be unwilling to perjure himself by submitting surveys which violated the law.

Dunmore replied to Washington on April 18, "The information you have received that the Patents granted for the Lands under the Proclamation of 1754 would be declared Null and Void, is founded on a report that the Surveyor who Surveyed those Lands did not qualify agreeably to the Act of Assembly directing the duty and qualification of Surveyors; if this is the Case the Patents will of Consequence be declared Null and void."[32] And there the matter rested (the Revolution having broken out almost immediately afterwards) for three years.

In 1778 the Virginia legislature passed an act providing that:

> All officers or soldiers, their heirs or assigns, claiming under the late governor Dinwiddie's proclamation of a bounty in lands to the first Virginia regiment, and having returned to the Secretary's office, surveys made by virtue

of a special commission from the president and masters of William and Mary shall be entitled to grants thereupon on payment of the common office fees. . . .[33]

No matter how vulnerable they may have been before, the patents issued to Washington on the basis of Crawford's surveys would now be validated if the people of Virginia succeeded in establishing the independence for which they were fighting.

Another important source of Washington's great western land holdings was the Royal Proclamation of 1763, directing governors of Virginia and other royal colonies in North America in which the Crown held ungranted land, to grant land, free of fees and of quitrent for ten years, to such "reduced" officers as had served in North America during the late war.[34] The term "reduced" officers meant those honorably retired from active service, commonly on the disbanding or contraction of the unit to which they belonged,[35] as, for example, the officers of Washington's old regiment who were retired when the regiment was disbanded after the close of the Cherokee war in 1762.[36] This clarifies what Washington had in mind in writing his brother Charles in 1770 "as you are situated in a good place for seeing many of the Officers at different times, I should be glad if you would (in a joking way, rather than in earnest, at first) see what value they set upon their lands"; but adding that he was interested in buying only "of those who continued in the Service till after the Cherokee Expedition."[37]

Washington having resigned voluntarily long before his regiment was disbanded, was, of course, not a "reduced" officer and hence was not entitled to any land under the Proclamation of 1763. But in 1773, he somehow induced Dunmore to issue a certificate to him for 5,000 acres,[38] the amount allowable to reduced colonels under this Proclamation.[39]

Thus, starting without right to any of the bounty land promised by either of the proclamations, Washington secured under them over 20,000 acres of land on his own account[40] in addition to land acquired by purchase of rights of others. The land in the Ohio valley owned by him at the time of his death in December, 1799, appraised by him in July of that year at approximately ten dollars an acre, constituted more than 40 per cent of the total appraised value of his estate.[41]

In considering Washington's ethics, there is, I think, a clear distinction between his getting land offered to reduced officers in the Royal Proclamation of 1763 and his getting land offered to enlisted men in Governor Dinwiddie's proclamation of 1754. Crown land was considered fair game by the colonists in general, and the only loser by Washington's obtaining land to which he was not entitled under the proclamation of 1763 was the Crown. But in the case of the land acquired under the proclamation of 1754, the more he got of the allotted 200,000 acres, the less was available for the enlisted men to whom it was promised.

Furthermore, Washington's engrossing the "cream" of the land at the expense of the officers who contributed to the cost of employing Crawford to make the surveys for their joint account is difficult to defend. Having agreed at the meeting of officers in March, 1771,[42] to act as agent for the group, he was in the position of a trustee and, as such, under obligation to see that his fellow contributors were apportioned a fair share of the best land.[43]

Though most of the charges made by Washington's enemies against him during the Revolution are demonstrably false or unsupported by any evidence, the statement in a biographical sketch published in London in 1779, that he was "avaritious under the specious appearance of disinterestedness—particularly eager in engrossing large tracts of land"[44]—apparently had considerable foundation.

CHAPTER FIFTEEN

Public Service in Civil Affairs

Washington's service in the Virginia House of Burgesses has generally been given relatively little attention by his biographers. Yet his many years of working with fellow members of the House, especially the work in committee, probably contributed more than anything to his understanding, patience, and tact in later dealing with the Continental Congress. And without these assets he could hardly have commanded, as he did, the unswerving support of a large majority of the Congress, essential to the success of the Revolution.

The earliest indication we have of Washington's ambition for a seat in the House of Burgesses is in a letter from him to his brother Jack in May 1755, stating:

As I understand your [Fairfax] County is to be divided, and that Mr. Alexander intends to decline serving it, I shou'd be glad if you could fish at Colo. Fairfax's Intentions, and let me know whether he purposes to offer himself a Candidate. If he does not I shou'd be glad to stand a poll, if I thought my chance tolerably good. . . . Parson Green's and Captn. McCarty's Interests in this wou'd be of Consequence; and I shou'd be glad if you cou'd sound their Pulse upon the occasion. Conduct the whole till you are satisfied of the Sentim'ts of those I have mention'd, with an air of Indifference and unconcern; after that you may regulate your conduct accordingly.[1]

Jack's report was apparently unfavorable, for Washington chose to run not in Fairfax but in the frontier county of Frederick, where he owned land, and, though not elected, polled a respectable vote.[2]

While serving in the Forbes campaign, Washington again ran in Frederick, and this time (July, 1758) led the poll, with a vote of 307 to 240, 199, and 45, respectively, for the other candidates.[3] Unable to attend himself, he had an agent on hand to provide entertainment to the tune of 66 gallons and 10 bowls of rum punch, 58 gallons of beer and 35 gallons of wine, 8 quarts of hard cider and three and a half pints of brandy.[4] Whether the other candidates were equally bountiful does not appear. He was elected for Frederick county again in 1761,[5] but in 1765 chose to run for his home county, Fairfax, and was elected.[6] Repeatedly re-elected, he continued to serve Fairfax county as one of its representatives until the Revolution.[7]

At the time of his first election, the House consisted of one hundred and six members, two for each county, one each for the boroughs of Jamestown, Norfolk, and Williamsburg and one for the College of William and Mary. By 1775 the membership had increased to one hundred and twenty-six by reason of the establishment from time to time of ten additional counties.[8]

At his first session Washington was appointed a member of the Committee of Propositions and Grievances, which was called upon to consider a wide range of matters. These included petitions for the better defense of Augusta county; establishment of ferries over the Dan, Staunton, Roanoke, and Rapidan rivers; change in the location of various public warehouses for the inspection of tobacco; better control of stray animals in Halifax county; dissolution of the vestries of several parishes; and continuation of acts regulating the militia and fixing the fees of various public officials. The committee also dealt with the regulation of "pedlars of furs" on the frontier; a proposed act forbidding slave-owners to let their slaves trade on their own account; establishment of towns in Culpeper, Lunenburg, Halifax, and Essex counties; reconstruction of dams by the owners of mills on the Rapidan to permit the passage of fish up the river; and regulation of pilotage fees.[9]

Washington was appointed to this busy committee again in 1762, when much the same type of questions came before it as in 1759, but with the variation of considering proposed acts for changing the boundaries of several counties and for the exemption of justices of the peace from serving in the militia.[10]

At the November, 1766, session of the legislature, Washington was appointed to the Committee of Privileges and Elections, whose duties considered chiefly in considering and making recommendations to the House whether returns of writs of election for burgesses in the several counties were in proper form and which candidate was to be seated in contested elections.[11] A bitter contest seemed in prospect when William Fitzhugh of Stafford county challenged the seating of Thomas Mason, brother of Washington's neighbor and friend George Mason; but the matter was settled before the committee heard the evidence by the withdrawal of Fitzhugh's protest.[12]

This must have been a painful session to Washington, because much of it was taken up with problems raised by the discovery of the embezzlement by his friend John Robinson, Treasurer of the colony as well as Speaker of the House, of over £100,000 of the public funds, lent to relations, friends, and members of the House (not, however, including Washington) and of the Council.[13]

So far as is known, Washington took no active part in colonial opposition to the encroachments by the British Crown and Parliament on colonial self-government from

1759 to 1764. No word of his has been found protesting against the Crown's peremptory order to Governor Fauquier of August 29, 1759, severely limiting the power of the Virginia legislature to amend or repeal existing acts of the colony; against the Act of Parliament of 1764, for the first time levying taxes clearly for revenue on the colonies; or against any other British measures before 1765.[14] He did, indeed, protest against the Stamp Act of 1765, but even his protests against this act were relatively mild.[15]

However, Parliament's passage of the Townshend Act of 1767, levying additional duties for revenue on colonial imports,[16] followed in 1769 by proposals in Parliament to ship leaders of the colonial opposition to Great Britain for trial as traitors,[17] evidently convinced Washington that the colonists must unite to combat British measures threatening the rights or privileges they had long enjoyed. He now spoke out in a powerful letter of April 5, 1769, to George Mason, suggesting the adoption of a non-importation agreement in Virginia similar to those adopted in the northern colonies,[18] engaging the subscribers not to import any of the articles taxed by the Townshend Act and a wide range of other articles customarily imported into the colonies, until the act was repealed. The object, of course, was to put pressure on British merchants and manufacturers to secure repeal.

> At a time [wrote Washington] when our lordly Masters in Great Britain will be satisfied with nothing less than the deprication of American freedom, it seems highly necessary that some thing shou'd be done to avert the stroke and maintain the liberty which we have derived from our Ancestors; but the manner of doing it to answer the purpose effectually is the point in question.
> That no man shou'd scruple, or hesitate a moment to use a—ms in defence of so valuable a blessing, on which all the good and evil of life depends, is clearly my opin-

ion; yet A—ms I wou'd beg leave to add, should be the
last resource, the denier resort. . . . Upon the whole,
therefore, I think the Scheme a good one, and that it
ought to be tryed here, with such alterations as the exi-
gency of our circumstances render absolutely necessary. . . .[19]

Heartily agreeing with Washington, Mason sent him
a proposed form of agreement,[20] presumably to take with
him to the session of the Virginia legislature which was
about to meet in Williamsburg. The House of Burgesses
was dissolved by Governor Lord Botetourt for its spirited
resolutions against the obnoxious measures of Parliament
in 1767 and 1769 referred to above, before action could
be taken in the House on non-importation;[21] but, immediately after dissolution, the recent members adopted a
non-importation agreement, proposed by a committee of
which Washington was a member,[22] which was similar to
Mason's draft.[23]

In the ensuing election of a new House, Washington
was again chosen as a representative for Fairfax,[24] and
attended the session which opened in November, 1769.
He was again appointed to the Committee of Privileges
and Elections and also to the Committee for Religion,
whose activities consisted chiefly of considering petitions
concerning parish boundaries, personnel of the parish
vestries, and land belonging to the parish.[25] This pattern
of service continued until 1775,[26] when, having been
elected by the House as a delegate to the Second Continental Congress, he was absent from the last (June, 1775)
session of the pre-Revolutionary House.[27]

Most of the relatively few bills in the Virginia House
of Burgesses with which Washington's name is associated
as proposer or otherwise were purely local or private. But
the minutes of the House of December, 1769, record that

he and Richard Henry Lee were authorized to bring in an important bill for clearing the Potomac to make it navigable from the great falls of the river, a little above Alexandria, to Fort Cumberland.[28]   Nothing came of the project at that time; but Washington, together with Thomas Johnson of Annapolis, Maryland, and George Mason, gave much time and thought to it, and, after the Revolution, it came to fruition in the establishment of the well-known Potomac Company, of which Washington long was president.[29]

In addition to his service as burgess, Washington had long experience as a vestryman of his local parish, Truro. The vestry in Virginia had charge not only of the temporal affairs of the established Church of England in the parish, but of various non-ecclesiastical matters including the care of the local poor.[30]   Elected in 1762, he faithfully attended vestry meetings until he left for service in the first Continental Congress in 1774.[31]

He also served for many years as a member of the County Court of Fairfax county, to which he was appointed by the Governor in 1768.[32]   The county court, made up of local justices of the peace, not only exercised wide judicial power as a court of common law, equity, and probate, but had a variety of administrative duties, including supervision of public buildings, laying out and improving roads, and levying taxes.[33]

Thus, though Washington was known nationally only for his early military services, he had had long and varied experience in civil affairs when chosen as one of the Virginia delegates to the first Continental Congress.

CHAPTER SIXTEEN

The Intolerable Acts and the First Continental Congress

Following repeal in 1770 of all the more important duties levied by the Townshend Act of 1767 except the duty on tea,[1] the Virginia non-importation agreement of 1769, referred to in the preceding chapter, was relaxed,[2] and for the next three years the relations between Great Britain and most of the colonies were greatly improved. But in 1773 Parliament again raised a storm in the colonies by an act to refund the British import duty on tea re-exported to the colonies, and to permit the British East India Company, previously required to sell its tea exclusively by auction in England, to export tea directly to the colonies.[3]

One of the objects, perhaps the main object of the act, was to help the company's finances by enabling it to undersell smuggled Dutch tea in the colonial market. But since it would have been equally helpful to the company to retain the old duty payable in England on tea re-exported and repeal the colonial duty of three pence a pound on tea levied by the Townshend Act, the act was apparently also designed to secure payment of the colonial duty and thus maintain and strengthen the British claim of right to tax the colonies for revenue.

As every one knows, the first of the company's shipments of tea to reach the colonies was thrown overboard by a band of men at Boston in December, 1773. Whereupon Parliament retaliated in 1774 by passing a number of acts, the so-called Intolerable Acts, the first of which, the Boston Port Act, shut the port of Boston to all commerce except the importation of fuel and provisions sufficient for Boston itself, with provision for rigorous enforcement by British warships.[4]

When news of this act reached Virginia, the House of Burgesses, which Washington was attending, adopted a resolution denouncing the act "as a hostile invasion of Boston" and appointing June 1 as a day of prayer "to implore the divine interposition, for averting the heavy Calamity which threatens destruction to our Civil Rights, and the evils of Civil War; [and] to give us one heart and one Mind firmly to oppose, by all just and proper means, every injury to American Rights. . . ."[5]

On learning of these resolutions, Governor Lord Dunmore dissolved the House,[6] whereupon its late members met as an extra-legal body and adopted resolutions (May 27, 1774) denouncing the Boston Port Act as "a most dangerous attempt to destroy the constitutional liberty and rights of all North America," declaring the attack on Massachusetts "to compel submission to arbitrary taxes" as "an attack made on all British America," and strongly recommending cessation of all purchases of East Indian products except saltpeter and spices until colonial grievances were redressed. The resolutions also called for an annual meeting of deputies from the several colonies "to deliberate on those general measures which the united interests of America may from time to time require" and threatened to cut off all commercial intercourse with Great Britain if Parliament persisted in taxing the colonies without their consent.[7]

Though Washington disapproved of the destruction of the tea at Boston,[8] he was fully in sympathy with the resolutions he had signed, as we know from a forceful letter of July 4, 1774, to Bryan Fairfax, son of his old friend and patron William Fairfax, challenging the view that petitioning the King for relief should be tried before resorting to another boycott:

> I would heartily join you in . . . petition to the throne, provided there was the most distant hope of success. But have we not tried this already? Have we not addressed the Lords, and remonstrated to the Commons? And to what end? Did they deign to look at our petitions? Does it not appear, as clear as the sun in its meridian brightness, that there is a regular, systematic plan formed to fix the right and practice of taxation upon us? Does not the uniform conduct of Parliament for some years past confirm this? Do not all the debates, especially those just brought to us, in the House of Commons on the side of government, expressly declare that America must be taxed in aid of the British funds, and that she [Great Britain] has no longer resources within herself?
>
> Is there any thing to be expected from petitioning after this? Is not the attack upon the liberty and property of the people of Boston, before restitution of the loss to the India Company was demanded, a plain and self-evident proof of what they are aiming at? Do not the subsequent bills (now I dare say acts), for depriving the Massachusetts Bay of its charter, and for transporting offenders into other colonies or to Great Britain for trial, where it is impossible from the nature of the thing that justice can be obtained, convince us that the administration is determined to stick at nothing to carry its point?[9]

Washington further showed where he stood by presiding at the meeting of the inhabitants of Fairfax county at Alexandria on July 18, which adopted the famous Fairfax resolves, reinforcing in even stronger language than that of the late burgesses, the resolutions recently adopted by them.[10]

The usefulness of a general congress was voiced by several colonial assemblies besides the Virginia House of Burgesses, and Philadelphia was fixed upon as the place of a meeting to be held early in September.[11]

Washington's long service in the Virginia House of Burgesses, his high standing in the province, and his recent outspoken opposition to British measures obnoxious to the colonies led naturally to his election by a provincial convention held at Williamsburg early in August, 1774,[12] as one of the Virginia delegates to the proposed intercolonial congress. His fellow delegates were Peyton Randolph, Speaker of the House of Burgesses, Richard Henry Lee, Patrick Henry, Richard Bland, Benjamin Harrison, and Edmund Pendleton.

At the so-called First Continental Congress, which convened at Philadelphia on September 5, 1774, Washington, who was shy of speaking,[13] apparently played only a very minor part. There is no evidence that he initiated any of the measures, including a petition to the King for the redress of colonial grievances, a resolution that if efforts were made to enforce the Intolerable Acts all America ought to support the people of Massachusetts in opposing them, and agreements for the non-importation and non-exportation of various products, adopted by the Congress. Nor was he elected to any important committee.[14] But, even at this early date, legend had begun to gather around him.

According to John Adams' diary, Thomas Lynch, a delegate from South Carolina, "told us that Coll. Washington made the most eloquent Speech at the Virginia Convention that ever was made. Says he, 'I will raise 1000 Men, subsist them at my own Expence, and march my self at their Head for the Relief of Boston,' " and Silas Deane, a delegate from Connecticut, wrote his wife that, when serving in Braddock's army, Washington had been "the means of saving the remains of that unfortunate army"[15]—neither of which apparently was true.[16] It is in this letter to his wife that Deane gave the well-known description of Washington as "nearly as tall a man as Col. Fitch, and almost as hard a countenance; yet with a very young look, and an easy, soldier like air and gesture."[17]

After adopting a resolution recommending another intercolonial congress to be held at Philadelphia on May 10, 1775, if the grievances set forth in the petition to the King were not redressed by that date, the First Congress dissolved itself on October 26,[18] and Washington was home by the thirtieth.[19]

Following his return from the First Congress, Washington spent much of his time promoting and organizing the non-importation association resolved upon at Philadelphia.[20] But he was also deeply involved in preparations for the defense of Virginia in case of war.

On January 17, 1775, he presided at a meeting of a military committee for Fairfax county at which it was resolved that "the defenceless state of this County renders it indispensably necessary that a quantity of Ammunition should be immediately provided" and that "such of the inhabitants of this County as are from sixteen to fifty years of age, . . . form themselves into Companies . . . [and] provide themselves with good Firelocks, and use their utmost endeavours to make themselves masters of the Military Exercise, published by order of his Majesty in 1764, and recommended by the Provincial Congress of the Massachusetts Bay, on the 29th of October last."[21] His correspondence and diary entries in the winter of 1774-1775 also disclose his great activity in drilling the Fairfax county military company and similar companies in other counties organized pursuant to the foregoing resolutions.[22]

Furthermore, Washington represented Fairfax county at the important convention of delegates from all over Virginia, held in Richmond in the last week of March, 1775, which adopted a resolution that the colony "be immediately put in a position of defence," chose a committee, including Washington, to implement this resolution, and re-elected the Virginia delegates to the First Continental Congress to represent the colony at the Second, conditionally scheduled to meet on May 10.[23]

CHAPTER SEVENTEEN

The Second Congress and Washington's Election as Commander-in-Chief

The fighting at Lexington and Concord on April 19, 1775, news of which reached Virginia nine days later,[1] banished any doubt as to the necessity for a second Continental Congress, and, on May 4 Washington again set out for Philadelphia, where he arrived May 9.[2]

With war actually begun, and a large British army reported on its way to America, the proceedings of the Second Continental Congress, which convened the day after Washington reached Philadelphia,[3] were naturally in most respects very different from those of the First. Then, plans centered chiefly on how to obtain redress without fighting, now they were centered on how the colonies were to defend themselves against approaching invasion, and in this changed atmosphere Washington immediately began to play an outstanding part in the proceedings.

The most urgent problem was to prevent the British from occupying New York, the strategic center of the colonies, and as soon as the tardy arrival of a majority of the New York delegates made it practicable for Congress to act, a committee was chosen (May 15) to deal with this emergency.[4] Washington headed this important committee, and the same was true of the other three most important committees on military affairs established during the next few weeks—committees on means to supply the colonies with ammunition, to bring in an estimate of the money necessary to be raised for military supplies, and to bring in a draft of regulations for the government of the army.[5]

On June 14 Congress took the first step to establish an army under its immediate direction and control by voting to enlist and pay ten companies of riflemen, of eighty-one officers and men each, to serve in "the American continental army" for one year, unless sooner discharged,[6] and, the following day, resolved that "a General be appointed to command all the continental forces, raised, or to be raised, for the defence of American liberty" with an allowance for pay and expenses of five hundred dollars a month.[7]

According to statements of John Adams written many years later, until he spoke up in Congress for the election of Washington, many if not most of the delegates were opposed to his election and favored Artemas Ward, Commander-in-Chief of the Massachusetts forces investing the British troops in Boston.[8] But Adams' recollections as to his speech in support of Washington, the opposition to the latter's election, and the strong support for Ward are unsupported by any known contemporary evidence,[9] and there is strong circumstantial evidence that from the time a Continental Commander-in-Chief was first considered, the great majority of members favored Washington for the command.

As shown by his election as head of the military committees previously referred to, Washington's fellow members in the Second Continental Congress evidently thought highly of him as a military man, and the approving description of him by Eliphalet Dyer, delegate from Connecticut, as "discreet and virtuous, no harum Starum ranting Swearing fellow but Sober, steady and Calm"[10] probably represented the general impression of him as a person.

Ward, on the other hand, was unknown to most if not all of the members except those from Massachusetts; few probably had even heard his name before his recent election (May 19) as Commander-in-Chief of the Massachusetts troops.[11] True, he had served in the field during one of the campaigns of the French and Indian War, but he had not distinguished himself then or in his recent brief command of the Massachusetts troops.[12] Furthermore, leading members of the Provincial Congress in Massachusetts had written to the colony's delegates at Philadelphia that they wished Washington was with the troops there and had no "doubt the New England generals would acquiesce in . . . making him generalissimo."[13]

In addition, there was, from the very beginning, strong reason for choosing someone from outside New England as Commander-in-Chief because of the fear, to quote Dyer again, that "an Enterprising eastern New England Genll. proving Successful, might with his Victorious Army give law to the Southern or Western Gentry"—[14] a fear based on the recent aggressiveness of New England settlers in disputes with New York and Pennsylvania,[15] whose bounds overlapped those claimed by three of the four New England colonies.[16]

Some months before the opening of the First Continental Congress, Judge Jared Ingersoll in Philadelphia wrote his nephew in Connecticut that "the people here begin to consider the Northern New England men as a Set of Goths & Vandals who may one day overrun these Southern Colonies unless thoroughly opposed . . .,"[17] and, in the meanwhile, there had been further acts confirming this apprehension.[18] General Nathanael Greene of Rhode

Island was doubtless honest in assuring "the Gentlemen to the Southward that there could not be anything more abhorrent proposed than a Union of these [the New England] Colonies for the purpose of Conquering the Southern Colonies";[19] but the existence of the fear, even if mistaken, was real, and nothing could do more to allay it than choosing a Commander-in-Chief from outside New England.[20]

Returning to the journals of Congress we find, immediately after the adoption on June 15, 1775, of the resolution for a commander of the continental forces, that "George Washington Esq. was unanimously elected"[21] to the command. The following day he accepted in a formal letter to John Hancock, Randolph's successor as President of the Congress:[22]

> Mr. President, Tho' I am truly sensible of the high Honour done me in this Appointment, yet I feel great distress from a consciousness that my abilities and Military experience may not be equal to the extensive and important Trust: However, as the Congress desires I will enter upon the momentous duty, and exert every power I Possess In their Service for the Support of the glorious Cause: I beg they will accept my most cordial thanks for this distinguished testimony of their Approbation. . . .
>
> As to pay, Sir, I beg leave to Assure the Congress that as no pecuniary consideration could have tempted me to have accepted this Arduous employment I do not wish to make any proffit from it: I will keep an exact Account of my expences; those I doubt not they will discharge and that is all I desire.

This letter, often quoted for its modesty, is no less significant for its waiver of any pay beyond the amount needed for expenses. This was characteristic of Washington's whole future conduct. Many sought and some found the opportunity to profit financially from the war and establishment of the national government which followed

the attainment of independence; but, from the time of
his election to the chief command, Washington dedicated
himself unreservedly to service of the public; first to the
winning of the war and from then on to establishment of
a nation designed to perpetuate the ideals for which he
and his soldiers had fought.

A week after his election, accompanied by Major Generals Charles Lee and Philip Schuyler, Washington left
for Cambridge.[23] Just before leaving, he wrote a tender
farewell to Martha in one of the few of his letters to her
which have survived:

> My Dearest: As I am within a few minutes of leaving
> this city, I could not think of departing from it without
> dropping you a line, especially as I do not know whether
> it may be in my power to write again till I get to the
> camp at Boston. I go fully trusting in that Providence,
> which has been more bountiful to me than I deserve and
> in full confidence of a happy meeting with you some time
> in the Fall. I have no time to add more as I am sur-
> rounded with company to take leave of me. I retain an
> unalterable affection for you which neither time or dis-
> tance can change. My best love to Jack and Nelly and
> regards for the rest of the family; Conclude me with the
> utmost truth and Sincerety, Your entire[24]

Reaching New York June 25,[25] Washington spent a
couple of days there on various matters,[26] and then hastened, by way of New Haven and Wethersfield, Connecticut, Springfield, Marlborough, and Watertown, Massachusetts, to Cambridge,[27] where he arrived on July 2.[28]
The next day, without fanfare, he took command of the
troops investing the British in Boston.[29]

The Virginia period was ended; a new period, the
period of Washington's great leadership of the Continental Army[30] in the War of the American Revolution,
had begun.

APPENDIX TO
CHAPTER ELEVEN

Washington's Illnesses from
1749 to 1769

As pointed out in Chapter 8, one of the most admirable aspects of Washington's service to the American Revolution was his remaining constantly with his troops throughout the whole eight years of the war. This was made possible by his remarkably good health, which was in striking contrast to his ill health in earlier years, as described by him or others writing for him:

Before, probably shortly before, Nov. 7, 1749—"Aguee and Feaver . . . to Extremety," *W* I 18.

Nov. 17, 1751—"strongly attacked with the small Pox"—in Barbados, *W* I 20.

May 20, 1752—"taken with a violent pleurisie, which has reduced me very low," *W* I 22.

June 14, 1755—"seized with violent Fevers and Pains" lasting for nine days, when "immediate ease" was given by "Doctor James Powder" prescribed by Gen. Braddock, *W* I 141. But W was still "weak and feeble" as late as Aug. 14, same 160.

Nov. 27, 1757—For over three months, "Bloody Flux," and more recently, "bad Fevers . . . Stitches & violent Pleuritick Pains"—which repeated bleedings failed to relieve, *Letters to W* II 231. Continued indisposition as late as March 4, 1758, "with my disorder at times returning obstinately upon me," *W* II 166.

Dec. 9, 1758—"My present Disorder," *W* II 316, was later described as having been for "Many months . . . an inveterate disorder in his Bowels," same XXIX 48.

July 27, 1761—"A violent cold" since the middle of May, 2 *W & M Q* XXII (1942) 223, with "fevers" and "pains," *W*

II 365, which seems to have hung on into November, same 373-374.

March 3, 1768—"Lax, Griping and violent straining," lasting for about a week, *W Diaries* I 256.

Sept. 22, 1769—"An Ague upon me," lasting apparently only two days, *W Diaries* I 345-346.

So far as I know this was Washington's last illness during our period except for an indisposition mentioned but not described in a letter of December 26, 1774 (*W* III 253), which was evidently mild since his diary shows he was up and about the whole time he said he had been unwell, diary for Dec. 2 to 30, 1774, *W Diaries* II 172-175.

Washington's Letter of August 28, 1762, to Burwell Bassett

Freeman challenges this letter on the ground that "the literary style . . . arouses suspicion," the letter being "written lightly, almost facetiously, and in a tone and spirit wholly different from that employed in Washington's authenticated letters to his friend Bassett or to anyone else."[1]

I find this reasoning utterly unconvincing. In the first place there is a letter, undisputed by Freeman, from Washington to Bassett (February 15, 1773) in much the same vein, stating "Our celebrated fortune, Miss French, whom half the world was in pursuit of, bestowed her hand on Wednesday last, being her birthday (you perceive I think myself under a necessity of accounting for the choice) upon Mr. Ben Dulany. . . . Mentioning one wedding puts me in mind of another, tho' of less dignity; this is the marriage of Mr. Henderson (of Colchester) to a Miss More (of the same place) remarkable for a very frizzled head, and good singing, the latter of which I shall presume it was that captivated our merchant."[2]

Furthermore, there are letters to others proving that Washington was occasionally in the mood to write "lightly, almost facetiously," as illustrated by the following amusing letter of December 20, 1784, to the Reverend William Gordon. "I am glad to hear," wrote Washington, "that my old acquaintance Colo. Ward is yet under the influence of vigorous passions. I will not ascribe the intrepidity of his late enterprize to a mere *flash* of desires, because, in his military career he would have learnt how to distinguish between false alarms and a serious movement. Charity therefore induces me to suppose that like a prudent general, he had reviewed his *strength,* his arms, and ammunition before he got involved in an action.   But if these have been neglected, and he has been precipitated into the measure, let me advise him to make the *first* onset upon his fair del Toboso, with vigor, that the impression may be deep, if it cannot be lasting, or frequently renewed."[3]

And what about the well-known paragraph in Washington's letter of May 10, 1786, to Lafayette, concerning Royal Gift, a young jackass recently received as a present from the King of Spain? "The Jack," he wrote, "in appearance is fine; but his late royal master, tho' past his grand climacteric, cannot be less moved by female allurements than he is; or when prompted, can proceed with more deliberation and majestic solemnity to the work of procreation"[4]—a theme which Washington repeated, with amusing variations, to several other correspondents.[5]

Washington's Diary Entries in 1760 and 1768

The following diary entries for the first six weeks of 1760 and of 1768 respectively, taken from Fitzpatrick's *The Diaries of George Washington 1748-1799* I 107-125 and 245-254, are given not only for the light they throw on the nature of Washington's day to day activities at Mount Vernon, but on the change in the pattern of living there between the two periods covered by these sets of entries. The days of the week, bare weather reports, and passages which throw no light on the activities at Mount Vernon are omitted.

Washington himself made his entries for 1768 under three headings, "Where & how my time is spent," "Remarks of the Weather," and "Observations"; for the convenience of the reader I have consolidated these into single daily entries. Those interested in identifying persons and places mentioned in the diary will find such identification, when identification is possible, in Fitzpatrick's editorial notes.

1760

January

1. Visited my Plantations and receivd an Instance of Mr. French's great love of Money in disappointing me of some Pork, because the price had risen to 22/6 after he had engaged to let me have it at 20/.

Called at Mr. Possey's in my way home and desired him to

engage me 100 Bar'ls of Corn upon the best terms he could in Maryland.

And found Mrs. Washington upon my arrival broke out with the Meazles.

2.   Mrs. Barnes who came to visit Mrs. Washington yesterday returned home in my Chariot the weather being too bad to travel in an open Carriage, which, together with Mrs. Washington's Indisposition, confined me to the House and gave me an opportunity of Posting my Books and putting them in good order.

Fearing a disappointment elsewhere in Pork I was fein to take Mr. French's upon his own terms and engaged them to be deliv'd at my House on Monday next.

3.   The Weather continuing Bad and the same causes subsisting I confind myself to the House.   Morris [an overseer] who went to work yesterday caught cold and was laid up bad again, and several of the Family were taken with the Measles, but no bad Symptoms seemed to attend any of them.

Hauled the Sein and got some fish, but was near being disappointed of my Boat by means of an Oyster Man, who had lain at my landing and plagued me a good deal by his disorderly behaviour.

4.   The Weather continued Drisling and Warm, and I kept the House all day.   Mrs. Washington seemg. to be very ill wrote to Mr. Green this afternoon desiring his Company to visit her in the Morng.

5.   Mrs. Washington appeard to be something better.   Mr. Green however came to see her at 11 oclock and in an hour Mrs. Fairfax arrivd.   Mr. Green prescribd the needful, and just as we were going to Dinnr. Capt. Walter Stuart appeard with Doctr. Laurie.

The Evening being very cold, and the wind high, Mrs. Fairfax went home in the Chariot.   Soon afterwards Mulatto Jack arrivd from Fred[eric]k [county] with 4 Beeves.

6.   The Chariot not returng. time enough from Colo. Fairfax's we were prevented from Church.

Mrs. Washington was a good deal better to day; but the Oyster Man still continuing his Disorderly behaviour at my Landing I was obliged in the most preemptory manner to order him and his compy. away, which he did not Incline to obey till next morning.

7. Accompanied Mrs. Bassett to Alexandria and engaged a Keg of Butter of Mr. Kirkpatrick, being quite out of that article.

Wrote from thence to Doctr. Craik to endeavor, if possible, to engage me a Gardener from the Regiment and returnd in the dusk of the Evening.

8. Directed an Indictment to be formd by Mr. Johnston against Jno. Ballendine for a fraud in some Iron he sold me.

Got a little Butter from Mr. Dalton, and wrote to Colo. West for Pork.

In the Evening 8 of Mr. French's Hogs from his Ravensworth Quarter came down, one being lost on the way—as the others might as well have been for their goodness.

Nothing but the disappointments in this Article of Pork which he himself had causd and my necessities coud possibly have obligd me to take them.

Carpenter Sam was taken with the Meazles.

9. Killd and dressd Mr. French's Hogs, which weighd 751 lbs. neat.

Colo. West leaving me in doubt about his Pork yesterday obligd me to send to him again to day, and now no definitive answr was receivd—he purposing to send his overseer down tomorrow, to agree abt it.

Colo. Bassett's Abram arrivd with Letters from his Master appointing Port Royal [on the lower Rappahannock] and Monday next as a time and place to meet him. He brought some things from me that Lay in Mr. Norton's Ware house in York Town.

10. Accompanied Mrs. Bassett in a Visit to Belvoir. She this day determind on setting of for Port Royal on Saturday.

Colo. West wrote me word that he had engagd his Pork. Killd the Beeves that Jack brought down two of which were tolerable good.

11. Deliverd Stephen's two Hogs in part of his Year's Provisions, weight, 69, 90. . . . He had one before of 100 lbs. weight. Two Hogs were also reservd for Foster that were cut out and salted makes up 719 lbs and accts. for Mr. French's

8 Hogs; showing the loss of weighing meat so soon killd, which cannot be less than 5 pr. Ct.

12. Set out with Mrs. Bassett on her journey to Port Royal. The morning was clear and fine, but soon clouded and promised much rain or other falling weather, which is generally the case after remarkable white Frosts as it was to day. We past Occoquan without any great difficulty, notwithstanding the wind was something high and lodged at Mr. McCraes in Dumfries, sending the Horses to the Tavern. Here I was informd that Colo. Cocke was disgusted at my House, and left because he see an old Negroe there resembling his own Image.

13-16. [Account of trip to Port Royal, with a visit to his mother en route.]

17. The Snow had turnd to Rain and occasiond a Sleet, the Wind at No. Et. and the Ground coverd abt. an Inch an half with Snow, The Rain continued with but little Intermission till noon and then came on a Mist which lasted till Night.

Abt. Noon I set out from my Mother's and Just at Dusk arrived at Dumfries.

18. Continued my Journey home, the Misting continuing till noon, when the Wind got Southerly, and being very warm occasioned a great thaw. I however found Potom[ac]k River quite covered with Ice, and Doctr. Craik at my House.

19. ....Recd. a Letter from my Overseer Hardwick, informing me that the Small Pox was surrounding the Plantation's he overlookd, and requiring working Tools.

Bought 4 Hogs weighing—1—103, 2—102, 3—130, 4—108— 442 lbs. @ 22/. and deliverd them to Richd. Stephens, wch. fully compleats his own and Son's allowance of Provision's.

20. My Wagon, after leaving 2 Hogsheads of Tobo. at Alexandria, arrivd here with 3 sides of sole Leather and 4 of upper Leather, 2 Kegs of Butter, one of which for Colo. Fairfax and 15 Bushels of Salt which She took in at Alexandria.

Visited at Belvoir to day, carrying Doctr. Craik with us, who spent the Evening there. . . .

21. The Ice in the River almost gone. The Rains that fell last night, and today in some measure hardned the Ground from the Rotten condition it appeared in Yesterday.

22. The wind continued No.wardly, the weather clear and cold, the ground hard froze and the River blockd up again.

Killed 17 more Hogs which were bought of Mr. French, who was here ready to see them weighd and to receive his money. Doctr. Craik Dind here. Hogs wd. 1722 lbs nett.

23. Clear and more moderate than Yesterday—but the g[roun]d etca. still hard frozen. Abt. Noon the wind (what little blew) came Westerly and Inclining South.

My Waggon set of for Frederick with Sundry's that were wrote for by the Overseer there

Doctr. Craik left this for Alexandria and I visited my Quarters and the Mill. According to Custom found young Stephen's absent.

[24. Weather only.]

25. . . . . Went to Alexandria and saw my Tobo. as it came from the Mountns. lying in an open shed, with the ends of the Hhds. out and in very bad order. Engaged the Inspection of it on Monday.

Wrote to Doctr. Ross to purchase me a joiner, Bricklayer, and Gardner, if any Ship of Servants was in.

Also wrote to my old Servt. Bishop to return to me again, if he was not otherwise engaged. Directed for him at Phila. but no certainty of his being there.

26. Rode to Williamson's Quarter—the overseer not there. A very remarkable circle round the Moon—another indication of falling Weather.

[27. Weather only.]

28. The River clos[d] again and the ground very knobby and hard.

The wind got So. about and blew fresh which allmost cleard the River of Ice.

Visited my Plantation. Severely reprimanded young Stephen's for his Indolence, and his father for suffering of it.

Found the new Negroe Cupid ill of a pleurisy at Dogue Run Quarter and had him brot. home in a cart for better care of him.

29. . . . . Darcus, daughter to Phillis, died, which makes 4 negroes lost this Winter; viz, 3 Dower Negroes namely—Beck,

—appraisd to £50, Doll's Child born since, and Darcus . . . , and Belinda, a Wench of mine, in Frederick.

30. Cupid was extreame Ill all this day and at night when I went to Bed I thought him within a few hours of breathing his last.

31. He was somewhat better, the wind continued at No. West all day, very cold and clear.

February

1. . . . . Snow till 9 oclock then cleard and became tolerable warm. Visited my Plantations, found Foster had been absent from his charge since the 28th. Ulto. Left Order's for him to come immediately to me upon his return, and reprihended him severely.

Mr. Johnston and Mr. Walter Stewart came here this afternoon.

2. The Gentlemen went of after Breakfast and I rid out to my Plantns. and to my Carpenter's. Found Richd. Stephen's hard at Work with an ax—very extraordinary this: Desird him to see after Wm. Nation's Rent, who died t'other day.

The wind for the most part was northerly yet the Day was mild, the Evening fine and promisd settled Weathr.

Mrs. Possey and 2 of her children came and stayd the night here.

3. Very white Frost and wind shifting from So. to East.

Breechy was laid up this Morning with pains in his breast and head attended with a fever.

Mrs. Possey went home and we to Church at Alexandria: dind at Colo. Carlyle's and returnd in the Evening.

One Newell offerd himself to me to be Overseer, put him of to another day.

4. White frost and So'ly Wind, Sometimes cloudy and sometimes clear. the Frost seemd to be getting out of the Ground.

Dispatchd Foster to Occoquan to proceed from thence in Bailey's Vessel to Portobacco for Barr'ls of Corn wch. Capt. Possey purchasd of Mr. Hunter the Priest for my use; sent money to pay for the Corn, viz. 37 pistoles and a Shilling, each pistole weighing 4 ds. 8 gr.

Breechy's pains Increasd and he appeard extreamely ill all the day, in Suspense whether to send for Doctr. Laurie or not.

Visited my Plantations and found two Negroes sick at Williamson's Quarter, viz. Greg and Lucy; orderd them to be Blooded. Step[he]ns. at W[or]k.

Colo. Fairfax giving me notice that he should send up to Frederick in the morning; sat down and wrote to my Overseer there.

5. Breech[y]'s Pain Increasg. and he appearing worse in other Respects inducd me to send for Dr. Laurie. Wrote to Mr. Ramsay Begging the favour of him to enquire into the price of Mr. Barne's Sugar Land Tract and he informd me the value set on it by Mr. Barnes was £400.

Visited my Plantation and found to my great surprise Stephens const[an]t[ly] at Work. Greg and Lucy nothing better.

Passing by my Carpenters that were hughing I found that four of them viz. George, Tom, Mike and young Billy had only hughd 120 Foot Yesterday from 10 oclock. Sat down therefore and observd. Tom and Mike in a less space than 30 Minutes cleard the Bushes from abt. a poplar, Stocklind it 10 Foot long and hughd each their side 12 Inches deep. . . .

Colo. Fairfax, his Lady, and Doctr. Laurie dind here. The Dr. went away afterwards but the others stayd the Evening.

6. . . . .Colo. Fairfax and Mrs. Fairfax Dind here.

The Dr. sent his Servant down with things to Breechy, Grig came here this afternoon, worse, and I had 15 Hogs arrivd from Bullskin.

7. The Hogs which arrivd yesterday were killd—weighg . . . 1614.

Out of which Jno. Foster recd. the remainder of his Year's Provisions, viz. 177 lbs. He had before 173, making 350, the years allow[anc]e.

Doctr. Laurie's Man attended the sick this day also.

I went to Mr. Craigs Funeral Sermon at Alexandria, and there met my waggons with 4 Hhds Tobo. more. Unloaded and sent them down to Mt. Vernon.

One of the Boys that came down with them and the Hogs (Nat) was taken with the Meazles last Night.

The Wind was Southerly, and very warm and drying, but the Earth extremely Rotton.

8. The Wind had got to No. West, but as it did not blew fresh, so neither was it cold.

Rode to my Plantatns. and ordered Lucy down to Home House to be Physickd.

9. . . . .Visited my Plantations before Sunrise and forbid Stephen's keeping any horses upon my Expence.

Set my Waggon's to draw in Stocks and Scantling, and wrote to Mr. Stuart of Norfolk for 20 or 30 or more thous'd Shingles, 6 Barr'ls Tar, 6 of Turpentine and 100 wt. of Tallow or Myrtle wax, or half as much candles. remarkable fine day but the wind at No. Et.

10. The Wind got to North, and often clouded up and threatend Rain but in the Evening at Sunsetting it cleard and seemd to promise fair Weather.

Captn. Possey, and Mrs. Possey dind here, He obliqu'ly hinted a design of selling his 145 acres of Wood Land on Muddy hole.

Orderd all the Fellows from the different Quarters to assembly at Williamson's Quarter in the Morning to move Petit's House.

11. Went out early myself and continued with my People till 1 oclock in which time we got the house abt. 250 yards. Was informd then that Mr. Digges was at my House, upon which I ret'd finding him and Doctr. Laurie there.

The Ground being soft and Deep we found it no easy matter with 20 hands, 8 horses and 6 Oxen to get this House along.

Exceeding clear and fine, wind Northwardly.

12. A Small Frost happening last Night to Crust the Ground causd the House to move much lighter, and by 9 oclock it was got to the spot on which it was intended to stand.

Visited at the Glebe the day being very fine clear and still. no wind blowing from any Quarter perceivably.

Sett Kate and Doll to heaping the Dung abt. the Stable.

Recd. a Letter and Acct. Currt. from Messrs. Hanbury, the former dated Oct. 1, 1759, the other Sept. 1st, same year.

1768

January

1. Fox huntg. in my own Neck with Mr. Robt. Alexander, and Mr. Colvill. Catchd nothing. Captn. Posey with us.
    Neck People clearing a piece of ground which was begun the 23d of Decr. Doeg Run People working in the Swamp which they began to clear this Fall. Muddy hole People (except two threshing) clearing the Skirt of Woods within ye Fence, 4 Men and 2 Women from Doeg Run assisting. Mill People also clearing.
    Ground exceedg. hard froze, but this day calm and moderate.

2. Surveying some Lines of my Mt. Vernon Tract of Land. Moderate—Wind Southwardly—thawing a little

3. At Home with Doctr. Rumney.

4. Rid to Muddy hole, D: Run, and Mill Plantns.

5. Went into the Neck.

6. Rid to Doeg Run and the Mill before Dinner. Mr. B. Fairfax and Mr. Robt. Alexander here.
    Doeg Run People finishd grubbing ye Swamp they were in and proceeded to another adjacent.

7. Fox hunting with the above two Gentn. and Captn. Posey. Started but catchd nothing.

8. Hunting again in the same Comp'y. Started a Fox and run him 4 hours, took the Hounds off at Night.
    Clear, frosty and still.

9. At Home with Mr. B: Fairfax.

10. At Home alone.

11. Running some Lines between me and Mr. Willm. Triplet.
    Clear with the Wind at West—Evening very cold and Wind Northwardly—severe Frost—River froze across.

12. Threshing Wheat at all Plantations. Ground being too hard froze to Grub to any advantage.
    Wind at No. West and exceedingly cold and frosty.

Attempted to go into the Neck on the Ice but it wd. not bear. In the Evening Mr. Chs. Dick, Mr. Muse and my Brother Charles came here.

13. At Home with them. Col. Fairfax [and] . . . .Lady.

14. Ditto—Do. Colo. Fx and fam'y went home in the Evening.

15. At Home with the above Gentlemen and Shooting together.
Clear and pleasant. Wind Southwardly—thawed a good deal.

16. At home all day at Cards*—it snowing.
Finishd my Smith's Shop—that is the Carpenters work of it.
Constant Snow the whole day from the Northward.

17. At Home with Mr. Dick, &ca.

18. Went to Court and sold Colo. Colvil's L[an]d, returnd again at Night.
Carpenters went to Saw Plank at Doeg Run for finishing the Barn there.
Will put new girders into my Mill where they had Sunk.

19. Went to Belvoir with Mr. Dick, my Bro'r, and Mike, Tom and Sam went abt. the Overseer's House at Muddy hole.

20. Returnd from Do. by the Mill, Doeg Run and Muddy hole.
Plantations chiefly employd in getting out Wheat.
Clear, still and warm. Thawd a great deal.

21. Surveyd the Water courses of my Mt. Vernon Tract of Land, taking advant. of the Ice.
Very warm and still. Snow dissolving fast.

22. Fox hunting with Capt. Posey, started but catch'd nothing.
Davy, George, Jupiter and Ned, finishd sawing at Doeg Run and joind Mike, etca. abt. Overseer's House at Muddy hole.
Warm, still, and clear again—Snow almost gone.

23. Rid to Muddy hole, and directed paths to be cut for Fox hunting.

* Cards—whist and loo—seem to have been Washington's favorite indoor pastime, his winnings and somewhat greater loses at which are detailed in Hughes *Washington* II 206-209.

No Frost last Night—warm, and clear in the forenoon—cloudy with some Rain in the afternoon—afterwards clear again—Ice broke in the River.

24. Rid up to Toulston in order to Fox hunt it.

Lowering Morning, but very fine and Warm till 7 in the Afternoon, when the Wind shifted to No. East from So.

25. Confind by Rain with Mr. Fairfax and Mr. Alexander.

26. Went out with the Hounds but started no Fox. Some of the Hound run of upon a Deer.

Wind at No. West—cloudy and cold, with Spits of Snow.

27. Went out again. Started a Fox ab. 10, Run him till 3 and lost him.

28. Returnd Home—found Mr. Tomi Elsey there.

Wind at No. West and very cold.

29. Went to Belvoir with Mrs. Wn. &ca. after Dinner—left Mr. Ellzey at home.

River froze up again last Night.

30. Dined at Belvoir and returnd in the afternoon. Borrowed a hound from Mr. Whiting, as I did 2 from Mr. Alexr. the 28th.

Very hard frost last Night, Morng cold but more moderate afterwards. Wind gettg. Southwardly.

31. At Home alone all day.

Lowering—Wind Southwardly and moderate—Ice breaking and dispersing.

February

1. Rid round into the Neck and directed the running of a Fence there.

Carpenters all (except Will) went to Sawing Pailing for a Goose yard.

2. Rid to Muddy hole, Doeg Run and Mill

3. Fox hunting with Captn. Posey and Ld. [Lund] Washington. Started but catchd nothg.

4. Snowing all day, but not very fast—at home.

5. At home alone till Mr. Robt. Alexander came in the Evening.

6. Fox hunting with Mr. Alexander and Captn. Posey. Started but catchd nothing.

7. At home alone.

8. Rid to Muddy hole, Doeg Run and Mill, and in returng. met Mr. Alexander, Mr. Stoddard and Captn. Posey, who had just catchd 2 foxes. Returnd wt ym. [with them] to Dinner.

9. Went out Hunting again. Started a fox, run him four hours, and then lost him. Mr. Stoddard went home. Alexr stayd.

10. Rid to Muddy hole, Doeg Run, and Mill, Mr. Alexander going in the Morng. as Mr. Magowan did, to Williamsburg.

11. Went into the Neck and returnd to Dinner.

12. Fox hunting with Colo. Fairfax, Captn. McCarty, Mr. Chichester, Posey, Ellzey and Manley, who dind here, with Mrs. Fairfax and Miss Nicholas—catchd two foxes.

Misleading Statements of Washington Concerning his Bounty Land

I think that the failure of Washington's biographers to give an accurate account of his acquisition of the land under Governor Dinwiddie's proclamation of 1754 is attributable chiefly to the defect mentioned in my Introduction, of assuming that Washington's statements are necessarily true.[1]

There are two well-known statements of Washington concerning his acquisition of this land.

The first, dated March 12, 1773, in reply to an inquiry from a person interested in land allotted to Andrew Waggener, one of the officers in Washington's Virginia regiment, states:

"I did not on the one hand, pick the Surveys that were assigned me, either from the excellency of the Land, or convenience of situation; If I had, I should have avoided the largest Tract I now have (composing a full moiety of my quantum) as every inch of it, from the Surveyor's account, is subject to be overflowed . . . [and] I might add without much arrogance, that if it had not been for my unremitted attention to every favorable circumstance, not a single acre of Land would ever have been obtained."[2]

The second, dated April 25, 1798, to a person who apparently considered himself entitled to some of the proclamation land, states:

"The burthen of obtaining the Grants for 200,000 acres of land under Governor Dinwiddie's Proclamation of 1754, and indeed the greater part of the expence attending this business, from the first move that was made therein until the issuing of the Patents, were thrown upon me, nor has the latter been re-embursed to this day.

"It was with great difficulty after Peace was established

in the year 1763, that I could obtain a recognition of the above proclamation; and then, instead of assigning a district, and permitting every Claimant to locate his own quantum therein, we were compelled to take the *whole* quantity in twenty Surveys; or rather not allowed to exceed that number. This it was that occasioned so many names to be jumbled together in the same Patent and has caused the difficulties which have since occurred to the Patentees, to obtain their respective quantities. The same happened to myself; but rather than be at the trouble and expence of dividing with others, I bought, and exchanged, until I got intire tracts to myself."[3]

These letters, it will be observed, state or clearly imply the following:

1. The "greater part" of the expense of obtaining the 200,000 acres for the officers and soldiers was thrown on Washington and not reimbursed.

2. Washington was on the same footing as his officers and soldiers in having his allotments "jumbled together" in large tracts with those of other claimants.

3. He did not pick the surveys covering the land allotted to him for the excellence or convenient situation of the land.

4. Except for his efforts, no one would have obtained any of the land promised in Dinwiddie's proclamation.

The first two statements set forth above are demonstrably untrue, the third is extremely dubious in the light of other evidence, and the fourth is uncorroborated and open to serious question.

1. As to the contributors and amounts contributed to the expense of securing the grants, the minutes of a meeting of the Governor and Council on November 6, 1771, give the following figures:

Total direct contributions   £180.6

Washington's share of the direct contributions   £26.5
In addition, an item of "£12 or £15 for Postage of Letters" is listed. Assuming this was paid by Washington as the person in charge of preparing and submitting the claims, it brings his share to, say, £41.5 out of a total of £195.6[4] or about one-fifth. The correctness of this estimate is confirmed by Washington's petition to the Governor and Council of November 5,

1773, for a distribution of 18,900 additional acres among those who had contributed to the expense of the undertaking, in which he states his share to be 3,500 acres,[5] or about one-fifth of the total. In short, about a fifth, not the "greater part," of the expense seems to have been paid by Washington.

2. As to Washington's allotments being included with those of others in large surveys the evidence is perfectly clear that his original allotments, constituting much the large part of the land allotted to him, were in four surveys, each of which was to him alone,[6] and that the additional allotment to him in November, 1773, of 3,953 acres was not "jumbled together" with a large number of others but with only one other allotment—an allotment to George Muse.[7]

3. It is obviously impossible to prove conclusively the untruth of Washington's statement that he did not pick his surveys "from the excellency of the Land, or the convenience of the situation." But, considering that he was familiar with land values and had inspected the land for which he asked patents, it is almost incredible that sheer luck brought him what he described, and with apparent truth, as "the cream of the Country."[8]

4. Washington's statement that but for him "not a single acre of Land would ever have been obtained" may well be true as to himself and his fellow officers, but it seems improbable as to the enlisted men, since there is no evident reason to assume that, but for Washington's solicitation, the Governor and Council would have failed to carry out Governor Dinwiddie's promise to the men within a reasonable time after it became practicable to do so.

NOTES

PREFATORY NOTE

In my footnotes, W stands for Washington, or, when no additional initial or name is given, for George Washington.

Where authors' last names or abbreviated titles are used in the following notes, the reader may find full identification by consulting the Listing of Publications and Documents Cited, pp. 197-210.

FOREWORD

1. "To dissemble was for him [W] an impossibility," Stephenson and Dunn *Washington* (1940) I 33. For a somewhat similar recent statement, Freeman II 384.

CHAPTER ONE

1. In his statement of "lineage" dated May 2, 1792, W gave the date of his birth as "February 11th. (old style) 1732" and the place as "Westmoreland County," W XXXII 28 and 29. The date is confirmed by an entry in the W family Bible now at Mount Vernon in which the year is more accurately described as "1731/2." There is a facsimile of this entry in the frontispiece of Freeman I. W's reputed birthplace, later called Wakefield, was on Pope's Creek, near the Potomac, same 35-36, 46-47.

2. W wrote that his father was forty-nine at the time of his death, April 12, 1743, in W's statement of "lineage" May 2, 1792, W XXXII 28. As to Mary W, the *Gazette of the United States* (New York City) of Sept. 13, 1789, reporting her death on August 25, gives her age as eighty-two. In writing of their mother's death to his sister Elizabeth Lewis Sept. 13, 1789, W spoke of her as "four score," W XXX 399.

3. As to Augustine W's great grandfather, the Reverend Lawrence W, a Church of England clergyman of Essex county, England, Hoppin I 1-247, and as to Augustine's grandfather John W, John's son Lawrence W, and their respective wives, Ford *Washington Family* 70-81 and 85-90. George W wrote William A. W Feb. 27, 1798, that John W came to Virginia in 1657, W XXXVI 173; but Hoppin I 147 gives reasons to believe the date was late in 1656.

4. Augustine W's plantations and crops are mentioned in his will made in 1743, Ford *Washington Family* 94-96.

5. As to the Principio Company, Whitely "Principio Company," 63-68, 190-198, 288-295, and May *Principio to Wheeling* 39-47. As to Augustine W's connection with the company, trips to England on company matters, and his share in the company, Freeman I 37-42 and 55-56. (Note, however that Freeman's statements on p. 55 as to British restriction on co-

lonial export of bar iron and on the making of iron castings are mislead-
ing. No such restrictions were imposed until after Augustine's death.)

6. Augustine W a justice of the peace and vestryman, Freeman I 34, 41,
47 n. and 53, and sources there cited.

7. Hughes *Washington* I 21, for example, states that Augustine W
represented Prince William county in the House of Burgesses; but the
footnote cited for the statement gives no evidence to support it, and there
is no record in the journals of the House of Burgesses of his having
represented this or any other constituency.

8. Augustine W's move to Little Hunting Creek was some time between March 25, 1735, when he was still referred to in a deed of that
date "of Westmoreland County," Paullin "Birthplace of George Washington" 5, and Nov. 18, 1735, when he was admitted to the vestry of Truro
parish, Prince William (later Fairfax) county, Truro Parish Vestry Book,
Nov. 18, 1735, Slaughter *Hist. of Truro Parish* 9.

9. Augustine W's move to the plantation on the Rappahannock in
Brunswick parish, King George (now Stafford) county, in November, 1738,
is fixed by two deeds, the first a deed to him of this (the former Strother)
plantation dated November 2, 1738, in which he is still described as of
Prince William county, Hoppin "House" 81, the other a later deed to
him of an adjoining tract of land, dated Dec. 1, 1738, in which he is
now described as "of King George county," King "Washington's Boyhood
Home" 268.

10. Augustine W's death April 12, 1743, W's statement of "lineage,"
May 2, 1792, *W* XXXII 28. Augustine's will dated April 11, 1743, was
probated May 6, Ford *Washington Wills* 50, 51.

11. W's brothers and sisters, W's statement of "lineage" May 2, 1792,
W XXXII 28. Augustine's first wife, the mother of Lawrence and Augustine Jr., was Jane Butler, daughter of Caleb Butler of Westmoreland
county Virginia, same.

12. Mary W continued to live at the Ferry Farm until 1771 or 1772,
Freeman III 595-598 and sources there cited.

13. For a detailed account of Augustine W, based largely on the
reminiscences of George Washington Parke Custis, W's step-grandson, who
was not born until many years after Augustine's death, Freeman I 71-72 and
72 n.

14. W's mention of his father, W to the Mayor and Commonalty of
Fredericksburg Va. Feb. 14, 1784, *W* XXVII 332; W's statement of "lineage" May 2, 1792 *W* XXXII 26-30, 32; W's "Remarks" on a biographical
sketch of him by David Humphreys, probably written soon after Humphreys' stay at Mount Vernon in the summer of 1786, *W* XXIX 36. (My
surmise as to the approximate date of the "Remarks" is based on W's
correspondence with Humphreys in 1785 and W's diary entries in 1786,
W XXXVIII 203 and *W Diaries* III 97-108.)

15. Early biographers in praise of Mary W, *Sparks* (1837) I 4-5; Irving
Washington (1855) I 23; and Custis *Recollections* (1860) 131-140.

16. In his *Young Washington* 10-11, republished in *By Land and
By Sea* (1953) 164, Morison wrote of Mary W, ". . . the cold record of
her own and her sons' letters shows her to have been grasping, querulous
and vulgar. She was a selfish and exacting mother, whom most of her
children avoided as soon and as early as they could; to whom they did
their duty, but rendered little love, . . . [who] opposed almost every-

thing that he [George] did for the public good . . . [and whose] selfishness lost George an opportunity to become midshipman in the Royal Navy. . . ."

17. Examples of disparagement of Mary W by others than Morison are Freeman I (1948) xix-xx, 193, 195, rebutted in my review of his first two volumes, 3 *W. & M. Q.* VI (1949) 114-118, and Ford *True Washington* 17-18. I think the biographers who denigrate Mary W as of this early period are unduly influenced by the evidence that when she was old and thought herself impoverished, she was querulous and a great trial to W, as to which see same 18-21. (By 1787 Mary was afflicted with cancer of the breast, Dr. Charles Mortimer to W May 4, 1787, and Burgess Ball to W Aug. 25, 1789, Washington Papers L.C.)

18. W's diaries and books of account indicate that he continued to live with his mother until the winter of 1754-1755. The only time he spoke of living elsewhere before 1755 was in an undated, early letter stating "my Place of Residence is at present at his Lordships," i.e. at Lord Fairfax's, *W* I 15-16; but there is no reason to suppose this was long continued. So long as Lawrence lived, George may well have visited often at Mount Vernon, which was "about 7 Hours and a half" from Fredericksburg, *W Diaries* I 298.

19. Correspondence concerning sending George to sea, William Fairfax and Robert Jackson to Lawrence W Sept. 10 and 18, 1746, Conway *Barons* 237-240; Joseph Ball to Mary W May 19, 1747, Freeman I 198-199. I have found no evidence supporting the intimation in Hughes *Washington* I 33-34 that George had been in some kind of a "scrape" at this time or the statement in Weems *Washington* 47 that the "rank of midshipman was procured for him on board a British man of war" which his mother dissuaded him from accepting.

20. Mary W's alarm over W's joining Braddock, W to Capt. Robert Orme April 2, 1755, *W* I 109.

21. Mary W's "uneasiness" over W's intention of re-entering the army, W to Mary W Aug. 14, 1755, same 159.

22. Legal papers in the records of Hanover county Virginia for 1733 disclose that over four-fifths of men signing these papers signed their names, while 41 of 57 women signed by mark, Meade *Henry* 44.

23. A typical letter of Mary W—to her brother Joseph Ball, July 2, 1760—is in Conway *Washington* p. xliii. For letters similar to Mary's in defective punctuation and spelling, Abiah Franklin, Benjamin Franklin's mother, Jane Mecom, his sister, and Deborah Franklin, his wife, Van Doren *Franklin-Mecom Letters* 45, 74, 137; Anna Ray Ward to Gov. Samuel Ward of R. I. (1765) Knollenberg *Ward* 18-19 and Martha W in Chapter 12 of this book.

24. In 1787 W wrote of his "revered Mother by whose maternal hand . . . I was led from Childhood," W to the Mayor and Commonalty of Fredericksburg Feb. 14, 1784, *W* XXVII 332. I have found no reason to doubt the sincerity of this statement as applied to the period here under consideration. As to Mary being a trial to George in later life, see note 17 above.

25. For conventional accounts of W's schooling, see, for examples, Ford *True Washington* 63; Hughes *Washington* I 21; Freeman I 64 n., 74 n.

26. W's early exercise books are described and illustrated in *W* I 1-5. For the famous "Rules of Civility and Decent Behaviour" copied by W

from Francis Hawkins' *Youth's Behaviour,* see Moore *George Washington's Rules.*

27. As to "Piper," George Mason to W June 12, 1756, "I take the Liberty to address You on Behalf of my Neighbour & Your old schoolfellow Mr. Piper," *Letters to W* I 277. I have not found W's reply if any. Perhaps Piper was Harry Piper of Alexandria, Va., often referred to in W's correspondence and diaries.

28. In his statement of "lineage" May 2, 1792, W said Lawrence W was "about 34" when he died, *W* XXXII 28, which was in July, 1752, thus indicating that Lawrence was about fourteen when W was born.

29. William Fairfax to Lawrence W Sept. 9, 1746, as "to putting Him [George] to sea with good Recommendation," Conway *Barons* 238. Morison *Young Washington* 11 states that Mary W's "selfishness lost George an opportunity to become midshipman in the Royal Navy. . . ." But Morison cites no source for this statement as to W's having an opportunity to become a midshipman, and I have found none except an assertion to this effect by Parson Weems of cherry tree fame (Weems *Washington* 47), whose statements are to be taken with a large grain of salt.

30. Joseph Ball to Mary W May 19, 1747, acknowledging Mary's letter of Dec. 13, 1746, and opposing the proposal to send George to sea, Freeman I 198-199.

31. Lawrence W's attendance at school at Appleby, Westmoreland county, England, Hoppin I 244; Richard Yates to Lawrence W Nov. 13, 1748, Conway *Barons* 108.

32. Lawrence W's commission, now at Mount Vernon, is endorsed by Governor William Gooch of Virginia as delivered to him on July 10, 1740. I have not found any evidence of how long Lawrence had been back in Virginia when the commission was delivered. The minutes of the Virginia Council Aug. 6, 1740, record Gooch as having "acquainted the Board that He proposed that Mr. Lawrence Washington, Mr. Charles Walker, Mr. Richard Bushrod and Mr. James Mercer should be Captains in the Forces raised here . . . ," *Va. Exec. Council Journals* V 22.

33. As to the American regiment in the expedition against Cartagena during the British-Spanish War or so-called War of Jenkins's Ear, Jones "American Regiment" 1-20.

34. Gen. Thomas Wentworth wrote Lawrence W April 17, 1743, that his letter of Jan. 17 "confirms the account of your safe arrivall in Virginia," Conway *Barons* 104, from which I deduce that he had arrived not long before Jan. 17, 1743.

35. Lawrence W's residence at his father Augustine's Little Hunting Creek plantation is indicated by a provision in Augustine's will dated April 11, 1743, leaving him "all that Plantation and Tract of Land at Hunting Creek . . . and all the household Furniture whatsoever now in & upon or which have been Commonly possessed by my said son . . . ," Ford *Washington Wills* 41.

36. Lawrence W was calling his plantation "Mount Vernon" by July 19, 1743, as we know from a letter to him from Richard Yates dated Nov. 13, 1743, stating "You tell me . . . on the 19th of July, that you had then taken your residence upon *Mount Vernon* . . . ," Conway *Barons* 106-107.

37. The supposition that Mount Vernon was named after Admiral Vernon is supported by the fact that Lawrence served with and liked

Vernon, as we know from a letter of May 30, 1741, from Lawrence to his father stating, "I have remained on board Admiral Vernon's ship ever since we left Hispaniola vastly to my satisfaction," *Mag. Am. Hist.* II (1878) 437. Also Robert Hunter, Jr., wrote in his diary of a visit to W on Nov. 16, 1785, that Lawrence W had named Mount Vernon after Admiral Vernon, "Washington and Mount Vernon" 21-22.

38. Lawrence W's inheritance under his father's will of the Little Hunting Creek (Mount Vernon) plantation and other property including his share in "the Iron works in which I am Concerned," Ford *Washington Wills* 41, 45.

39. Lawrence W appointed Adjutant General at a salary of £150 a year *Va. Exec. Council Journals* V 117, 136. The Adjutant General was responsible for "instructing the Officers and Soldiers in the Use and Exercise of their Arms . . . [and] bringing the Militia to a more regular Discipline . . . ," same 412.

40. Lawrence W was appointed a justice of the peace for Fairfax county, Oct. 21, 1743, *Va. Exec. Council Journals* V 132. Lawrence W was a member of the House of Burgesses at its session beginning Sept. 4, 1744, *Va. House Journals* 1742-1749 p. 78, but I have not found the date of his election. As to his service in the House, same 78-386 *passim*.

41. Lawrence W married Ann Fairfax, daughter of William Fairfax, July 19, 1743, W's statement of "lineage" May 2, 1792, W XXXII 28; Richard Yates to Lawrence Nov. 13, 1743, acknowledging Lawrence's letter of July 19, mentioning Mount Vernon, and adding, "You . . . give me to understand that in a few hours after writing you might probably be upon your *Mons Veneris*," Conway *Barons* 106-107; and William Beverly to Lord Fairfax July 27, 1743, referring to Lawrence's recent marriage, Ford "Beverly Letters" 235.

42. As to William Fairfax, Harrison *Landmarks* 340-341. He was issuing grants on behalf of Lord Fairfax as early as 1741, Land Office Records of the Proprietary of the Northern Neck, E 300, Va. State Library, Richmond. He was appointed to the Virginia Council in 1744, *Va. Exec. Council Journals* V 140, and on the death of Thomas Lee in 1751 became the senior member of the Council, as evidenced by the order of procedure at meetings of the Council Oct. 1751 to May 2, 1752, same 354-396 *passim*.

43. W to John Augustine W, May 28, 1755, *W* I 129, as to W's particular obligations to William Fairfax. The term "Old Gentleman" was probably used to distinguish William from his son George William Fairfax.

44. As to Governor Robert Dinwiddie, *D.A.B.* and Koontz *Dinwiddie passim*. Dinwiddie was actually lieutenant-governor; the governorship of Virginia was generally a sinecure held by some English or Scottish nobleman who never even came to the colony.

45. As to the Ohio Company, Bailey *Ohio Company* (1939); Mulkearn *Mercer Papers* (1954); James *Ohio Company* (1958). As to Lawrence W's partnership in the company from its formation in 1747 until his death in 1752, when his executors sold his interest to Lunsford Lomax, Mulkearn *Mercer Papers* 2-3, 176. Lawrence's brother Augustine was also a partner from the beginning. He sold his interest in 1753, same 2, 178. There is no evidence that George W was ever a partner in the company.

46. Dinwiddie bought a share (one-twentieth interest) in the Ohio Company March 27, 1750, same 5, and there is no evidence that he ever sold his share.

47. Dinwiddie to Lawrence W March 20, 1751, to be delivered by William Fairfax, commenting on the death of Thomas Lee, pointing out that the management of the Ohio Company would now devolve on Lawrence if his health permitted, and sending his and his wife's "kind respects" to Lawrence and his wife, Conway *Barons* 278-279.

48. W's early surveying, *W Col. Traveller* 5-7. He bought a Gunter scale, presumably for use in surveying, Sept. 20, 1747, same 7. Some surveying instruments were among the items inventoried in Augustine's estate, King "Washington's Boyhood Home" 271, and these may well have been allotted to George as part of the share of his father's estate to which he was entitled under Augustine's will, Ford *Washington Wills* 44. There are several facsimiles of W's early surveys in Sawyer *Washington* Part 1, I 104 and 106 and Martin *Washington Atlas* 3, 19, 20, 21.

49. W's diary entries March 11 to April 13, 1748, captioned "A Journal of My Journey over the Mountains begun Fryday the 11th of March 1747/8," *W Diaries* I 1-12.

50. W's diary entry March 23, 1748, describing the Indian war dance, same 7.

51. W's appointment as Surveyor of Culpeper county July 29, 1747, Howe *Hist. Coll. of Va.* 237.

52. W's survey for Richard Barnes in Culpeper county, July 1749, *W, Col. Traveller* 22.

53. As to W's extensive surveying from the fall of 1749 to 1751, same 24-32 and *W* I 18. In W's surveys in Frederick county for Barnaby Mc-Hantry and William Baker, dated Nov. 9, 1749, John Lonem and Edward Corder were his chainmen, and William Baker his marker, Washington Papers, L.C. There are five Frederick county surveys of W for various persons from March, 1750, to March, 1751, in the deCoppet Collection at the Princeton U. Lib.

54. W to "Richard," undated (probably *ca.* November, 1749) stating "a Doubloon is my constant gain . . . [weather permitting] and sometimes six Pistoles," *W* I 17. W valued a doubloon at £4.6.7 in Oct., 1748, and two pistoles at £2.3.2 in 1749, *W. Col. Traveller* 18, 21. This was presumably in terms of Virginia currency, which normally was worth 80 per cent of sterling, Wright *Am. Negotiator* p. lxii.

55. See Sparks II 422-423 for details of Lawrence W's illness. I have not found any reference to the precise nature of the illness, but seeking relief in a mild climate, the lingering nature of the malady, the nature of the treatment and George's reference to Lawrence's "Cough," *W* I 13, indicate that he was suffering from tuberculosis of the lungs.

56. Barbados trip, W's diary entries Oct. 4, 1751, to Feb. 4, 1752, *W Diaries* I 17-36 supplemented by fragments of entries Sept. 28 to Oct. 3, 1751, in Toner *Daily Journal of Washington in 1751-1752* 21-23. Curiously, I have seen only one reference to W being pock-marked—in a letter from "a gentleman of Maryland" published in London in 1780 and attributed to John Bell, Baker *Early Sketches of Washington* 77. Portraits of W I have seen show no pockmarks.

57. W's meeting with Dinwiddie, *W Diaries* I 35. The date of the entry concerning this meeting is torn off; but the sequence of events described, following the entry for Jan. 26, 1752, indicates that the date of the meeting was Jan. 28. (While W was in Barbados, Mary McDaniel was convicted of "robing the Cloaths of Mr. George Washington when

he was washing in the river some time last Summer" and was sentenced to fifteen lashes on her bare back, Spotsylvannia County Order Book Dec. 3, 1751, *Tyler's Quarterly* VII [1926] 176-177.)

58. W's resumption of surveying (March, 1752) on return from Barbados and purchase of 552 acres of land on Bullskin Creek, a western tributary of the Shenandoah, for £115 *W. Col. Traveller* 38. W had previously (1750) acquired land on this Bullskin Creek, Freeman I 243-244.

59. W to William Fauntleroy May 20, 1752, *W* I 22, enclosing letter to "Miss Betsy," Fauntleroy's daughter. I have not found the enclosed letter. As to William Fauntleroy and his family, Freeman I 262.

60. Betsy Fauntleroy and her husband Bowler Cocke, same 262 n.

61. Lawrence W's return to Virginia by June 20, 1752, is known by the fact that his will of that date was witnessed by neighbors in Virginia, Ford *Washington Wills* 78. George Mason to George W or one of his brothers July 29, 1752, speaks of Lawrence W as having just been buried, *Letters to W* I frontispiece.

62. W to Dinwiddie June 10, 1752, soliciting appointment as one of the proposed district adjutants, *W* XXXVII 477.

63. Division of the Adjutancy into four districts, W's appointment to the Southern District Dec. 13, 1752, and statement of rank and pay, *Va. Exec. Council Journals* V 412-413. W to Dinwiddie Aug. 21, 1754 *W* I 99 discloses that by this time he had been transferred to the Northern Neck (his home) District.

64. Washington wrote the Reverend G. W. Snyder Sept. 25, 1798, that, far from "Presiding over the English lodges in this Country," as Snyder supposed, he had not even been in a Masonic lodge "more than once or twice, within the last thirty years," *W* XXXVI 453.

65. W was initiated a Mason in the lodge at Fredericksburg, Va., Nov. 4, 1752, Freeman I 267 and Hayden *Washington and His Masonic Compeers* 23.

CHAPTER TWO

1. Gov. Dinwiddie to the Board of Trade June 16, 1753, concerning French encroachments in the upper Ohio Valley on territory claimed by the British, C.O. 5; 1327:639-640, Pub. Rec. Office.

2. Royal instruction for delivery of message to the French Aug. 28, 1753, Labaree *Royal Instructions* I 414-415. (Dinwiddie had previously sent William Russell with a letter of inquiry to the French but it had not been delivered, Minutes of the Va. Council, June 14, 1753, *Va. Exec. Council Journals* V 433-434, and Dinwiddie to the Board of Trade Nov. 17, 1753, Sparks II 430).

3. Lord Holderness (often spelled Holdernesse) to Dinwiddie Aug. 28, 1753, Bailey *Ohio Company* 201-203.

4. Dinwiddie's presentation of the royal instruction to the Va. Council, attended by William Fairfax Oct. 22, 1753, *Va. Exec. Council Journals* V 442.

5. W's offer was presented to the Council and accepted Oct. 27, 1753, and the papers, prepared by a committee of the Council headed by Fairfax, were delivered to W at a Council meeting on Oct. 31, same 444-445. The message to the French commandant, dated Oct. 31, is in *N. Y.*

Col. Doc. X 258; the commission and instructions dated Oct. 30, and the undated passport are in Sparks II 428-429.

6. W's instructions of Oct. 30, 1753, as to obtaining information, same 428.

7. W's journal of his journey to Fort Le Boeuf is published in *W Diaries* I 41-67. W's statement as to its preparation from his "rough Minutes" is at same 41. The minutes themselves have not been found.

8. Christopher Gist's diary of his trip to Fort Le Boeuf is in Darlington *Gist* 80-87, 147.

9. W's diary entries Oct. 31 to Nov. 25, 1753, concerning the first leg of his trip to the French Commandant and arrival at Logstown, *W Diaries* I 43-46. The fact that W traveled by horseback appears from a diary entry of Dec. 23, same 63.

10. Intelligence obtained by W at Logstown on Nov. 25, 1753, same 46-48. Washington's interpreter Jacob Van Braam apparently thought that, in speaking of Illinois, the French deserters said "Isles Noires," since W's diary entries relating to Illinois are to the "Black-Islands."

11. Trip from Logstown to Venango and intelligence obtained by W there, Nov. 30 to Dec. 7, 1755, same 54-57.

12. Trip from Venango to Fort Le Boeuf and presentation of Dinwiddie's letter to the commander Dec. 7 to 12, 1755, same 58-59.

13. Le Gardeur de St. Pierre's reply to Dinwiddie Dec. 15, 1753, the French original, *8 Pa. Arch.* V 3642-3643; English translation *London Magazine* for June, 1754, XXIII 275.

14. W's description of Fort Le Boeuf and the French forces there, Dec. 13, 1755, *W Diaries* I 59.

15. Le Gardeur's supplying of W with food, liquor, and a canoe, and W's trip from Fort Le Boeuf to Venango Dec. 15 to 22, 1753, same 61-62.

16. The Indian's shooting at W and Gist Dec. 27, 1753, same 64. Gist's account of this incident differs from W's; Gist says the Indian was alone.

17. Mishap of the raft on the Allegheny, Dec. 28, 1753, *W Diaries* I 65. W wrote that Gist and he crossed at "Shannapins." The location of Shannapins is shown in the map referred to in note 19 below.

18. Journey to Frazier's and Williamsburg Dec. 29, 1753, to Jan. 16, 1754, *W Diaries* I 65-67.

19. W's map of the region traversed by him on his trip to Fort Le Boeuf is discussed in Ford "Washington's Map of the Ohio," *Mass. Hist. Soc. Proc.* LXI, 71-79, and a fine reproduction of it is in the pocket at the back of that volume. A less good reproduction is in *W* I facing p. 31.

20. W's diary entries for Nov. 23 and 24, 1753, concerning the superiority of the Forks of the Ohio as a site for a fort over that proposed by the Ohio Company, *W Diaries* I 44-45.

21. Distribution of W's diary, Dinwiddie to the Board of Trade Jan. 29, 1754, and to Lord Holderness, Secretary of State for the Southern Department, March 12, referring to his earlier letter of Jan. 29, Sparks II 431 and *Dinwiddie* I 93; Dinwiddie to many of the colonial governors, same 85-91, *passim.*

22. As to the printing and reprints of the diary entitled *The Journal of Major George Washington sent by the Hon. Robert Dinwiddie . . . to*

the *Commandant of the French Forces on the Ohio* . . . (Williamsburg, 1754), Ford "Washington's Map of the Ohio" *Mass. Hist. Soc. Proc.* LXI 72-74. Extracts from the diary are in the *London Magazine* for June 1754, XXIII 271-274.

CHAPTER THREE

1. Capt. William Trent's commission and instructions dated Jan. 26, 1754, are in *Mercer Papers* 82-83. W's commission has not been found but a letter of Gov. Dinwiddie to Trent dated Jan. 27, refers to W's having a commission, same 81.

2. Undated instructions to W., *Dinwiddie* I 59.

3. Vote of funds, Acts of Feb., 1754, Session Ch. 1, Hening *Va. Statutes* VI 417-420, and appointment of Fry and number of men, Dinwiddie to Secretary of State Lord Holderness, March 10, and to Board of Trade May 12, *Dinwiddie* I 93-96, and 101. The three hundred men were exclusive of seventy men raised by Capt. Trent, Dinwiddie to Gov. James Hamilton of Pa. March 21, same I 120. Fry's commission dated Feb. 27, and his instructions dated "March 1754" are in Toner *W Journal in 1754* 13-14. The *D.A.B.* has a good biographical sketch of Fry.

4. W's commission as lieutenant-colonel has not been found, but, according to his diary, it was dated March 15, 1754, *W Diaries* I 73. As to his seeking the commission, W to Richard Corbin, a member of the Va. Council, March 1754, and Corbin to W, undated, *W* I 34-35, 35 n.

5. Information of proposed French descent of Ohio and Dinwiddie's order to W, March 15, 1754, *Dinwiddie* I 106-107.

6. W's departure for the Ohio April 2, 1754, *W Diaries* I 73-74.

7. W to Charles Lawrence April 26, 1763, giving his measurements, *W* II 395-396. Similar statements by W as to height in 1759 and 1761, same 339, 372. I cannot account for the discrepancy between these statements and Tobias Lear's note of Dec. 15, 1799, that W's corpse measured "6 ft. 3¼ inches exact," Ford XIV 252.

8. Uniform of Virginia officers described by W in regimental orders Sept. 17, 1755, as a "blue . . . Coat to be faced and cuffed with Scarlet and trimmed with Silver: A Scarlet waistcoat, with Silver Lace; blue Breeches, and a Silver-laced Hat," *W* I 176.

9. French expel Virginians from Forks of Ohio, Ensign (Second Lieutenant) Edward Ward's report of May 9, 1754, in *Virginia Gazette* of May 10, Mulkearn *Mercer Papers* 85-88. Ward's deposition of May 7, Darlington *Gist* 275-278; W to Gov. Horatio Sharpe of Md. April 27, *W* I 43. Contrecoeur's summons of April 17 is in 1 *Mass. Hist. Soc. Coll.* VI 141-142.

10. W to Dinwiddie, April 25, 1754, Ward's report "this day," *W* I 40. (W's diary, *W Diaries* I 75 and Donald H. Kent *Contrecoeur's Copy of George Washington's Journal for 1754* (1952) 15, says April 22.)

11. W to Dinwiddie April 25, 1754, and to Gov. Sharpe April 27, as to his change of plan, *W* I 41 and 43-44.

12. Contrecoeur's summons dated May 23, 1754, Virginia State Library, and his orders to Jumonville, also dated May 23, as to delivery of the summons and other matters, Leduc *Washington* 163-165 (English translation in same 83-85).

13. W learns from the Indian chief, the Half King, and from Christopher Gist of an approaching French party of fifty men said to be in-

tending to attack the English, W to Dinwiddie May 27, 1754, *W* I 53-54 and W's diary for May 27, *W Diaries* I 86-87.

14. Message received by W from the Half King on the night of May 27, 1754, that he believed the French party reported by Gist was camped about six miles from W, W to Dinwiddie May 29, *W* I 63 and W's diary for May 27, *W Diaries* I 87.

15. Attack on Jumonville's party, W to Dinwiddie May 29, 1754, *W* I 64, 66. A letter from W to his brother Jack on May 31, concerning the attack adds nothing of importance, but contains the oft-quoted statement "I heard the bullets whistle, and, believe me, there is something charming in the sound," same 70. W to Dinwiddie June 3, says there were only thirty-three Virginians and seven Indians "with arms" in the attack, same 73.

16. Report on Jumonville affair, Contrecoeur to the Marquis Du Quesne June 2, 1754, Leduc *Washington* 93-95, and Druillon, one of the French prisoners, to Dinwiddie June 17, *Dinwiddie* I 225. (I have not found Druillon's first name.)

17. Trevelyan's and Freeman's glorification of W, Trevelyan *American Revolution* I 53; Freeman I 351, 373.

18. French prisoners sent under guard first to Winchester and then to Alexandria, W to Dinwiddie May 29, 1754, *W* I 67; Dinwiddie to W June 1 and 2, *Dinwiddie* I 186 and 189; Gov. Sharpe to Dinwiddie Dec. 10, *Sharpe* I 142; and Dinwiddie to Sir Thomas Robinson Oct. 1, 1755, *Dinwiddie* II 227.

19. French prisoners, other than a Monsieur La Force, shipped to England, Dinwiddie to Robinson Oct. 1, 1755, same II 227-228. (La Force, who was alleged to have robbed some of the British colonial frontier settlers, was still a prisoner as late as August, 1756, same II 228, 484).

CHAPTER FOUR

1. Proposed inclusion in the expedition of the North Carolina troops under Col. James Innes and of three independent companies of British regulars, Dinwiddie to various correspondents May 4, June 17, and June 20, 1754, *Dinwiddie* I 146, 200, and 213. As to Innes' royal commission as captain, Dinwiddie to Henry Fox, Secretary at War, July 24, 1754, same 246.

2. Innes' commission from Dinwiddie as Commander-in-Chief, June 4, 1754, same 194-195. Even before Fry's death, Dinwiddie had apparently contemplated giving Innes this post on his arrival in Va., Dinwiddie to Innes March 23, same 126.

3. Dinwiddie's hope that the appointment of Innes would avoid disputes over right of command, Dinwiddie to Gov. Horatio Sharpe of Md. June 20, 1754, same 213.

4. As to the death of Col. Joshua Fry May 31, 1754, sketch of Fry in *D.A.B.* He was fatally injured by a fall from his horse, Gov. Sharpe to John Sharpe April 19, 1755, *Sharpe* I 198. W was appointed colonel of the Va. regiment and Major George Muse was promoted to lieutenant colonel soon after Fry's death, Dinwiddie to W June 4, 1754, *Dinwiddie* I 193. I have not found W's commission.

5. W's letter of thanks to Dinwiddie June 10, 1754, *W* I 74.

6. W to Dinwiddie June 15, 1754, concerning his dispute with Capt. James Mackay, *W* I 80-83. (W's letter is undated but the date is determinable from W's statement that he would continue his march to Redstone "tomorrow," which his diary records as taking place June 16, *W Diaries* I 93.

7. Mackay was commissioned ensign or cornet (second lieutenant) in the British regular army, March 17, 1737, War Office Lists 1736-1754, Index 5436 fol. 110 Pub. Rec. Office, London.

8. W to Dinwiddie June 15, 1754, as to Mackay's position, *W* I 81, 83.

9. In replying June 27, 1754, to W's letter concerning the dispute with Mackay, Dinwiddie, saying he was "excessively hurried," suggested that W consult Col. Innes, *Letters to W* I 13-14. Dinwiddie's puzzlement appears from his letter of July 24 to Henry Fox, *Dinwiddie* I 246. An order issued by George II Nov. 12, 1754, *Letters to W* I facing p. 56, though ambiguous, apparently meant that captains holding a royal commission should outrank all provincial officers, even generals.

10. Building of fort (later called Fort Necessity) at the Great Meadows from May 30 to June 3, 1754, W's diary for May 30, *W Diaries* I 90, and W to Dinwiddie June 3, *W* I 73. As to the location of the Great Meadows, see the map in Showalter "Travels of W" 12.

11. Arrival of Lieut. Col. George Muse with the last body of troops of the Virginia regiment, W's diary for June 9, 1754, *W Diaries* I 92. (As the Muse's recent promotion from major to lieutenant-colonel, note 4, above.)

12. W's advance as far as Gist's plantation and distance from the Great Meadows, W's minutes of a Council of War June 28, 1754, *Letters to W* I 16-17. As to the location of Gist's plantation, Showalter "Travels of W" 12. As to leaving Mackay's company at the Great Meadows, W to Dinwiddie June 15, *W* I 83.

13. Lord Albemarle, British Ambassador to France, to Sir Thomas Robinson, Secretary of State, Aug. 21, 1754, reporting a French protest concerning the "treacherous" killing of Jumonville, but adding he had been assured that DuQuesne had been instructed, despite the provocation, "to behave in the most moderate manner," Pease *Anglo-French* 49-50.

14. Capt. Claude Contrecoeur, commander at Fort Duquesne, sends Capt. Louis Coulon de Villiers with four hundred French and a number of allied Indians to retaliate Jumonville's death, Villiers' journal June 28, 1754, *Olden Time* II 210-213.

15. W receives report of proposed French expedition, W's minutes of council June 28, 1754. These indicate that the receipt of the report of the French force and the decision to retreat both took place on that date, *Letters to W* I 16-17. An undated letter of Maj. Adam Stephen in the *Maryland Gazette* of Aug. 29, indicates that the report was received June 29, the retreat was decided upon June 30, and the fort was reached July 1, Ambler *Washington* 214.

16. W's minutes of council of war June 28, 1754, states "We had only about 25 head of Live Cattle . . . for 400 men," *Letters to W* I 17. Innes to Gov. James Hamilton of Pa. (undated), published in the *Maryland Gazette* of Aug. 1, Ambler *Washington* 213, said of the 400 men, including "a good many . . . sick and out of Order." Dinwiddie to Board of Trade July 24, said the combined British forces were but "few more than 300 Men," *Dinwiddie* I 239.

17. All of W's Indian allies had left him, Robert Callendar to Gov. Hamilton July 16, 1754, Gipson *British Empire* VI 45 n. The Indian chief, Half King, later complained that W "took upon him to Command the Indians as his Slaves," Conrad Weiser's journal Sept. 3, Wallace *Weiser* 367.

18. French attack on July 3, 1754, and British casualties, *Virginia Gazette* July 19, 1754, in Ambler *Washington* 211 and Dinwiddie to Board of Trade July 24, *Dinwiddie* I 239-241. The supposed French and allied Indian loss of six hundred killed and wounded mentioned by Din-widdie (I 240) was apparently grossly exaggerated. According to Villiers, his losses were only two killed and seventy wounded, Villiers' journal July 3, *N.Y. Col. Doc.* X 262.

19. Articles of Capitulation July 3, 1754, Leduc *Washington* 219-227, English translation, *Sharpe* I 78-79.

20. Criticism, Gov. Sharpe of Md. to Lord Baltimore Aug. 8, 1754, *Sharpe* I 80. *The Present State of North America* (London 1755) de-nounced the capitulation as "the most infamous a British Subject ever put his Hand to," Wroth *Am. Bookshelf* 40-41.

21. W to unidentified correspondent as to mistranslation by his inter-preter, Jacob Van Braam, March 27, 1757, Sparks II 464 with *W Diaries* I 72. See also Sharpe to Lord Bury Nov. 5, 1754, *Sharpe* I 116. (In "Col. Stephens life written by himself for B. Rush in 1775" *Pa. Mag. Hist.* XVIII [1894] 43-50, Stephen asserted that he had refused to sign the Articles because of their change of "Assassination." I disregard this state-ment, indicating that there was no mistranslation, as worthless because made long after the event and also because it conflicts with a statement of Stephen soon after the capitulation, Ambler *Washington* 215).

22. I was led to question the truth of this explanation not only because of the circumstantial evidence discussed in the text but by the fact that, in studying W's later career, I had found evidence of his having on two occasions thrown the whole blame on others for decisions, one disastrous in its consequences, the other threatening disaster, in which he had participated, Knollenberg *Washington and the Revolution* 134-139, 157-165.

23. W's recommendation of Van Braam for a captaincy, W to Din-widdie June 12, 1754, *W* I 78.

24. Dinwiddie to Board of Trade July 24, 1754, concerning the capitu-lation, *Dinwiddie* I 239-241. (There is a further, possible relevant though inconclusive circumstance, namely that soon after the capitulation, while Van Braam was held as a hostage by the French, the Va. House of Burgesses in effect censured him by omitting his name from a resolution of thanks to officers of the Va. regiment, Aug. 30, 1754, *Va. House Journals* for 1752-1755 p. 198; but on receipt of a letter (now missing) from Van Braam, after his release, presumably presenting his side of the story, the House voted him back pay, a bonus, and recommendation for pro-motion, March 10, 1760, and March 24 and 30, 1761, same for 1758-1761 pp. 166, 227, and 238.)

25. Only 150 men of Va. regiment remain and N.C. force disbanded for lack of funds, Dinwiddie to Sharpe Sept. 6, 1754, and to Lord Gran-ville, Sept. 23, *Dinwiddie* I 304 and 331.

26. Washington in Alexandria, Va., to recruit, and period he remained there, Letters of W from Alexandria to William Fairfax and to Din-

widdie Aug. 11 and 20, 1754, *W* I 89, 96, and Col. Innes to W Sept. 27, referring to a letter (now missing) of W from Alexandria dated Sept. 22, *Letters to W* I 47.

27. Arrival of Gov. Arthur Dobbs of N. C. in early Oct., 1754, with funds for Dinwiddie and commission and orders for Gov. Sharpe, Sharpe to Lord Baltimore, to Cecilius Calvert and to Sir Thomas Robinson Oct. 25, *Sharpe* I 102-104 and Dinwiddie to Robinson Oct. 25, *Dinwiddie* I 352-354.

28. Sharpe's royal commission as lieutenant-colonel dated July 5, 1754, is in *Md. Arch.* XXXI (1911) 52. His orders are in Robinson to Sharpe, July 5, same 52-53.

29. Conference of Dinwiddie, Sharpe, and Dobbs at Williamsburg Oct. 19 to 25, 1754, and plan of operations, Sharpe to Robinson Oct. 25 and to William and John Sharpe Nov. 3, *Sharpe* I 104-106 and 109; undated "Plan of Operations" enclosed in Dinwiddie to Lord Halifax Oct. 25, *Dinwiddie* I 367.

30. I have not found Dinwiddie's order dissolving the regimental organization of the Virginia regiment; but William Fitzhugh to W Nov. 4, 1754, *Letters to W* I 54-55, indicates that such an order had been issued before that date.

31. W's threat to resign is indicated by Fitzhugh's letter cited in the preceding footnote.

32. W to Fitzhugh Nov. 15, 1754, refusing to reconsider resigning, *W* I 104-106.

33. Dinwiddie to Sir Thomas Robinson Nov. 16, 1754, stating "Colo. Washington . . . has resigned his Commission," *Dinwiddie* I 403.

34. Adam Stephen's remaining in service after W's resignation is evident from Dinwiddie to Stephen Nov. 18, 1754, same 411.

35. As to Stephen's appointment as commander, Dinwiddie to Stephen, Dec. 12, 1754, same I 420. Stephen had succeeded Muse as lieutenant-colonel on the latter's resignation the preceding July, Dinwiddie to Stephen Aug. 1, same I 263. (Muse had incensed his fellow officers, after the surrender at Fort Necessity, by stating that he and the rest of the officers, without exception, had been guilty of cowardice there, Capt. William la Peyronie to W Sept. 5, *Letters to W* I 40).

CHAPTER FIVE

1. I have not found the exact date when W moved to Mount Vernon, but a letter from him to Robert Orme dated March 15, 1755, is headed "Mount Vernon," *W* I 107.

2. Devise of the Mount Vernon (Prince William county) property in the will of George's father, Augustine W, dated April 11, 1743, Ford *Washington Wills* 41, 47. In W's statement of quitrents for 1761, this property is listed as having 2,126 acres, *W* II 390.

3. Since Lawrence W's will, naming his daughter Sarah as a beneficiary, was dated June 20, 1752, only five weeks before he died (July 26), his daughter presumably was still living at the time of his death—a presumption confirmed by the memorandum cited in footnote 5, below.

4. Lawrence W's devise of a contingent remainder interest in Mount Vernon (now in Fairfax county after a division of Prince William county)

to George W, with remainder over in fee to Lawrence's brother Augustine, same 74, 75-76.

5. Sarah W's death is referred to in a memorandum of agreement of Dec. 10, 1754, signed by her mother, Ann Lee (formerly Mrs. Lawrence W), quoted in Freeman II 3. The agreement indicates that Sarah had no issue.

6. The lease to W of Mount Vernon, dated Dec. 17, 1754, is in Conway *Washington,* p. lxii. The lease included the use of eighteen slaves.

7. Ann, widow of Lawrence W, died March 14, 1761, Lee *Lee of Virginia* 140.

8. Edmund Pendleton's legal opinion dated July 3, 1769, Ford *Washington Wills* 53-55.

9. W's brother Augustine W died on some unknown date between Feb. 16, 1762, when he signed a codicil to his will, and May 25, 1762, when his will was probated, Westmoreland County Deeds & Wills No. 14 1761-1768, pp. 131-132.

10. W's will dated July 9, 1799 (by mistake written 1790) and probated Jan. 20, 1800, left Mount Vernon to Martha W for life and then to Bushrod W, Ford XIV 271-308. As to Bushrod W, biographical sketch of him in *D.A.B.* (Conceivably, of course, W may have purchased Augustine's remainder interest from him or his heir or assigns; but I have found no evidence of this.)

11. Conway's statement as to William Augustine W's complaint concerning W's devise of Mount Vernon, Conway *Washington,* p. xcii.

12. Prussing's suggestion, *Estate of Washington* 201.

13. Devise of "all my lands" (with unimportant exceptions) by Augustine W to his son William Augustine, Augustine W's will probated May 25, 1762, Westmoreland County Deeds & Wills No. 14 1761-1768 p. 127.

CHAPTER SIX

1. Lord Albemarle to the Duke of Newcastle, First Lord of the Treasury, Sept. 11, 1754, as to sending regular officers to the colonies, Add. MSS 32850: 289-291, Brit. Museum Lib.

2. Decision to send two regiments of British regular troops from Ireland with Major General Edward Braddock in chief command, George II's non-secret Instructions to Braddock Nov. 25, 1754, Sargent *Braddock Expedition* 393-394. As to Braddock's background, McCardell *Braddock* 3-134.

3. Braddock's arrival at Hampton, Va. Feb. 19, 1755, Dinwiddie to Maj. John Carlyle Feb. 20, *Dinwiddie* I 511.

4. George II's secret Instructions to Braddock Nov. 25, 1754, *N. Y. Col. Doc.* VI 920-922. As to the establishment in 1754 of a base at Will's Creek, present Cumberland, Md., Dinwiddie to Col. James Innes Aug. 30 and Oct. 5, and to Gov. Horatio Sharpe of Md. Sept. 6, 1754, *Dinwiddie* I 296, 305, and 346.

5. Nine Va. companies, including two of carpenters, presumably for clearing roads and building bridges, and one of light cavalry, Dinwiddie to Sir Thomas Robinson, March 17, 1755, *Dinwiddie* I 525.

6. W goes on Braddock's expedition as his aide, W to Orme March 15, 1755, and to William Byrd April 20, *W* I 107 and 114, with Braddock's

order of May 10, 1755, Lowdermilk *History* p. xxx. W to William Byrd April 20, states that he would not accept a commission from Braddock in the regular army even if offered one because "I am told a Compa. [Company] is the highest Comn. that is now vested in his gift," *W* I 114.

7. W to John Robinson April 20, 1755, same 112, as to his reason for joining Braddock. To similar effect W to William Byrd and to Carter Burwell April 20, same 114, 115.

8. W to Orme March 15, 1755, stating he had "some little time ago" written Braddock congratulating him on his safe arrival, same I 108. I have not found this letter to Braddock.

9. Orme to W March 2, 1755, as to Braddock's understanding of W's desire "to make the Campaigne" with him, *Letters to W* I 57.

10. W to Orme March 15, 1755, as to his reasons for wishing to accompany Braddock, *W* I 107.

11. W to John Augustine (Jack) W May 14, 1755, as to the opportunity to make useful acquaintances by serving with Braddock, same 124.

12. As to W's leaving Jack W to manage Mount Vernon, reference in W's will dated July 9, 1799, Ford *Washington Wills* 108. Jack had apparently taken up residence at Mount Vernon before the end of May 1755, and was still there as late as Sept., 1758, W to Jack W May 28, 1755, and Sept. 25, 1758, *W* I 129 and XXXVII 483.

13. As to W's joining Braddock at Frederick (Frederick Town) Md. on or about May 1, 1755, W to Augustine W May 14, *W* I 124, with *W Col. Traveller* 72.

14. W's arrival at Fort Cumberland May 10, 1755, same 73.

15. Braddock sends W to Williamsburg for funds on May 15, 1755, W's undated memorandum and letter to John Hunter of May 16, *W* I 125. As to when he returned, W in "Camp at Wills Creek," i.e., Fort Cumberland, to William Fairfax June 7, 1755, stating he arrived there May 30, same 133.

16. W to William Fairfax June 7, 1755, as to Braddock's obstinancy, same 133.

17. Later letters indicating good relations between W and Braddock, Capt. Roger Morris to W June 19, 1755, *Letters to W* I 66; W to Jack W June 28, and to Orme June 30, *W* I 141-146 and 146-147.

18. Braddock's Return of Forces, June 8, 1755, enclosed in Braddock to Adjutant-General Robert Napier June 8, Pargellis *Military Affairs* 84-92. My figures exclude about 150 sick, the civil branch of the artillery detachment, and over 100 officers, but include non-commissioned officers and drummers.

19. The thirty sailors, "Sea-Men," with four officers and two boatswains mates, are included in the Return of Forces, same 90-91. As to taking big guns for the expedition from the British warships and the detachment of sailors to handle them, Gipson *British Empire* VI 79.

20. First contingent leaves May 28, 1755, W's memorandum dated May 30, but obviously written, at least in part, later, *W* I 131-132, with Sharpe to Dinwiddie June 8, *Sharpe* I 215.

21. March of successive detachments from Fort Cumberland, Orme's journal, Sargent *Braddock's Expedition* 326-327.

22. W's illness and Braddock's division of his army on W's advice, W to Jack W June 28, 1755, *W* I 141-143.

23. Braddock's promise to W to bring him to the front before beginning the attack on Fort Duquesne, W to Jack W June 28, 1755, and to Orme June 30, same 144, 146.

24. W, though still very weak, brought to the front in a covered wagon on June 8, undated memorandum of W, same 147.

25. Washington underestimated the number of French and Indians in the attack. There were 108 French regulars, 146 Canadian militia, and over 600 Indians, Gipson *British Empire* VI 91-92.

26. W to Mary W July 18, 1755, concerning the battle and defeat of July 9, *W* I 150-152. In writing Dinwiddie a similar account (July 18, 1755) W added the well-known passage as to the officers being no more able to control their frightened men than "if we had attempted to have stop'd the wild Bears of the Mountains," same 148-150.

27. Further light on Braddock's expedition and defeat is given by Pargellis "Braddock's Defeat" 253-269; Hamilton *Braddock's Defeat, passim*; Gipson *British Empire* VI 56-97; Freeman II 36-83; Sargent *Braddock's Expedition* 193-389; Pargellis *Military Affairs* 98-106; Keppel *Keppel* I 213-221; *Shirley* II 311-313; McCardell *Braddock* 209-265; and Nichols "Braddock's Army" 126-147. The subsequent retreat and Braddock's death are described in detail in Dinwiddie to Lord Halifax, Oct. 1, 1755, *Dinwiddie* II 221-222.

28. W's undated account of the battle written after July 1, 1785, *W* XXIX 41-43. I deduce the dating from a passage in a letter of July 27, 1785, from W to Col. David Humphreys, for whom the account was written, same XXVIII 203-204.

29. W's contemporary letters and other contemporary evidence say nothing of his alleged suggestion to Braddock. The nearest approach to confirmatory evidence I have found are belated statements made the following October by two of Braddock's officers that some of the provincial troops and officers predicted that if they "engaged the Indians in their European manner of fighting they would be beat," *Shirley* II 313, and by Dinwiddie that Braddock "did not allow our Men to go to Trees to attack the Indians in their own way . . . ," *Dinwiddie* II 221.

30. See Bancroft *History* IV 170 and Wright *Atlantic Frontier* 313 for examples of statements as to Braddock's obstinacy. The other chief source, I think, contributing to Braddock's seemingly unjust reputation for obstinacy is Walpole's *Memoirs of Geo. II* 29, describing him as "obstinate in his sentiments"; but Walpole gives no evidence to support this statement. Gipson *British Empire*, VI 84-85 has a favorable and, I think, just sketch of Braddock.

31. Orme to W Aug. 25, 1755, concerning Braddock, *Letters to W* I 84. Orme wrote W on March 2, 1756, "I was told . . . you had writ several Letters to England speaking in very disrespectful terms of General Braddock. I absolutely denied it could be so as I had Letters from You of a very different Language," same 198. I have found no letters of W to England speaking disrespectfully of Braddock; but Fairfax may well have written English correspondents quoting W's letter to him of June 7 (*W* I 133) accusing Braddock of obstinacy.

32. Orme to Sharpe, July 18, 1755, as to W's bravery, *Sharpe* I 253, and to similar effect, Charles Lewis to W Aug. [no day] 1755, and William Fairfax to W July 26, *Letters to W* I 73 and 75.

33. Establishment of Va. Regiment, Acts of Aug., 1755, session, ch. 1 sec. 7, Hening *Va. Statutes* VI 521-530.

34. W's commission as "Colonel of the Virginia Regiment and Commander-in-Chief of all the Forces now raised or to be raised for the Defense of this His Majesty's Colony" is dated Aug. 14, 1755 [misprinted 1775], *Dinwiddie* II 184. Dinwiddie, of course, did not, and could not, unless otherwise ordered by the King, abdicate supreme command over the Virginia troops conferred by the King's commission to him as lieutenant-governor of the colony, July 4, 1751, C.O. 324: 38:287-289, Pub. Rec. Office.

CHAPTER SEVEN

1. Col. Thomas Dunbar's withdrawal of all the British regulars except the sick and wounded, Gov. Dinwiddie to Sir Thomas Robinson Aug. 20, 1755, *Dinwiddie* II 162-163.

2. As to the Va. frontier of over 350 miles, "Plan of Forts," enclosed in W to Dinwiddie Nov. 9, 1756, showing the distance between each of the frontier forts and a total distance of 360 miles, *W* I 490, 496. W wrote Gen. John Stanwix Oct. 8, 1757, that the Va. frontier was over 350 miles long, same II 145.

3. The proceedings of the very important session of the Va. legislature from Aug. 5 to 23, 1755, are in *Va. House Journals* for 1752-1755, pp. 297-315.

4. Ch. 1 of Va. Acts of Aug., 1755, session, Hening *Va. Statutes* VI 521-530, appropriated £40,000 for 1,200 men to defend the Va. frontier.

5. Division of the regiment into sixteen companies of sixty men each, Dinwiddie's instructions to W undated, *Dinwiddie* II 185, and W's instructions to recruiting officers Sept. 3, 1755, *W* I 163. As to the four unregimented companies of rangers, Dinwiddie's commission and instructions to captains of three of the companies Aug. 13, 14, and 20, and his letters of Sept. 6 and 20, to Lord Halifax and Gen. William Shirley, *Dinwiddie* II 158-159, 195, and 210. A list of most of the officers of the regimental companies, dated Sept. 17, 1755, and a complete roster dated Jan. 9, 1756, are in *W* I 176 and 272-274.

6. As to W's command of all the Va. forces, Commission from Dinwiddie to W Aug. 14, 1755, and undated Instructions, *Dinwiddie* II 184-185.

7. Appointment of Lieut. Col. Adam Stephen, and Major Andrew Lewis and of Capt. George Mercer as W's aide, W's orders, Sept. 17, 1755, *W* I 176.

8. Rendezvous of troops at Fredericksburg, Alexandria, and Winchester, and designation of Winchester as W's headquarters, Dinwiddie's undated Instructions to W, *Dinwiddie* II 185.

9. Remnants of Va. companies at Fort Cumberland following Braddock's defeat, Dinwiddie to Sir Thomas Robinson Aug. 20, 1755, same II 162-163.

10. W left Williamsburg about Sept. 3, 1755, *W Col. Traveller* 81-82.

11. As to W's trip to and arrival at Fort Cumberland, W's correspondence and orders Sept. 6 to 17, 1755, *W* I 169-175. W reached Fort Cumberland on or before Sept. 15, 1755, *W Col. Traveller* 84. On his way he visited the recruiting centers at Fredericksburg, Alexandria, and Winchester, same 82-84.

12. W's orders at Fort Cumberland Sept. 17 to 20, 1755, *W* I 175-182.

13. As to W's inspection trip from Fort Cumberland to Fort Dinwiddie, his orders there to Capt. Peter Hogg Sept. 24, 1755, and W to Dinwiddie Oct. 11, same 182 and 206-207. The location of the fort, same 182 n. My statements of distances, unless otherwise noted, are as the crow flies; distances by road or trail were, of course, greater.

14. W overtaken Oct. 7, 1755, as he was nearing Williamsburg by a messenger reporting Indian depredations, W's undated memorandum and W to Dinwiddie, Oct. 8, same 187 and 188.

15. W to Dinwiddie Oct. 11, 1755, reported his arrival in Winchester the day before, same 200.

16. W's activities at Winchester, including marching about a hundred men to strengthen the garrison at Fort Cumberland, W's orders and his letters to various persons Oct. 11 to Oct. 29, 1755, same 200-233.

17. W's notice to settlers Oct. 13, 1755, of his having "great reason to believe that the Indians who committed the late Cruelties . . . are returned Home," since they had "not been seen or heard of these ten days past," same 208.

18. Dinwiddie to W Oct. 18, 1755, asking him to come to Williamsburg to help secure needed military legislation, *Dinwiddie* II 247. The legislature was in session from Oct. 27 to Nov. 8, *Va. House Journals* for 1752-1755, pp. 319-332.

19. Dinwiddie to Gen. William Shirley Nov. 4, 1755, reporting W's arrival in Williamsburg "last night," *Dinwiddie* II 261.

20. W arrived in Fredericksburg from Williamsburg Nov. 16, 1755, and stayed there at least until Nov. 18, W to Adam Stephen Nov. 18, *W* I 235.

21. W's stay chiefly in Alexandria from Nov. 28, 1755, to Feb. 2, 1756, and his activities there, W's orders and his letters to various persons between those dates, same I 240-297. He spent about three weeks in Winchester in Dec., 1755, and Jan., 1756, same 256-285.

22. W arrived in Williamsburg from his trip to Boston on or shortly before March 30, 1756, same 95.

23. News of renewed Indian raids reached Williamsburg soon after W's arrival there, W to Gov. Robert Hunter Morris of Pa. April 9, 1756, *W* I 309.

24. W apparently left Williamsburg April 2, 1756, *W Col. Traveller* 95 and 96. He wrote Dinwiddie April 7, that he had reached Winchester the day before, *W* I 300.

25. W to Dinwiddie as to frontier conditions and urgent need for help, April 7, 16, 18, 22 and 24, 1756, same I 300-331 *passim*. In similar vein, W to John Robinson, Speaker of the Va. House of Burgesses, April 7, 16, and 24, same 304-336 *passim*.

26. An offensive against Fort Duquesne as the best protection for Va., W to John Robinson April 24, 1756, and to Dinwiddie Aug. 4, *W* I 333 and 423; Dinwiddie to Gen. Lord Loudoun, Shirley's successor as Commander in Chief in North America, July 1 and Aug. 9, *Dinwiddie* II 455-456 and 474; to Sir Charles Hardy and Col. Clement Read July 1, Sept. 8, same 454, 503; to W May 8, July 12 and Nov. 16, *Letters to W* I 245 and 313, and II 3-4.

27. As to the legislative committee chosen to supervise the expenditure of funds for the defense of Va., John Robinson, its chairman, to W Aug.

19, 1756, same I 349-350. See also Robert Carter Nicholas, a member of the committee, to W Aug. 18, and John Kirkpatrick, W's secretary, to W Aug. 19, same 336, 341.

28. W to John Robinson April 24, 1756, pointing out the reasons it was impracticable to take the offensive without help from "the neighbouring colonies," *W* I 333. As to an unsuccessful offensive against the Shawnee by Virginia troops alone in 1756, Draper "Expedition" 61-76.

29. As to the little prospect of outside help, W to Dinwiddie Feb. 2, 1756, saying he understood Pa. would act only on the defensive, *W* I 296, and Gov. Sharpe of Md. to Gov. Morris of Pa. March 22, saying he doubted if the Md. Assembly would pass even an act for defense that he could properly sign, *Sharpe* I 379. The Md. legislature eventually passed and Sharpe signed an act appropriating funds for an attack on Fort Duquesne, but only on condition that Pa. and Va. do likewise, and Pa. refused to act, Sharpe to John Sharpe May 27, 1756, same 430.

30. W to Dinwiddie April 7, 1756, disagreeing with the House of Burgesses' "sentiment" in favor of a chain of small frontier forts because of the inordinate number of men required for such a project but suggesting no alternative plan of defensive war, *W* I 301. (The House, which had convened on March 25, sat until May 5, *Va. House Journals* for 1752-1758, pp. 335-397.)

31. W to John Robinson, April 24, 1756, giving his views as to the necessity for a chain of frontier forts, *W* I 332-336.

32. W to Robinson April 24, 1756, stating he wished "the Assembly had given two thousand men, instead of fifteen hundred," same 332. To similar effect W to Dinwiddie April 24, same 330.

33. W had obtained only 321 "effectives" by May 1756, Freeman II 193, and even by August, after the drafting of men had been voted, he had only 926 in his regiment, W to Stephen Aug. 5, 1756, *W* I 437. In a letter to Gen. Lord Loudoun Aug. 9, Dinwiddie gave the number as less than 600, exclusive of three companies of scouts ("rangers"), *Dinwiddie* II 474. The draft law was defective in permitting draftees to escape service on payment of £10, which many paid to avoid serving, Dinwiddie to Loudoun July 1, same 455.

34. The bill for frontier defense, including provision for the chain of forts, which became Ch. 1 of Va. Acts of March to May 1756, Hening *Va. Statutes* VII 1-32, passed the House of Burgesses April 24, 1756, *Va. House Journals* for 1752-1758, p. 382.

35. Resolution by House of Burgesses May 3, 1756, for a strong fort at Winchester, same 393, and Robinson to W May 3, advising him of this, *Letters to W* I 239. W's recommendation to Robinson for a strong fort at Winchester had been reinforced by a similar recommendation from W to Dinwiddie April 27, *W* I 342, which was laid before the House on May 3, *Va. House Journals* for 1752-1758, p. 393.

36. As to the "Gentlemen Associators" or "Gentlemen Volunteers," Robinson to W May 3, 1756, Dinwiddie to W May 3, and William Fairfax to W May 9, *Letters to W* I 239, 241-242, and 251.

37. Dinwiddie to W May 27, 1756, reported that the Gentlemen Associators had left for Winchester, same 268, but there is no evidence that they made any inspection tour or made any determination of where the forts were to be located. The last mention of them in W's surviving papers is in a letter of W to Capt. Robert Stewart June 2, indicating that

the "Associators" had not yet arrived, *W* I 390. When they tardily arrived they apparently left it to W and his officers to make the decision as to locations.

38. Minutes of the Council of Officers at Fort Cumberland July 10, 1756, *Letters to W* I 301-304. These minutes say the forts south of Fort Dinwiddie were to be "two or thirty" miles apart; but instructions from W to Capt. Peter Hogg, dated July 21, show that the distance was to be twenty to thirty miles, *W* I 400. Dinwiddie to W June 12, gave him general discretion as to locating the forts, and on July 1, approved W's calling a council of officers to determine the matter, *Letters to W* I 275, 295.

39. As to the successful French operation in 1756 to capture Fort Oswego, which was surrendered Aug. 14, Gipson *Brit. Empire* VI 192-200.

40. The only heavy French and Indian raid on the Virginia settlements in 1756 after March of that year of which I have found any evidence is a raid in Augusta county on Sept. 11 to 14, in which forty-four men, women, and children were killed and many others captured, *Va. Mag.* II 401. No mention of the raid was made in W to Dinwiddie, dated at Mount Vernon Sept. 23, *W* I 466-471. W probably was on his way to Mount Vernon on some private affairs, referred to in this letter, when news of the raid reached Winchester.

41. Dinwiddie to W May 3, 1756, and July 1, as to using militia to help build the projected forts, *Letters to W* I 241 and 296-297. Dinwiddie wrote Loudoun Aug. 9, 1756, that seven hundred of the militia were apportioned to "small Forts on our Frontiers," *Dinwiddie* II 474—both as builders and as garrisons, I presume.

42. The duration of W's tour of the frontier forts is somewhat uncertain, but apparently it was a little over three weeks. He wrote Stephen from Winchester Sept. 28, 1756, that he was setting out the next day, *W* I 476, and an entry of Sept. 29 in his Ledger A of expenses on the road, *W Col. Traveller* 101, evidences that he in fact left as planned. It is the date of his return which is uncertain. He wrote Stephen from Winchester Oct. 23, that he had returned "last night" from his tour of inspection, *W* I 482, and this is confirmed by orders issued by W at Winchester on Oct. 23, same 485. But on Nov. 9, he wrote John Robinson "I am just returned" from the tour of the frontier, same 499.

43. W to Dinwiddie Nov. 9, 1756, enclosing a list of fifteen frontier forts, in addition to the fort at Winchester, same I 490 and 496. The approximate location of most of these forts and the route followed by W on his tour of inspection are shown on maps in Freeman II 229 and 215, and a description of some of them is given in Koontz *Virginia Frontier* 111-148.

44. W to Dinwiddie Sept. 23, 1756, recommending that the chain of undermanned small forts be abandoned in favor of four strong forts amply garrisoned *W* I 468-469, doubtless because of the great deficiency of men, as to which W wrote Capt. Thomas Waggener Aug. 5, "I have so . . . great calls for men, and so little prospect of getting any, that I find it impossible to comply with the act of Assembly, and opinion of the Council of War, in building the chain of forts on the frontiers," same 435.

45. Dinwiddie to W Sept. 30, 1756, personally approving the proposed change of plan as to the frontier forts but informing him that his letter had unfortunately arrived too late, the legislature, which would have to

approve the change, having risen before the letter reached Williamsburg, *Letters to W* I 373.

46. W to Dinwiddie Nov. 9, 1756, enclosing a plan of frontier forts, listing fifteen already built or under construction and four more to be built, and a statement of the number of men to garrison each fort, *W* I 490 and 496.

47. Dinwiddie to W Nov. 16, 1756, "establishing of Regulars would be very agreeable," but asking how they could be had, *Letters to W* II 3. In W's reply of Nov. 24, he commented on other portions of Dinwiddie's letter, but gave no answer to Dinwiddie's question on this vital point, *W* I 507-511.

48. W's difficulties and problems are described by him in letters to various correspondents from April 7 to Dec. 19, 1756, *W* I 300-530 *passim*, and to Lord Loudoun in an undated letter, enclosed in W to Capt. James Cunningham Jan. 28, 1757, same II 4, 7-17.

49. See, for example, the accusation in Baker-Crothers *Virginia and the French War* 101 that Dinwiddie largely contributed to W's difficulties.

50. The evidence of Dinwiddie's excellent co-operation with W is well presented in Koontz *Dinwiddie* 301-351 *passim*.

51. Gov. Sharpe to John Sharpe May 27, 1756, outlining the limited use he was permitted to make of the troops recently voted by the Md. legislature, *Sharpe* I 424.

52. W to Dinwiddie Jan. 13 to Sept. 23, 1756, repeatedly recommending withdrawal from Fort Cumberland, *W* I 286-468 *passim*. W had suggested this to Dinwiddie as early as November 1755, W to Stephen Nov. 28, 1755, same 241.

53. Dinwiddie to W Aug. 19, 1756, declining to abandon Fort Cumberland, *Letters to W* I 344.

54. Dinwiddie to W Sept. 30, 1756, authorizing him to call a council of officers concerning Fort Cumberland, and, if the council so advised, to withdraw the Virginia garrison after demolishing the fort, bringing the ammunition and stores to Winchester and destroying everything else that might be of service to the enemy, same 372.

55. Minutes of the council of officers Oct. 30, 1756, Lieut.-Col. Adam Stephen presiding, recording the unanimous decision of the sixteen officers present not to give W any advice one way or the other because the decision on so important a question as abandoning "the *only* fort belonging to His Majesty on this Quarter" ought to be made by Dinwiddie or Lord Loudoun, *Letters to W* II 6-9. W forwarded the minutes to Dinwiddie Nov. 9, with a statement of his reasons for continuing to favor withdrawal, *W* I 487-490 and 498.

56. Minutes of Va. Council, Dinwiddie presiding, Nov. 15, 1756, voting unanimously not to abandon the fort and to reinforce it by a hundred men from Winchester, enclosed in Dinwiddie to W stating his concurrence and ordering W to act accordingly, Nov. 16, *Letters to W* II 5 and 12.

57. W to Dinwiddie, Fort Loudoun, Dec. 2, 1756, against stripping this fort (at Winchester) to strengthen Fort Cumberland, *W* I 511-514.

58. Minutes of Va. Council Dec. 9, 1756, reaffirming the advice to hold and strengthen Fort Cumberland, but to do so by withdrawing troops from the smaller forts, *Letters to W* II 16-17. Dinwiddie had laid before the Council a letter of Oct. 25, from Loudoun desiring that Fort Cumber-

land be held and strengthened. I have not seen the letter but its date is known from Dinwiddie's reply of Dec. 18, *Dinwiddie* II 568. The passage of Loudoun's letter relating to Fort Cumberland is in Dinwiddie to W Dec. 10, same 559-560.

59. Dinwiddie to W Dec. 10, 1756, ordering him to hold and reinforce Fort Cumberland, *Letters to W* II 18, and W's reply of Dec. 19, saying he had immediately given the required orders, *W* I 522.

60. Gov. Sharpe to Dinwiddie May 5, 1757, "Capt. [John] Dagworthy has taken Possession of that place [Fort Cumberland] with a Detachment of 150 effective Men from the Troops in the Pay of this [Md.] Province," *Sharpe* I 548. Dinwiddie on April 7 had ordered W to withdraw the Va. troops and stores from Fort Cumberland as soon as the Md. troops arrived, *Letters to W* II 62. As to the Md. act of 1757, enabling Sharpe to garrison Fort Cumberland temporarily, Sharpe to Dinwiddie May 9, *Sharpe* I 552-553.

61. William Fairfax to W April 14, 1756, as to disapproval of his appointment of an aide-de-camp and a secretary, *Letters to W* I 216, and John Robinson and Dinwiddie to W April 13 and 17, 1756, concerning complaints as to misconduct of officers in his regiment, same 213 and 221. I suppose the disapproval of W's appointments was because of the extra expense these might entail.

62. W to Dinwiddie April 18, 1756, defending his conduct, *W* I 317.

63. As to W's thought of resigning, W to Dinwiddie April 18, 1756, same 317 and Landon Carter and Charles Carter to W April 21 and 22, 1756, *Letters to W* I 223-226. I have not found W's letter to Charles Carter to which both Carters refer in their letters to him. They assured him that the charges of misconduct were not at all leveled against him and that he was in high favor among all except perhaps a few who were envious of him.

64. Article by "The Virginia-Centinel" published Sept. 3, 1756, republished Ford *Washington and "Centinel"* X 3-9. The name of the writer is unknown.

65. Augustine W to W Oct. 16, 1756, saying he was held in high esteem and urging him not to resign, *Letters to W* I 375-377. To similar effect, William Ramsay Sept. 22, 1756, John Kirkpatrick Sept. 22, and John Robinson Nov. 16, same I 368-369, 370-371 and II 1-2.

CHAPTER EIGHT

1. W's sick leave in 1756-1757 and his resignation in 1758, are dealt with in Chapters 9 and 11.

2. W to William Byrd April 20, 1755, as to his unwillingness to accept a royal commission that was not higher than a captaincy, *W* I 114. In his autobiographical "Remarks," written much later, W said that Gen. Braddock had offered him a brevet captaincy, "the highest Grade he had it in his power to bestow," *W* XXIX 41.

3. The price for royal commissions in North America fixed by Gen. Jeffery Amherst in 1759 was £200 sterling for an ensign's (second lieutenant's) commission, £300 for a first lieutenant's, and £1200 for a captain's, Pargellis *Loudoun* 308 n., and judging from the relative prices of different grades in England, a majority in North America would cost about £2000 sterling. (William Fairfax's son, William Henry, wrote W Dec.

9, 1757, that he had paid £200 sterling for a commission as ensign, *Letters to W* II 253).

4. W to William Fitzhugh Nov. 15, 1754, "My inclinations are strongly bent to arms," *W* I 107.

5. An account of W's many illnesses from 1749 to 1758 is given in an Appendix to Chapter 11.

6. W to Dinwiddie as to advantage of a royal commission, May 29, 1754, *W* I 62.

7. Captain John Dagworthy and his royal commission and command of a company of Maryland provincial troops, Gov. Sharpe of Md. to Cecilius Calvert Sept. 2, 1754, *Sharpe* I 95; W to Dinwiddie, Jan. 14, 1756, *W* I 290.

8. Dagworthy's claim of right to command the Va. troops stationed at Fort Cumberland, Dinwiddie to Gen. William Shirley Nov. 4, 1755, *Dinwiddie* II 261; W to Dinwiddie Dec. 5, and to Lieut. Col. Adam Stephen Dec. 28, 1755, and W to Dinwiddie Jan. 14, 1756, *W* I 248-290 *passim*.

9. W disputes Dagworthy's claim of command, and Sharpe supports Dagworthy, W to Dinwiddie Dec. 5, 1755, and Jan. 14, 1756, same 249 and 289-290; Dinwiddie to Shirley Jan. 24, 1756, *Dinwiddie* II 329-330.

10. Dinwiddie to Shirley requesting royal brevet commissions for W, Lieut. Col. Adam Stephen and Maj. Andrew Lewis of the Va. regiment, Nov. 4, 1755, and Jan. 24, 1756, same II 261 and 330. (The letters as printed read "Private" commissions; but Dinwiddie's letter book at the Va. Hist. Soc. reads "Brevet" in both letters.)

11. Shirley to Dinwiddie Dec. 4, 1755, saying he had ordered Sharpe to remove the difficulties between W and Dagworthy. This letter is missing, but its contents are known from Dinwiddie's reply of Jan. 2, 1756, same 311.

12. Sharpe to Dinwiddie Jan. 4, 1756, saying he had ordered Dagworthy not to "assume any authority over the Virginians" posted at Fort Cumberland, *Sharpe* I 334-335. Sharpe was subject to Shirley's orders as a lower ranking officer (lieutenant colonel) in the regular army.

13. W to Dinwiddie Jan. 14, 1756, threatening to resign his commission rather than yield to Dagworthy's claim of command, and asking for leave to go and see Shirley, *W* I 289. W, who was at Alexandria, Va., had apparently not yet learned of Sharpe's order to Dagworthy.

14. Dinwiddie to W Jan. 23, 1756, giving him leave to go and see Shirley, W's setting out for Boston on Feb. 4, and the persons accompanying him, *Dinwiddie* II 327 and W's "Ledger of Accounts," Feb. 4 *W* I 297 n. and 298. Shirley was governor of Mass. as well as Commander-in-Chief of the British forces in North America in succession to Gen. Braddock.

15. The earlier description of W, often quoted (e.g., Freeman III 6), as having "dark brown hair," "blue-grey penetrating eyes," and a large nose and mouth is from a supposed copy of a letter of George Mercer to an unidentified correspondent some time in 1760. Judging from W's portraits and a letter published in 1780 (Baker *Early Sketches of Washington* 77), the description seems accurate. But since no one, much less an expert, so far as is known, has ever seen the original of Mercer's supposed letter, it cannot, I think, be accepted as evidence.

16. Capt. David Kennedy's description of W in Gen. Loudoun's diary Feb. 27, 1757, Loudoun Papers, Huntington Library.

17. W's northern trip which took him from Feb. 4 to the end of March, 1756, can be followed from his expense accounts in *W Col. Traveller* 92-95 and *W* I 298-299.

18. Shirley's order of March 5, 1756, as to precedence, *Letters to W* I 201. The assumption that brevet commissions were refused is based on a letter of Dinwiddie to Gen. James Abercromby May 28, 1756, *Dinwiddie* II 425, and on W's contemplated resignation after his interview with Shirley, *W* I 310.

19. W's thought of resigning, W to Gov. Robert Hunter Morris of Pa. April 9, 1756, same 310.

20. Decision to remain in service, W to Morris April 9, 1756, mentioning his being "diswaded . . . at least for a time" from resigning, same 310.

21. Proposed expedition, Shirley to Sharpe Feb. 23, 1756, *Shirley* II 396-398.

22. Sharpe to Shirley concerning W, April 10, 1756, *Sharpe* I 389.

23. Shirley to Sharpe concerning W, May 16, 1756, same 416.

24. Declaration of War dated May 17, 1756, *Shirley* II 450-453. Diplomatic relations had been broken ten months before, Pease *Anglo-French* lvi. The immediate causes of the Declaration were an attack on French naval vessels by Admiral Edward Boscawen followed by a French attack on the island of Minorca, at that time a British possession, Lewis *Walpole* XX 484-486 and 559-572. War was declared in Va. the following August, Dinwiddie to W Aug. 19 and 21, *Letters to W* I 348-349 and 356, and W to Dinwiddie Sept. 8, *W* I 463-464. W's address accompanying his reading of the Declaration to his officers and men is in same 446-447.

25. George II's commission to Gen. Lord Loudoun March 17, 1756, superseding Shirley, Pargellis *Loudoun* 57-58. Loudoun had authority to grant royal commissions up to and including the rank of lieutenant colonel, under a royal instruction dated May 7, LO [Loudoun] 1124A, Huntington Lib. As to Shirley's knowledge by May 16, that he had been superseded by Loudoun, with Gen. Abercromby as second in command, Shirley to Gov. Morris April 18, 1756, *Shirley* II 428.

26. W's letter to Dinwiddie of May 23, 1756, requesting a recommendation to Loudoun is missing but its substance is deducible from Dinwiddie's reply of May 27, *Letters to W* I 269. Sailing from England on May 22, Loudoun landed at New York City on July 23, Pargellis *Loudoun* 81-82.

27. Dinwiddie to Abercromby May 28, 1756, recommending W for a royal commission and stating he "is a person much beloved here and has gone through many hardships in the Service, and I really think he has great Merit, and believe he can raise more Men here than any one present that I know," *Dinwiddie* II 425. Dinwiddie did not mention what rank in the regular army W was now seeking, and I have found nothing on this point.

28. Loudoun was appointed Governor of Va. Feb. 20, 1756, Andrews "Commissions" 522.

29. Dinwiddie to W Feb. 2, 1757, reluctantly granting him leave of absence to see Loudoun in Philadelphia, *Letters to W* II 45.

30. The exclamation point is W's own.

31. I question W's statement that Braddock had assured him of preferment agreeable to his wishes, because of an earlier statement by W to

William Byrd, *W* I 114, that "as to any prospect of obtaining a Commission I . . . am pretty well assur'd it is not in Genl. Braddock's [power] to give such a one as I wou'd accept . . . ," and a later statement by him that Braddock had offered and he had refused "a Captain's Commission by brevet (which was the highest Grade he had it in his power to bestow)," same XXIX 41.

32. W to Loudoun, undated, concerning the military situation in Va., and hinting at a royal commission, same II 6-19. W's covering letter to Capt. James Cunningham Jan. 28, 1757, is in same 4-6. An opening statement in the letter to Loudoun indicates that it was to have been presented to Loudoun on an expected earlier visit to Va., as to which see Dinwiddie to W Aug. 19, 1756, *Dinwiddie* II 481, and W to Dinwiddie Sept. 8, *W* I 462.

33. As to W's trip to Philadelphia starting about Feb. 14, 1767, *W Col. Traveller* 106-108, Freeman II 234-241 and sources there cited.

34. Loudoun's proposed conference at Philadelphia with Pennsylvania and southern governors beginning Feb. 17, 1757, and his long delay in arriving, Dinwiddie to Loudoun Jan. 29, *Dinwiddie* II 587-588, and Gov Sharpe to Lord Baltimore March 23, *Sharpe* I 533. As to reasons for the delay, Pargellis *Loudoun* 218 n.

35. Loudoun's diary for March 20, 1767, concerning his interview with W, HM 1717 vol. 3, Huntington Lib.

36. W was back in Va. about April 1, 1757, *W Col. Traveller* 107-108. W to Dinwiddie April 5, *W* II 20, indicates that he had arrived at Alex andria on or before that date and was about to set out for Fort Loudoun.

CHAPTER NINE

1. W's desire for Indian auxiliaries, W to Dinwiddie April 7, 24, and 27 and Sept. 8, 1756, and May 30, 1757, *W* I 301-302, 330, 341, 463-464 and II 41 and to Col. John Stanwix June 28, 1757, same 82. As to Stanwix, who was appointed to command the southern military district, *D.N.B.* and *N. Y. Col. Doc.* VII 280 n. Dinwiddie avoided a possible clash over jurisdiction by directing W to obey Stanwix in case the latter's orders differed from his own, W to Dinwiddie June 10, 1757, questioning what to do, *W* II 50-51, and Dinwiddie's reply of June 24, *Letters to W* II 119.

2. Six Cherokees had recently reached Winchester, W to Dinwiddie Dec. 19, 1756, *W* I 526, and over a hundred Catawbas arrived early the next year, W to Dinwiddie April 5, 1757, same II 20.

3. Loudoun had raised two thousand men and taken an outstanding part in suppressing the rebellion in Scotland in 1745, and he had been colonel of the 50th regiment of infantry since 1750, sketch of Loudoun (John Campbell 1705-1782), in *D.N.B.* Shirley had had no experience in the field, sketch of Shirley in *D.A.B.*

4. The British and British colonial troops not only failed to take either Louisbourg or Quebec in 1757, but lost Fort William Henry, Pargellis *Loudoun* 211, 231-252.

5. Usefulness of the Indian auxiliaries, W to Dinwiddie May 24 and 29, June 12, Oct. 24, and Nov. 5, 1757, *W* II 36, 39, 57-58, 152-153 and 157-158; and W to Stanwix June 28, same 82.

6. Vexing problems in dealing with the Indian auxiliaries, W to Din-

widdie May 24, May 30, June 12, and Oct. 5, 1757, same II 36, 40, 58, 140; W to Stanwix July 30, same 114-115; Edmund Atkin, Superintendent of the Southern Indians, to George Croghan June 8, same 53 n.; William Fairfax to W Aug. 6, *Letters to W* II 167. As to Atkin, for whom W seems to have had little esteem (*W* II 84, 97, 114 and 123), Alden *Stuart* 68-100 and 134-135.

7. Accounts of French and Indian raids on the Va. frontier in 1757, and the death and capture of many settlers and the terrorizing of those who escaped, W to Dinwiddie June 27, Aug. 3 and 27, Sept. 17, Oct. 5, and to Stanwix Oct. 8, *W* II 77, 118, 121, 129, 143 and 144, and Dinwiddie to W Aug. 8, *Letters to W* II 169.

8. W had 432 men in May, and only about 700, including draftees, in Sept., W to Dinwiddie July 11 and Sept. 17, 1757, *W* II 94 and 127. These figures presumably were exclusive of two companies of about 100 men each sent to South Carolina under W's second in command, Lieut. Col. Adam Stephen. As to these, *W* II 27, 48 and *Letters to W* II 95, 173-181. Presumably because of the dearth of troops, only nine frontier forts, including Fort Loudoun, were now garrisoned, Minutes of Council of War June 16, 1757, same 96.

9. As to floggings and threats of death, W to Dinwiddie Jan. 12 and Aug. 3, 1757, and to Stanwix July 15, *W* II 1, 97 and 118. W erected a gallows forty feet high to frighten the men, W to Stanwix July 15, same 97. He later carried out the threat by hanging two of them, explaining he had hanged, not shot, them because this "conveyed more terror to the others," W to Dinwiddie, same 118.

10. W to Stanwix July 15, 1757, as to deserters at Fredericksburg from the recent draft, same 97. Thirty others had deserted at Winchester, but all of these had been recaptured except one who was killed. For further details W to John Robinson July 10, same 86, 88.

11. W to Gov. Sharpe of Md. July 20, 1757, protesting against the failure to return some Va. troops who had fled to Maryland and Sharpe's reply of July 27, enclosing a deposition of Sergeant Richard Davis April 20, 1757, that Capt. Christopher Gist had assured the men they were to serve only six months, same 99-100 and *Letters to W* II 161-164.

12. W to Dinwiddie Oct. 24, 1757, complaining of Dagworthy's conduct in retaining orders found on a French officer killed and scalped by a party of Indians sent out by W, *W* II 152-153.

13. I have not discovered the nature of the supposed "Scheme" with which W was charged. Perhaps it was thought that W was trying to promote unnecessary expenditures in order to enhance his profits under an arrangement with the legislative committee, headed by his friend Robinson, that he was to have a 2 per cent commission on all the money passing through his hands—an arrangement canceled by Dinwiddie in May, 1757, Dinwiddie to W May 16, 1757, *Letters to W* II 73. W still hoped for some commission on purchases of clothing for the soldiers, but Robinson discouraged this hope, W to Robinson July 10, *W* II 87-88, and Robinson's reply July 18, *Letters to W* II 153.

14. William Peachy to W Aug. 22, 1757, concerning W's alleged "Scheme" reported to him by Charles Carter of Shirley (not Charles Carter, burgess of King George county, mentioned in Chap. 7), same II 181-182. Carter had heard the story from Christopher Robinson, who said he heard it from Richard Corbin.

15. W to Peachy Sept. 18, 1757, acknowledging his letter and calling the story absurd, *W* II 134.

16. In his letters to W before Sept. 13, 1756, Dinwiddie customarily added a personal touch, as "Your friend," "with Esteem and regard," or "with Prayers for Your Protection," Jan. 22 to Aug. 21, 1756, *Letters to W* I 174-355 *passim*. His letters on and after that date are formal, *Dinwiddie* II 506-508 and 529-716 *passim*.

17. W to Dinwiddie Sept. 17, 1757, enclosing Peachy's letter and denouncing W's detractor and remarking on Dinwiddie's change of conduct towards him, *W* II 131-133. W seems to have been morbidly suspicious of Dinwiddie, having written to Robinson on June 10 that he was convinced Dinwiddie would be pleased to hear W "was involved in trouble," same 53—without, so far as Dinwiddie's letters or other known evidence reveals, any justification for the suspicion that Dinwiddie had any such wish.

18. Dinwiddie to W Sept. 24, 1757, reproaching him with ingratitude, *Dinwiddie* II 703.

19. W to Dinwiddie Oct. 5, 1757, in reply to Dinwiddie's reproach of ingratitude, *W* II 141.

20. Dinwiddie to W Oct. 19, 1757, replying to other parts of W's letters of Oct. 5, but saying nothing as to W's denial of ingratitude, *Letters to W* II 214-216. Dinwiddie referred to W's letter as "Yours of the 3d" but the contents of Dinwiddie's letter shows that it was in answer to W's of the 5th.

21. My conjecture that Dinwiddie had read or learned the contents of W's letter to Robinson of Aug. 5, 1756, is based not only on the general probability that the contents of such a letter would have been bandied about by Robinson, who was on bad terms with Dinwiddie, but on the fact that the change from friendliness to formality in Dinwiddie's letters to W began about a month after W's letter of Aug. 5, 1756, *Dinwiddie* II 506-508.

22. W to Robinson Aug. 5, 1756, complaining of Dinwiddie, *W* I 428. Fitzpatrick in his editorial comment on this letter, same 428 n., says "The original letter [from Dinwiddie to W quoted by him] is in the *Washington Papers*, and Washington's quotation is exact and correct." Fitzpatrick omits to point out that the passage quoted is immediately followed by a sentence which clears up what might otherwise have been ambiguous.

23. Dinwiddie to W June 12, 1756, about Fort Cumberland, *Letters to W* I 276.

24. W to Dinwiddie June 25 and Aug. 4, 1756, showing he clearly understood from Dinwiddie's letter that Fort Cumberland was not to be abandoned, *W* I 392 and 419. W also misrepresented Dinwiddie to Robinson, Oct. 25, 1757, complaining that Dinwiddie had refused (Dinwiddie to W Oct. 19, *Dinwiddie* II 707-708) to give him leave of absence to come to Williamsburg to settle his accounts and "to represent the melancholy situation of our distressed frontiers," *W* II 153. This latter, urgent reason makes Dinwiddie's refusal seem unreasonable. In fact, W had not mentioned the latter reason in writing Dinwiddie on Oct. 5, asking for leave, same 142.

25. As to the general clarity and definiteness of Dinwiddie's directions to W, see their correspondence from June, 1754, to June, 1756, *Dinwiddie*

I 218-436 and II 122-432 *passim* and *Letters to W* I 13-279 *passim*. W's misstatements concerning Dinwiddie have, I think, misled historians and biographers to denigrate the latter unfairly.

26. W to Dinwiddie Sept. 17, 1757, reporting that thirteen of the twenty-nine recently drafted men from Lunenburg county had deserted, *W* II 126.

27. Further Indian raids and the havoc done, W to Dinwiddie Sept. 17 and Oct. 24, and to Stanwix Oct. 8, 1757, same 129, 151 and 144.

28. W to Dinwiddie Sept. 24, 1757, as to parties sent out after raiders returning without having been able to kill or capture any of the enemy, same 135.

29. W to Dinwiddie Oct. 5, 1757, as to the Cherokees, Atkin and the Indian interpreter, same 140-141.

30. Capt. Robert Stewart to Dinwiddie Nov. 9, 1757, *Letters to W* II 231, and W to Dr. (the Reverend) Charles Greene Nov. 13, *W* II 159, concerning W's illness of three months' standing.

31. The statement in Freeman II 275 that W "turned over the command to Capt. Robert Stewart" should be amplified. Stewart, as senior officer at Fort Loudoun would, of course, assume command of the Va. troops there; but over-all command of the regiment would devolve upon Major Andrew Lewis, stationed at Fort Augusta. (Stephen, next in line to W, was in South Carolina in command of the Va. companies stationed there, Dinwiddie to Stephen Nov. 24, 1757, *Dinwiddie* II 718.)

32. Capt. Robert Stewart to Dinwiddie Nov. 9, 1757, as to W's malady and his leaving Winchester, *Letters to W* II 231. Dinwiddie replied to Stewart on Nov. 15, expressing his concern for W's health and approving his having accepted his doctor's advice without waiting to secure leave of absence, same 239-240. Dinwiddie himself was ill, and was planning to leave soon for Great Britain, Dinwiddie to W Nov. 2 and to Stephen Nov. 24, *Dinwiddie* II 713, 718. He sailed the following January, Acting Governor John Blair to W Jan. 25, 1758, *Letters to W* II 257.

33. W to Mrs. George William (Sally) Fairfax Nov. 15, 1757, stating he had arrived at Mount Vernon "Sunday last" (which was Nov. 13), *W* XXXVII 459.

34. W to Blair April 2, 1758, headed "On the road to Winchester," same II 168, indicates the date of his return to the army.

CHAPTER TEN

1. W to Sally (Mrs. George William) Fairfax Nov. 15, 1757, as to the regimen prescribed by Dr. Charles Greene, *W* XXXVII 479.

2. Absence of Jack's wife, Hannah W, and W's request to Sally Fairfax for help, W to Sally Nov. 15, 1757, same XXXVII 479. Jack W had married Hannah Bushrod in April, 1756, William Fairfax to W Apr. 14 and 26, 1756, *Letters to W* I 217, 232.

3. Sally (Sarah) Cary had married George William Fairfax in 1748, Cary *Sally Cary* 22.

4. William Fairfax died in Sept., 1757, W to Mary W Sept. 30, 1757, *W* II 137.

5. George William Fairfax had left for England on business in the fall of 1757, W to Richard Peters Sept. 30, 1757, *W* II 136. He wrote W

on Dec. 6, 1757, indicating that he would remain until spring, *Letters to W*
II 251. He was back at Belvoir before Aug. 5, 1758, as we know from a
letter of that date from him to W, same III 17. (This and later letters
from him to W are signed "Wm." in place of "George Wm." Fairfax, indicating that, following the death of his father, George William adopted
"William" as his first name, even though he had a younger half brother
[killed in 1759] named William, too.)

6. The reference to Mrs. Custis is the earliest known record of W's
engagement or supposed engagement to Martha Custis—if, as I believe,
W's supposed letter to Martha of July 20, 1758 (*W* II 242), is not authentic.

7. I suppose from the context and W's known attendance at dancing
assemblies that "A——B——s" refers to Assembly Balls.

8. Mrs. Spotswood was perhaps Mrs. John Spotswood, widow of a son
of former Governor Alexander Spotswood of Va.

9. I cannot identify "Captain" Gist. Lieutenant Nathaniel Gist of W's
regiment (W to Gen. John Forbes Nov. 18, 1758, *W* II 306) may have
been an acting captain and hence called Captain unofficially.

10. "Col. Mercer" presumably was Lieutenant-Colonel George Mercer
of the Second Virginia regiment.

11. W probably had proposed the gift of a carpet to the Fairfaxes in a
letter of Aug. 23, 1758, now missing, from W to George William Fairfax,
which is referred to in a letter of Fairfax to W Sept. 1, *Letters to W* III
67.

12. W's letter or supposed letter to Sally Fairfax dated Sept. 12, 1758,
was published in full in the New York *Herald* of March 30, 1877 (p. 2
column 5) with the statement that it was to be sold at auction "this afternoon." The next day's issue of the *Herald* carried a notice of the sale,
including sale of a letter of Washington for $13. The letter was re-
published (1889) in Ford II 95-98.

13. The supposition that W was engaged to Martha Custis is, at first
glance, supported by a tender letter of July 28, 1758, supposed to be from
W to Martha referring to "that happy hour when we made our pledges
to each other," *W* II 242. However, the original of this letter has not been
found, and I agree with Freeman in doubting its authenticity for the
reasons given by him, Freeman II 405-406.

14. Examples of treatment of the W-Sally Fairfax letter: (1) Passed
over in silence, Lodge *Washington* and Sawyer *Washington*; (2) interpreted as mere banter, Fitzpatrick in his *Washington* 110, who adds that
"to claim more than this requires an imagination unresponsive to the
niceties of honor and good breeding"; (3) authenticity questioned, Fitzpatrick in *W* II 289 n. and Stephenson "The Romantics and George
Washington" 274-275.

15. Rupert Hughes' treatment of the W-Sally Fairfax letter, Hughes
Washington I 398-419, 525.

16. Stephenson "The Romantics and George Washington," *A.H.R.*
XXXIX (1934) 274-275.

17. Inclusion of the W-Sally Fairfax letter by Fitzpatrick, with an
editorial caution, *W* II 286-289 and 289 n.

18. W-Sally Fairfax letter in Morrison *Catalogue* VI (1892) 387-388.

19. W-Sally Fairfax letter listed in item 1177 in the annotated catalogue

at the Yale U. Lib. of part 2 of the sale of the Morrison collection April 15-19, 1918, by Sotheby, Wilkinson & Hodge, as sold to Maggs Brothers.

20. The statement as to the authenticity of W's letter of Sept. 12, 1758, to Mrs. Fairfax is based on my own examination of it.

21. W to Sally Fairfax Sept. 25, 1758, as to his "true meaning," *W* II 292-294. In this letter W inserted "most unalterably," before his conventional closing, "Your Most Obedient & Obliged G. Washington."

22. The Fairfaxes' moving to England in 1773 is known from W to George William Fairfax Jan. 19, 1773, June 10, 1774, and May 31, 1775, *W* III 108, 221, 290; and Samuel Athawes to *W* April 8, 1774, and Fairfax to W March 2, 1775, *Letters to W* IV 367 and V 121-122.

23. W to Warner W Nov. 9, 1787, reporting the death of George William Fairfax, and that he, G. W., was named in Fairfax's will as one of the executors of his estate in Virginia, *W* XXIX 306.

24. W to Sally Fairfax May 16, 1798, as to the happiest moments of his life which he had enjoyed in her company, same XXXVI 263.

CHAPTER ELEVEN

1. W's return to duty, W to Acting Governor John Blair April 9, 1758, from his headquarters at Fort Loudoun, *W* II 171.

2. William Pitt to colonial governors and to Gen. James Abercromby, Commander-in-Chief in North America, Dec. 30, 1757, (Londoun had just been recalled) as to 1758 campaign and the new order as to rank, favorable to provincial officers, Kimball *Pitt Corresp.* I 136-143. Gov. Horatio Sharpe of Md. had received Pitt's circular letter before the end of March, Sharpe to Gen. John Forbes March 27, 1758, *Sharpe* II 162, and presumably Blair received a duplicate original of the letter about the same time.

3. Order as to rank, Dec. 13, 1757, *N.J. Col. Doc.* IX 19. George II had issued an order on May 12, 1756, more favorable to provincial officers than the order of Nov. 12, 1754, (*Letters to W* I facing p. 56) discussed in Chapter 4, by giving provincial general and field officers rank over regular captains, *Sharpe* I 413. The new order gave provincial generals rank over all regular field officers, and provincial field officers rank over regular field officers of lower grade. The new order was, however, limited in its effect by the King's advancing twenty-five regular lieutenant-colonels to the rank of colonel while serving in America, Pargellis *Loudoun* 93.

4. Expedition to be against Fort Duquesne and to be launched from Philadelphia, "Plan of Operations" Feb. 1, 1758, and Forbes to Gov. Sharpe April 4, *Forbes* 35 and 64. The choice of Philadelphia was probably influenced by the advice of Braddock, who had written Col. Robert Napier June 7, 1755, that it had been a mistake to start from Virginia rather than from Philadelphia, Pargellis *Military Affairs* 92.

5. Choice of Raystown as the forward base, Forbes to Bouquet May 20 to 29, 1758, *Forbes* 94-102—a decision based on the advice of Forbes' Quartermaster, Col. John St. Clair, Forbes to Bouquet July 23, 1758, same 156.

6. There are good biographical sketches of Forbes in *Forbes* pp. ix-xii and *D.A.B.*

7. List of troops under Forbes' command dated Sept. 25, 1758, gives about sixteen hundred British infantry, *Olden Time* II 284. Forbes wrote

Gen. James Abercromby, July 3, of a "small" amount of artillery with him, *Forbes* 168. See also Forbes to Pitt, May 1, same 77-78.

8. W's regiment continued and a second provided for, Laws of March, 1758, session, ch. 1 sec. 1, Hening *Va. Statutes* VII 163-164. Appointment of William Byrd III (1726-1777), as colonel, Gen. Forbes to Pitt July 10, 1758, *Forbes* 141-142. As to Byrd, son of the distinguished William Byrd II (1674-1744), Bassett *Byrd* pp. xxxvii-xxxviii.

9. Provision for three Pennsylvania regiments, act of April 22, 1758, ch. 431, *Pa. Statutes* V 337-339. I have not found the Governor's order or orders as to the use of the funds thus voted, but there is a list of the Pennsylvania troops by regiments, dated Sept. 25, 1758, in *Olden Time* II 284, and there are many references to the regiments in *Bouquet* II *passim.*

10. Maryland, North Carolina, and Delaware troops, List of Troops, Sept. 25, 1758, *Olden Time* II 284.

11. W to Gen. John Stanwix April 10, 1758, asking to be distinguished from the "common run" of provincial officers, *W* II 173. W wrote in similar vein to Col. Thomas Gage April 12, same 176-177. I have found no answer from either Stanwix or Gage. W wrote a flattering letter to Forbes himself on April 23, same 182. As to W's previous correspondence with Stanwix, May 1757 to March 1758, same 37-167 *passim.*

12. Activities of detachment from W's regiment to serve under Col. Henry Bouquet, Bouquet correspondence June 6 to Aug. 26, 1758, *Bouquet* II 41-431 *passim;* and Col. Adam Stephen to W Sept. 9, Sept. 13, *Letters to W* III 88, 96. As to Bouquet, sketch of him in *D.A.B.*

13. W to and from various correspondents April 9 to Sept. 25, 1758, concerning his activities at this period, *W* II 171-291 *passim* and *Letters to W* II 276-410, III 1-103 *passim.* Bouquet and Forbes were delighted with "the Indian dress" (*W* II 229) in which W clothed his men, Bouquet to W July 11, 14, *Letters to W* II 354, 361.

14. Forbes' preference for a direct route from Raystown to Fort Duquesne, Forbes to Bouquet July 14, 1758, and to Gen. Abercromby July 25, *Forbes* 145, 159.

15. Forbes estimated a saving of 86 to 96 miles, same 157. W estimated a saving of only 19 miles, *W* II 256, but, as pointed out later in the text, his method of computation was unsound. My estimate of a saving of at least 40 miles is based on analysis of the two contemporary estimates and an inspection of the two routes.

16. Forbes to Abercromby July 25, 1758, as to advantage of avoiding crossing of the Youghiogheny *Forbes* 159.

17. The fear of being delayed in crossing the Youghiogheny by heavy rains is evidenced by W's assurance to Bouquet in a letter of Aug. 2, 1758, that any difficulties on this score were "so trivial that they are really not worth mentioning," *W* II 254.

18. Correspondence of Forbes and Bouquet June 21 to July 31, 1758, and Forbes to Abercromby July 25, concerning conflicting reports as to routes, which apparently stemmed largely from Pennsylvania-Virginia rivalry, *Bouquet* II 123-291 *passim* and *Forbes* 159.

19. As to reasons for rivalry over the choice of route, W to Dinwiddie's successor, Gov. Francis Fauquier, Sept. 2, 1758, *W* II 281 and Forbes to Gen. Jeffery Amherst Jan. 26, 1759, *Forbes* 283. As to Fauquier, Dunbar "Royal Governors" 231-237 and sketch of him in *D.A.B.*

20. W to Bouquet July 25 and Aug. 2, 1758, and to Maj. Francis Hal-kett Aug. 2, urging that the Fort Cumberland route be chosen, *W* II 246, 252-258 and 260. The relative distances and routes of the two roads are given in the letter of Aug. 2, same 256.

21. W to Bouquet and to Halkett Aug. 2, 1758, protesting his disinter-estedness in urging the choice of the Fort Cumberland route, same 260, 261.

22. W to Bouquet Aug. 2, 1758, as to crossing the Youghiogheny pre-senting no material difficulties even in the case of heavy rains, same 254. Washington stated that he himself had crossed the Youghiogheny "after 30 odd days almost constant Rain," but failed to state the further material fact that he had been held up several days before he could cross. As to this, W to Dinwiddie May 18, 1755, *W* I 48 and W's diary for May 18 to 24, 1755, *W Diaries* I 82-85.

23. W to Bouquet July 25, 1758, that a road fit even for pack horses ("carrying Horses") was impracticable, *W* II 246.

24. Forbes' order to Bouquet to begin building the new, direct road from Raystown to Fort Duquesne, Halkett for Forbes to Bouquet July 31, 1758, *Bouquet* II 294. Forbes had just received a letter of July 26, from Bouquet, same 277, enclosing a letter of July 25, from Maj. George Armstrong of Pa. stating that, according to the reports of two guides sent ahead to explore, the direct route was practicable, same 271.

25. W to Speaker John Robinson, Sept. 1, 1758, as to his suspicion of Forbes and probable failure of the expedition, *W* II 277-278.

26. Other letters of W similar to the one to Robinson are W to Gov. Fauquier Sept. 2, 25, 28, and Oct. 30, 1758, same II 281, 291, 295, 300; to Sally Fairfax and to Jack W Sept. 25, 1758, same II 293 and XXXVII 483; and to various other of W's correspondents in letters now missing but whose substance is evident from the replies, *Letters to W* III 16, 30, 44, 50, 97, 110.

27. Forbes' correspondence June 27 to Aug. 11, 1758, concerning the proposed new road, indicating that he had no bias in favor of Pennsyl-vania, *Forbes* 124-173 *passim*.

28. Forbes' illness, Forbes to various correspondents July 23, to Sept. 6, 1758, *Forbes* 154-206 *passim*.

29. Forbes reached Raystown Sept. 15, 1758, and W conferred with him there the next evening, Forbes to Bouquet, Sept. 17, and Halkett to Gov. Sharpe, Sept. 16, *Forbes* 214, 209.

30. Forbes to Bouquet, Aug. 9, 1758, as to his unfavorable opinion of W, *Forbes* 171. W's letter referred to by Forbes was, I surmise, a letter of W to Halkett of Aug. 2, saying that unless Braddock's road was chosen "All is lost by Heavens! Our Enterprise Ruin'd; and we stop'd at the Laurel Hill this Winter . . . ," *W* II 260. My surmise is based on Forbes to Gen. Abercromby, Aug. 11, *Forbes* 173.

31. Forbes to Bouquet, Sept. 4, 1758, warning him to be cautious in accepting W's advice, same 199. On Sept. 23, 1758, Forbes wrote Bouquet that he had told both W and Col. William Byrd of his displeasure over their conduct concerning the choice of roads, same 219.

32. W wrote Fauquier from Raystown Sept. 25, 1758, "I marched to this Camp the 21st instant, by order of the General," *W* II 291.

33. Defeat of Maj. James Grant on Sept. 14, 1758, Grant to Forbes undated and Bouquet to Forbes Sept. 17, *Bouquet* II 499-504, 517-521; W to Jack W Sept. 25, *W* XXXVII 482-483; Forbes to Pitt Oct. 20, *Forbes* 238; Gipson *British Empire* VII 268-270; Freeman II 339-350. The French lost only sixteen killed and wounded, M. Daine to Marshal Belle Isle Nov. 3, 2 *Pa. Arch.* VI 423. The Va. troops in the engagement, though part of Stephen's detachment, apparently were under the immediate command of Major Andrew Lewis of Va.

34. The only evidence I have found of W's activities while stationed at Raystown is of his attending a conference of the colonels on the expedition at Forbes' headquarters Oct. 5, 1758, and his submission to Forbes on Oct. 8, of two beautifully executed plans of march, *W* II 295-298. I have not discovered if W's proposals were followed; Forbes to Bouquet Oct. 21, 1758, asking for a plan of march, *Bouquet* II 583, indicates that he was then still uncertain as to what plan to adopt.

35. Forbes to Bouquet Oct. 15, 1758, as to his having ordered W forward Oct. 14, *Forbes* 229, following receipt of word of an attack on the post at the Loyalhanna Oct. 12, described in Forbes to Abercromby Oct. 16, same 231-233.

36. W's arrival at the Loyalhanna Oct. 23 is noted in his itinerary from Raystown to there, *W* II 299 n. Gov. Sharpe to Pitt Nov. 28, 1758, states that Forbes reached the Loyalhanna Nov. 2, *Sharpe* II 303.

37. Robinson to W Nov. [misprinted September] 13, 1758, concerning the Virginia legislature's adverse action, *Letters to W* III 94. The act was ch. 1 of the Laws of September 1758 session, Hening *Va. Statutes* VII 172-173. (The legislature reversed its action at a special session in November, Robinson to W Nov. [misprinted September] 13, 1758, *Letters to W* III 94-95 and Laws of November, 1758, session ch. 1, Hening *Va. Statutes* VII 252-253, but Forbes had decided to advance before he could know this.)

38. Address of Va. House of Burgesses to Gov. Fauquier Oct. 11, 1758, *Va. House Journals* for 1758-1761, p. 44.

39. Council of war and advice by Forbes' officers not to advance, Minutes of Council of Officers at Pittsborough (as the post at Loyalhanna was temporarily named) Nov. 11, 1758, *Bouquet* II 600-601; and W to Gov. Fauquier Nov. 28, *W* II 308-309. As to the name Pittsborough or Pitsborough *Bouquet* II 600 and 603 and *W* II 306.

40. Forbes to Gen. James Abercromby Nov. 17, 1758, as to foray of Nov. 12, and importance of the intelligence obtained from prisoners taken, *Forbes* 255, and W to Gov. Fauquier Nov. 28, *W* II 308. W as the leader of the detachment that captured the prisoners was reported in the *Maryland Gazette* of Dec. 7, 1758.

41. W's letter of Nov. 28, 1758 to Fauquier implies that it was the intelligence from the prisoners which induced Forbes to proceed. (In his autobiographical "Remarks" in 1786, *W* XXIX 47, W said the arrival of "some seasonable supplies" was responsible for Forbes' decision to advance. I have found no contemporary evidence supporting this statement.)

42. Arrangement of troops, Forbes' Orderly Book, Nov. 14, 1758, Toner "Washington in the Forbes Expedition" 203, with Col. James Burd of Pennsylvania to Bouquet Nov. 20, Nixon *Burd* 65. Order of march, Sharpe to Pitt Nov. 28, 1758, *Sharpe* II 303 with W to Forbes Nov. 15, 16, and 17, *W* II 301-305. W was the senior provincial officer because his commission

as colonel, issued in 1755, long antedated those of Col. Byrd of Va. and the three Pennsylvania provincial colonels who were not commissioned until 1758.

43. W's statement that his brigade was "the leading one," "Remarks" in 1786, *W* XXIX 47.

44. As to Armstrong's party leading the advance, report in *Maryland Gazette* Dec. 5, 1758, confirmed by circumstantial evidence in W to Forbes Nov. 15, 16, 17, and 18, *W* II 301-306. Forbes' Orderly Book, Nov. 14, 1758, Toner "Washington in the Forbes Expedition" 203, lists Col. John Armstrong in Bouquet's, not in W's brigade. As to Armstrong, sketch of him in *D.A.B.*

45. French abandon and Forbes enters Fort Duquesne, Bouquet to Chief Justice William Allen of Pa. Nov. 25, 1758, *Bouquet* II 610-612; Capt. John Haslet of Delaware to Francis Alison Nov. 26, *Olden Time* I 184; W to Fauquier Nov. 28, *W* II 308; Forbes to Pitt Nov. 27, *Forbes* 267; Sharpe to Lord Baltimore Dec. 14, *Sharpe* II 312.

46. Col. Hugh Mercer of Pa. left in command, Forbes to Gen. Amherst Jan. 28, 1759, *Forbes* 287; Bouquet to Amherst March 11, 1759, *Bouquet Papers* Series 21634 p. 8. Mercer at Fort Pitt, Mercer to Bouquet Dec. 19 and 23, 1758, *Bouquet* II 635-636; 639-640 and Waterman *Mercer* 47-57. As to renaming Fort Duquesne, Fort Pitt, Forbes to Pitt Jan. 21, 1759, *Forbes* 269.

47. As to Forbes' leaving Fort Pitt Dec. 4, 1758, his arrival in Philadelphia Jan. 18, 1759, and his death there on March 11, same 270, 282, 301-302.

48. W's prompt return to Virginia from Fort Pitt, W to Fauquier Dec. 2, and 9, 1758, and to Forbes Dec. 30, *W* II 312-317.

49. W's "Remarks" concerning his resignation because of ill health, *W* XXIX 48-49. The "Remarks" as printed are dated "1783" but this is probably a misprint for 1786, when W was collaborating on a biography of himself (never published and probably never completed) by David Humphreys. W wrote Faquier on Dec. 9, 1758, of his "present Disorder," but did not indicate the nature of his illness, *W* II 316. His frequent illnesses from 1749 to 1758 are described in an appendix to this chapter.

50. The exact date of W's resignation is not known; but presumably it was as of Dec. 31, 1758.

51. The officers' regret is recorded in an affectionate and highly appreciative address dated Dec. 31, 1758, signed by nearly all the officers of W's regiment, *Letters to W* III 143-146.

52. There is a good account of the capture of Fort Niagara and Quebec in 1759 and of Montreal in 1760 in Gipson *Brit. Empire* VII 347-355, 400-425, and 444-463. By the Capitulation of Montreal of Sept. 8, 1760, the Marquis de Vaudreuil surrendered not only Montreal but all the remaining posts in Canada not yet in British possession, *S. & D. Doc.* I 25-36.

53. There is an admirable account of the French influence among the Cherokees and of the Cherokee War of 1760-1761 in Alden *Stuart* 88-133.

54. W's letters from 1759 to 1761 referring to the fighting still in progress, *W* II 318-373 *passim* and W to the Reverend Andrew Burnaby July 21, 1761, 2 *W & M Q* XXII (1942) 221-223.

CHAPTER TWELVE

1. W married Martha Custis Jan. 6, 1759, W's statement of "lineage," *W* XXXII 29. The probable place of the wedding is discussed in Freeman III 1-2. Martha was about nine months older than W, same II 292 n. Details of her property (acquired by W through his marriage) are given in Chapter 13. W's letter to Sally Fairfax of Sept. 12, 1758, quoted in Chapter 10, indicates that Martha and he were then reputed to be engaged.

2. That W and Martha wrote many letters to each other is known from references in their few surviving letters to each other and in letters of others to or from them, notably a letter from Mrs. Samuel Powell to W March 11 to 13, 1797, telling of her having found a whole packet of his letters to Martha in a writing desk she had bought from him, Carroll and Ashworth, *Washington* 449.

3. The known surviving letters are W to Martha W, June 18 and 23, 1775, *W* III 293-295, and 300-301, and Martha to W, undated postscript to letter of March 30, 1767, from Lund W to W, *Mount Vernon Report* for 1959, p. 40. I agree with Freeman, for the reasons stated by him, Freeman II 405-406, that W's supposed love letter to Martha of July 20, 1758, *W* II 242, is probably spurious.

4. In an introductory note to his editon of W's writings Fitzpatrick states that "a granddaughter . . . is authority for the statement that, shortly before her demise, Martha Washington destroyed her correspondence with the General," *W* I xlix. Lossing *Mary and Martha* 278 n. quotes W's step-grandson, George Washington Parke Custis, as saying that Martha destroyed her letters to and from W to avoid "desecrating their chaste loves," and because "perhaps some word or expression might be interpreted to his disadvantage."

5. Martha W's undated postscript to a letter of Lund W to W, dated March 30, 1767, *Mount Vernon Report* for 1959, p. 40, described there as *Photocopy from the original in the collection of Dr. Joseph Fields.*

6. Martha W's affectionate letter to her sister Mrs. Burwell Bassett Aug. 28, 1762, Wharton *Martha Washington* 56-57. "Mrs. Dawson," referred to by Martha, was probably Elizabeth Dawson of Williamsburg, widow of William Dawson. W apparently was disturbed by Martha's defective spelling, grammar, and punctuation, since he later wrote out letters for her to copy and sign as her own. See, for example, a letter of Martha to Mrs. Samuel Powell, May 20, 1767, in Carroll and Ashworth *Washington* between pages 99 and 100, and accompanying comments there.

7. Mercy (Mrs. James) Warren to Mrs. John Hancock concerning Martha W April 5, 1776, Freeman IV 77.

8. Abigail (Mrs. John) Adams to Mrs. Richard Cranch June 28 and July 12, 1789, describing Martha, Mitchell *Abigail Adams* 13-15. Henry Wansey, who met Martha in 1794, described her as "short in stature" and "rather robust," Decatur *Private Affairs of Washington* 174. Other descriptions of Martha are in Benjamin Latrobe's diary (1796); Albert Gallatin to his wife (1797); Julian U. Niemcewicz's diary (1798) and Joshua Brookes' journal (1799), Carroll and Ashworth *Washington* 395, 431 n., 511, and 564.

9. Scandal stories about W discredited, Fitzpatrick *The George Washington Scandals, passim.* The supposed "Kate the Washer-woman's Daughter" incident is fully disposed of in French "The First George Washington Scandal" 468-474.

10. My supposition as to the happiness of the marriage is based chiefly on the few letters between W and Martha and many letters from her to others. There is a large collection at Mount Vernon of Martha's letters to various correspondents, mostly after June, 1775. The only letters of hers in our period which I have seen are: June 1, 1760, to Mrs. Burwell Bassett, Hughes *Washington* I 458-459; August 28, 1762, to Mrs. Burwell Bassett, Wharton *Martha Washington* 56-57; Aug 10, 1764, to a milliner, Mrs. Sherbury, original at Mount Vernon.

11. W to Jonathan Boucher July 9, 1771, stating that Jacky would be seventeen "next November," *W* III 51, is equivalent to saying he was born in Nov., 1754. Hence, he was four years old when his mother married W in Jan., 1759.

12. As to employment of Walter Magowan as a tutor in 1761 and his residence with the Washingtons until 1768, *W* II 368 and 486-487 and *W Diaries* I 252-254.

13. W's order of books from Robert Cary & Co. of London Oct. 12, 1761 *W* II 370-371. The cost was to be divided equally between Jacky and Patcy Custis.

14. W to Boucher May 30, 1768, concerning Jacky Custis' study of Virgil and of the New Testament in Greek, same II 487.

15. W to Robert Cary & Co. May 10, 1768, stating that Magowan was leaving for England to take holy orders, same II 482-483.

16. Boucher to W July 15, 1768, indicates that Custis had entered the school not long before, *Letters to W* III 320. In 1768 Boucher's parish and school were in Caroline county, Va. but by Oct. 1, 1770, he had moved to Annapolis, Md., same IV 34.

17. W to Boucher May 30, 1768, as to Custis' good ability ("genius") and morals, *W* II 487-488. W added that he was particularly anxious to have Custis fit for useful purposes because he was "the last of his Family and will possess a very large Fortune."

18. Boucher to W Aug. 2, 1768, speaking very favorably of "Master Custis," *Letters to W* III 324-328.

19. Boucher to W July 20, 1769, and Dec. 18, 1770, speaking of Custis' laziness and his voluptuousness, same III 360 and IV 41-46.

20. W to Boucher Jan. 2, 1771, as to his preference concerning Custis' studies, *W* III 36.

21. W's order of July 25, 1769, to Robert Cary & Co. for books for Custis, same II 512, 515-517.

22. W's letter criticizing the composition of Custis' letters is missing but its contents are deducible from Custis' reply of Aug. 18, 1771, *Letters to W* IV 80. Other letters of Custis to W and Martha W are in same 31, 230, 232, and 336.

23. W to Boucher Feb. 3 and July 9, 1771, and Boucher to W May 9 and July 4, 1771, concerning a contemplated grand tour of England and continental Europe by Custis with Boucher as his tutor, *W* III 39, 49-51 and *Letters to W* IV 61, 69-73.

24. Boucher to W Nov. 19, 1771, discloses that W then had in mind sending Custis to college, same 83-84, 86.

25. Boucher favors William and Mary College for Custis, Boucher to W Nov. 19, 1771, same 86.

26. W's unfavorable opinion of William and Mary College, Boucher

to W Nov. 19, 1771, and Jan. 19, 1773, same 86 and 175, referring to letters of W which are missing but whose contents are evident from Boucher's replies. About this time (July 12, 1772) Richard Henry Lee wrote his brother William that he "never could bring" himself "to think of William and Mary" for his sons' education, because "there, so little attention is paid either to the learning or the morals of the boys . . . ," Ballagh *Lee* I 70. Probably these same considerations influenced W's decision.

27. W's favoring the college at Princeton or at Philadelphia appears from Boucher to W Nov. 19, 1771, and Jan. 19, 1773, *Letters to W* IV 83-84, 86, 175, and 179. W had previously volunteered to send the son of a distant relative to Princeton ("Jersey College"), W to William Ramsay Jan. 29, 1769, *W* II 499, sent Jacky's son there in 1797, and wrote highly of the college, same XXXV, 284, 510.

28. Boucher to W Jan. 19, 1773, conceding that the latter's careful "Enquiries on the Spot precludes all farther Doubt" as to "the Mismanagement" at William and Mary College, and urging that King's College be chosen instead, *Letters to W* IV 175-178.

29. W to Benedict Calvert April 3, 1773, as to the engagement of Custis and Nelly Calvert, *W* III 129-130.

30. Benedict Calvert was an illegitimate but recognized son of the fifth Lord Baltimore, deceased, former Proprietor of Maryland, Freeman III 318-319, and was the half-brother of Baltimore's legitimate daughter, Caroline Calvert, wife of Robert Eden (Horatio Sharpe's successor as Governor of Maryland), of whom there is a sketch in *D.A.B.*

31. Calvert was a member of the Maryland Council and Collector of the King's customs for the Patuxent District of Maryland, two highly important offices.

32. As to Nelly Calvert, W to Calvert and to Burwell Bassett, April 3, 1773, and June 20, *W* III 130 and 138, and Boucher to W April 8, *Letters to W* IV 192-193.

33. W to Calvert April 3, 1773, concerning a marriage settlement for Nelly Calvert, *W* III 130.

34. Calvert to W April 8, 1773, concerning a marriage settlement for Nelly, *Letters to W* IV 189-190.

35. W's trip to New York, diary entries May 8 to June 8, 1773, *W Diaries* II 110-114.

36. Custis' horse, suite of rooms, and "Joe," his combined valet and groom, Custis to W and to Martha W July 5, 1773, *Letters to W* IV 231, 233. As to number of students at King's College in 1773, *Columbia Register* 989.

37. Custis' courses of study and his complacent remarks, Custis to W and to Martha W July 5, 1773, *Letters to W* IV 230, 233.

38. President Myles Cooper of King's College and Prof. John Vardill to W Sept. 20, 1773, giving favorable reports of Custis, same 262-263 and W's replies Dec. 15, *W* III 167, 168 n.

39. W to Cooper Dec. 15, 1773, concerning Custis' prospective marriage, *W* III 167-168.

40. The marriage took place at the Calvert home Feb. 3, 1773, W's diary for that day, *W Diaries* II 140. The Custises had four children, the two younger of whom, George Washington Parke Custis (father-in-

law of General Robert E. Lee) and Eleanor Parke Custis, were virtually adopted by George and Martha W. As to them and the other children of Jack and Nelly Custis, see the Index, under "Custis" in Carroll and Ashworth *Washington* 692.

41. As to the guess concerning Patcy Custis' age, Freeman III 2. I have found no better evidence than that to which he refers.

42. W's sending for Dr. Rumney (William Rumney of Alexandria, Va.) for Patcy, June 14, 1768, *W Diaries* I 272.

43. Paid Joshua Evans £1 10 sh for the iron ring treatment, Feb. 16, 1769, Freeman III 210. Trip to Warm Springs, W's diary July to Sept. 1769, *W Diaries* I 336, 339-344. W to Thomas Johnson of Md., July 20, 1770, as to simples (herbs) from Dr. John Johnson "for Fitts," *W* III 20-21; Dr. John Carter of Williamsburg, May 7, 1771, £1 5 sh for "4 bottles of Fit Drops," *W Diaries* II 15 n.; "another large Cargo of Physic for Miss Custis," Boucher to W May 9, 1771, *Letters to W* IV 61.

44. W to Burwell Bassett, husband of Martha's sister, June 20, 1773, concerning Patcy Custis' death, *W* III 138.

45. W's visitors from 1760 to 1775, W's diaries for Jan. to May 1760, and Jan. 1, 1768, to June 19, 1775, *W Diaries* I 107-164 and 245-455 and II 3-199.

46. There are fourteen surviving letters of W to Robert Stewart and over fifty from him (1755 to 1768), twelve to William Henry Fairfax and nine from him (1755 to May 1775) and nine to Burwell Bassett and three from him (1762 to June, 1775). All of these are published in *W* I, II, III, and XXXVII and *Letters to W* I-V. (Dr. James Craik, too, was apparently a good friend, but there are few surviving letters between him and W, and W's only other considerable surviving correspondence in this period, that with his neighbor George Mason, is chiefly political.)

47. Stewart to W Oct. 13, 1763, speaks of Great Britain as "my native Isle," *Letters to W* III 259. This and much of the information in the text and the ensuing footnotes concerning Stewart is missing from the undocumented and inaccurate sketch of him in *Wisc. Hist. Coll.* XVIII (1918) 225 n.

48. Stewart served with distinction in a Virginia unit with Gen. Braddock in 1755, *Va. House Journals* for 1752-1755 p. 301 and Dinwiddie to Abercromby May 28, 1756, *Dinwiddie* II 425. He was a captain in W's re-established regiment, W to Stewart, Nov. 18, 1755, *W* I 238, and accompanied W on his trips to Gen. Shirley and Gen. Loudoun discussed in Chapter 8, Joseph Chew to W March 4, 1756, *Letters to W* I 200 and *W Col. Traveller* 107.

49. Stewart got a royal commission as a lieutenant in the 60th (Royal American) Regiment in Sept., 1758, Ford *British Officers* 96; but he was able to continue, on leaves of absence, as an officer in the Va. service for several years longer, Stewart to W May 14, 1760, Oct. 2, 1760, and April 6, 1761, *Letters to W* III, 181, 197, and 212. By 1762 he had become a lieutenant colonel in the Va. service, Stewart to W Nov. 15, 1762, same 240.

50. Stewart to W Jan. 14, 1764, telling of his recent arrival in England, *Letters to W* III 262.

51. Stewart to W March 10, 1768, from Jamaica telling of his appointment as Comptroller of Customs, same III 307. Stewart back in England by 1774, Robert Mackenzie to W Sept. 13, 1774, same V 50. W to George

Mercer April 5, 1775, saying he had written Stewart several letters, without receiving a reply, and now sending him "warmest wishes,"*W* III 288-289.

52. W to Stewart enclosing bills of exchange for £302 sterling as a loan, *W* II 399. As to the loan being without security and free of interest, W to Robert Cary & Co. July 25, 1769, same 512. (£302 sterling then was perhaps equivalent to about $8,000 today. See Knollenberg *Origin* 270.)

53. Stewart to W Jan. 25, 1769, thanking him for his kindness, *Letters to W* III 335. Stewart had written W March 10, 1768, telling him to draw for repayment, *Letters to W* III 308. Some difficulty arose over W's draft; but this was eventually cleared up, W to Robert Cary & Co. July 25, 1769, and Aug. 20, 1770, *W* II 512 and XXXVII 494.

54. W to Stewart Aug. 10, 1783, answering the latter's request for help in securing a government position in the U.S., *W* XXVII 88-90. W wrote that he "never interfered in any Civil Appointments" and that in any event, those who had exposed themselves "with Halters about their Necks, not only to common danger . . . but to the verge of poverty" should have priority.

55. As to W's attention to Fairfax's affairs after his leaving for England, W to Fairfax Oct. 15, 1773, June 10 and 25, 1774, and May 31, 1775, *W* XXXVII 501-502, III 221-225, 226 n., and 290-291. Fairfax and his wife, Sally, had left Virginia before Oct. 15, 1773, and had reached Dumfries, Scotland by Jan. 10, 1774, same XXXVII 501 and III 221.

56. W to Samuel Athawes Jan. 8, 1788, acknowledging the latter's letter of July 29, 1787, advising W of Fairfax's death and of W's appointment as an executor of the estate, same XXIX 360-361. W was too overburdened with his own and public affairs to accept.

57. W frequently spelled off "of"—a common spelling of the word in the eighteenth century.

58. W's jocular letter to Bassett Aug. 28, 1762, *W* XXXVII 484-485. Though accepted without question by Fitzpatrick in editing W's writings, this letter was challenged by Freeman (Freeman III 82 n.) as probably, at least in part, "spurious." For reasons given in an appendix to this chapter, I am not impressed by Freeman's grounds for questioning the letter. He seems determined to make Washington conform to a preconceived image or to fit his own standard of behavior instead of accepting Washington as he was.

59. W to Bassett June 19, 1775, as to his election as Commander-in-Chief, *W* III 296-297. W and Bassett remained warm friends until the latter's death in 1793, as to which see W to Henry Lee Jan. 20, 1793, and to Burwell Bassett Jr. March 4, *W* XXXII 310 and 373. W had by this time been drawn to the Bassetts closer than ever by the marriage of their daughter Frances to one of his favorite nephews, George Augustine W.

CHAPTER THIRTEEN

1. W's letters refer to many letters received from Robert Cary & Co., but I have found only one from them, a brief letter of Feb. 18, 1774, *Letters to W* IV 332.

2. The Mount Vernon acreage of 2,126 given in the text is from W's

list of quitrents paid in 1761, *W* II 390. (Freeman VI 388, for reasons there given, puts the acreage at 2,650, but I think these reasons fail to justify not accepting W's own figure.) As to the death of Lawrence W's widow in 1761, Freeman III 57.

3. The statement of W's probable land holdings at the time of his marriage in 1759 is based on "A List of Lands for which I paid Quit-Rents in the year 1761" in *W* II 390. The 1,806 acres listed as "bot. of Clifton," were acquired in May 1760, i.e., after his marriage, *W Diaries* I 163. The land listed in King George county was probably the unsold portion of land inherited by W from his father; the rest W had gradually acquired, Freeman I 243, 244, 260, and 269 n. W also may have had some town property at this time.

4. Under the common law rules of inheritance and coverture in force in Virginia, Martha became entitled to a life interest in one-third of these assets, and, when she married W, this interest passed to him, same III 20.

5. W to Robert Cary & Co. May 1, 1759, as to his being entitled to a share of the Dainel Parke Custis estate, *W* II 319. Custis had died intestate leaving 17,438 acres of land and about 300 slaves, Freeman II 300 and III 21.

6. Each of Custis' heirs received personal property and slaves valued at £1,617 sterling plus £7,618 Virginia currency, of which £2,986 Virginia currency was in slaves, same III 21. In his will W provided for eventual freeing of all his slaves. Ford *Washington Wills* 85-86, 96, but at this period his attitude towards and treatment of them seem to have been those of a typical slaveholder of the upper South. A suit against the Custis estate was long pending, same II 298-301, III 225-227, 248, 282, 287, 335, but apparently nothing came of it.

7. W to Robert Cary & Co. Nov. 10, 1773, saying he was entitled to half of over £16,000 due Patcy Custis at her death and to credit this to W's account *W* III 164-165.

8. As to W's additions to his holdings adjoining Mount Vernon, Freeman VI 388-390. The statement in same III 263 n. that Ledger A fol:257 gives W's holdings in Fairfax county in 1770 as 2,318 acres is a slip for 5,318. A detailed description of the Mount Vernon farms appears in an advertisement by W Feb. 1, 1796, *W* XXXIV 433-438.

9. My statement as to tobacco as the chief cash crop on W's plantations is based on his not mentioning the sale of other crops in his surviving letters before 1765. Wheat replacing tobacco as chief cash crop at Mount Vernon, W to Stewart & Campbell Sept. 4, 1766, to Carlyle & Adam, Feb. 15, 1767, and to Robert Cary & Co. June 1, 1774, same II 442, 445 and III 220. W's "Remarks" estimate that he was growing "about 7,000 Bushls. of Wheat"—apparently shortly before the Revolution, *W* XXIX 49.

10. As to the flour mill, W to various correspondents, same III 7-63 *passim*. Creswell's comments concerning the mill are in his journal for July 10, 1774, *Creswell's Journal* 26-27. W to Robert Cary & Co. June 1, 1774, stated that his "Force" was about confined to growing wheat and milling it into flour, *W* III 220.

11. W to Daniel Jenifer Adams July 20, 1772, as to shipment of musty flour to Barbados, same III 98. As to subsequent anxiety and litigation over this shipment, same 105-275 *passim*.

12. W to Robert McMickan of Jamaica May 10, 1774, and Jan. 7, 1775, as to shipment of flour to Jamaica and McMickan's failure to pay, same 213, 256.

13. Unless otherwise noted the statements in this and the following five paragraphs are based on a multitude of items in published letters of and to W, his diaries and his unpublished Ledger A covering the years 1759 to 1775. W's "Remarks" estimate that he was growing "about . . . 10,000 bushels of Indn. Corn"—apparently shortly before the Revolution, *W* XXIX 49.

14. For an illustrative contract of employment of a carpenter ("joiner") for one year, for keep and twenty-five pounds Virginia currency payable at the end of the term, between W and John Askew, dated Sept. 1, 1759, Ford *Washington as an Employer* 25-26.

15. The earliest evidence I have found of W's having a commercial distillery is in 1799, *W* XXXVII 2-461 *passim*. (Freeman III 78 states that W "ordered a new still in 1761," but this apparently was not primarily for commercial use, same 116.)

16. For a contract between Burgess Mitchell and W dated May 1, 1762, to act as overseer of W's "house Plantation" for six months for keep and six pounds Virginia currency payable at the end of the term, Ford *Washington as an Employer* 27-28.

17. Lund W came "to live with me" in 1764, W to Carlyle & Adam Feb. 15, 1767, *W* II 449. W's letters to Lund W from August 1775 to 1794, same III to XXXIV, are very interesting and important. Most of the letters of the same period from Lund W to W have not yet been published.

18. For a contract for the management of "Bullskin Quarters" for one year on a share basis between W and Edward Violet, dated Aug. 5, 1762, Ford *Washington as an Employer* 28-32.

19. W's order ("invoice of sundries") enclosed in W to Robert Cary & Co. Sept. 20, 1759, *W* II 330-336.

20. As to W's complaints of low prices for his tobacco shipped to Robert Cary & Co. and the high prices and poor quality of goods shipped by them to him, Nettels *Washington* 68-69. Typical of his complaints are those stated at length in W to Robert Cary & Co. Aug. 20, 1770, *W* XXXVII 491-493.

21. As stated in the Foreword, one of the great difficulties in dealing with W's life before 1775 is that nearly all of Robert Cary & Co.'s letters to him are missing. However, the fact that he continued to use the company as his chief factor from 1759 to 1774, when he ceased to ship tobacco, tends to indicate that it was able to give satisfactory answers to many if not most of his many complaints. Some Virginia planters were so heavily in debt to their factors that they were practically unable to shift to another factor, but this was not true of W.

22. W's companions and journey to Pittsburgh en route to the Great Kanawha River, Oct. 5 to 17, 1770, *W Diaries* I 404-409.

23. W's visit in and around Pittsburgh, trip down the Ohio, and observations concerning the land along the lower Great Kanawha Oct. 17 to Nov. 1, 1770, same 409 to 427.

24. W's diary entries concerning his trip on the Ohio and Great Kanawha Oct. 20 to Nov. 21, 1770, same 412-446.

25. W's return trip to Mount Vernon Nov. 4 to Dec. 1, 1770, same 429-452.

26. Initial members of the Dismal Swamp Company May 1763, Freeman III 95, 103. John Robinson, Speaker of the House of Burgesses, and Anthony Bacon & Co. of London had become members by the following November, "Articles of Agreement" Nov. 3, 1763, *Va. Mag.* XXXV (1929) 64-65. Freeman's well-documented account of W's Dismal Swamp venture is based largely on the Dismal Swamp Records and Accounts at the Library of Congress, cited by him as "Papers of the Dismal Swamp Company." For descriptions of the Swamp, W's diary for Oct. 15, 1763, *W Diaries* I 188-194; W to Dr. Hugh Williamson March 31, 1784, *W* XXVII 378-380; and sources cited in Freeman III 94 n.

27. The Commission from the King to successive Governors of Virginia authorized them, with the advice of the provincial Council, to grant Crown land in the colony "to any Person or Persons . . . as you, by and with the Advice aforesaid, shall think fit . . . ," e.g., Commission of Jan. 15, 1715, to Gov. Lord Orkney, published in *Va. Mag.* XX (1912) 345-346. This power was continued in the Commission of March 4, 1761, to Governor Gen. Sir Jeffery Amherst, under which Lieut. Gov. Francis Fauquier, Dinwiddie's successor, was acting, C. O. 5:1368:23-51. Various limitations on this broad power were imposed by the Governor's Instructions and Va. statutes.

28. Membership of William and Thomas Nelson and Robert Burwell in the Va. Council, *Va. Legislative Council Journals* III 1305.

29. An option was preferable to an outright grant, because the latter would have required immediate payment of a large fee for patenting the land and an annual quitrent to the Crown.

30. Petitions of May 25 and Nov. 1, 1763, for the exclusive right for seven years to survey and patent up to 180,000 acres of land in the Dismal Swamp area, Freeman III 95 and 102. Presumably in order to get around a royal instruction to the Governor not to grant more than 1,000 acres to any one person, Labaree *Royal Instructions* II 580, the real petitioners, as was commonly done, added the names of dummies, 138 of them in this case, to secure the total acreage desired, Freeman III 102-103.

31. Petition for the option was granted by the Governor and Council of Va. in Nov., 1763, and renewed in Nov., 1769, same 102, 240. Also in Jan., 1764, the syndicate secured introduction into the Va. House of Burgesses of a bill "to enable certain Adventurers to drain a large Tract of marshy ground in the Counties of Nansemond and Norfolk," *Va. House Journals* for 1761-1765 pp. 214 and 215-222 *passim*. The bill, promptly enacted into law, gave the right to construct canals and causeways across others' lands on payment of compensation to be determined by arbitration if the parties concerned could not otherwise agree, Va. Acts of Jan., 1764, Hening *Va. Statutes* VIII 18.

32. As to W's investment from 1763 to 1768 of at least £157 and the labor of some of his slaves in the Dismal Swamp project, entries in his books of account from May, 1763 to Jan. 1, 1772, *Letters to W* III 276-279 n. Payments of his quota of expenses of the syndicate at various times from Nov., 1763, to May, 1766, disclose that W then held a one-twelfth interest. In 1768 he purchased part of John Robinson's share, same 278 n.

33. Seven trips of W to the swamp are listed in his account of expenses incurred on the trips, same 276-278 n. His route to and from Williamsburg to the swamp can be worked out from various items in *W Col. Traveller* 165-227 *passim*. In W to Patrick Henry, Nov. 30, 1785, W said he had been "manager of that Company," *W* XXVIII 333.

34. W to John De Neufville Sept. 8, 1785, stating that "The war gave considerable interruption, indeed almost put an entire stop to the progress of the [Dismal Swamp drainage] business," *W* XXVIII 259. My conjecture that work on draining the swamp was not resumed after the Revolution is based on various letters of W from April, 1784, to Oct., 1785, concerning efforts to revive the project, *W* XXVII 391 and XXVIII 121, 127, 136, 259, 286, coupled with the absence of any later references to progress made. Additional details concerning the later history of the project are in Prussing *Estate of Washington* 277-289, 360; the Dismal Swamp Papers, 1784-1785, Duke U. Lib. and W's memorandum for Gov. Henry Lee Feb. 18, 1793, *W* XXXII 349-350.

35. As to the eventual value of the swamp because of its timber, Prussing *Estate of Washington* 278, 285. W valued his interest in the Great Dismal Swamp Company, in an inventory of his holdings of July 9, 1799, at "about $20,000," Ford *Washington Wills* 125-126.

36. Articles of Agreement of the Mississippi Company June 3, 1763, for the acquisition by each of the proposed fifty members of 50,000 acres in the Mississippi valley, *Critical Period* 19-22, with names of the nineteen founding members in Hulbert "Washington's Tour" 436-439. An undated list of members, sent to Lord Chatham by some unknown person on April 2, 1774, names thirty-eight members, *Critical Period* 22-23. Whether the quota of fifty members was ever filled does not appear.

37. By the Treaty of Paris Feb. 10, 1763, France relinquished to Great Britain all its claim to territory east of the Mississippi "except the town of New Orleans and the island in which it is situated," *S & D Doc.* I 116.

38. Articles of Agreement June 3, 1763, giving the framework and mode of procedure of the company, *Critical Period* 19-22.

39. Petition to the King for an option on 2,500,000 acres in a defined tract east of the Mississippi, adopted at a meeting of the company Sept. 9, 1763, attended by W and seventeen other members, same 25. Alvord *Miss. Valley* I 97 has a map of the area as bounded in the company's petition.

40. Minutes of the company's meeting Sept. 9, 1763, *Critical Period* 23-29. As to Thomas Cumming, sketch of him in *D.N.B.* and Gipson *British Empire* VIII 174-176 and 176 n. Mention of his "friendship for many members of the Company" in a letter to Cumming of Sept. 26, 1763, Carter "Documents" 315, suggests that he had been in Virginia. Perhaps he was a relative of Gov. Dinwiddie, whose mother's maiden name was Cumming, *Dinwiddie* I viii and xxii. (A few days after the meeting W wrote George William Fairfax suggesting that he and their friend Dr. James Cockburne join the company, *W* XXXVII 486; but I have seen no evidence of either of them having done so.)

41. The Executive Committee of the company to Cumming Sept. 26, 1763, Carter "Documents" 311-315 as to various matters. The letter and honorarium of 100 guineas for Cumming was to be delivered by Charles Digges, a member of the company, who was bound for London.

42. The Royal Proclamation of Oct. 7, 1763, reserved "for the present"

to the Indians "all the Lands and Territories lying to the Westward of the Sources of the Rivers which fall into the Sea [Atlantic Ocean] from the West and North West . . . ," *S. & D. Doc.* I 167. Probably because of his inability to do anything immediately useful for the company, Cumming declined to accept the 100 guineas tendered him by the company, as appears from the Executive Committee to him March 1, 1767, referring to his generous refusal of the honorarium, Carter "Documents" 316. Cumming became a member of the company, *Critical Period* 23, but when, and whether by gift or purchase, I have not discovered.

43. For later efforts to revive the Mississippi Company project, including a revision of its petition in 1768 to substitute land farther east than that covered in its original petition, Carter "Documents" 315-319; *W Diaries* I 185 n; Alvord *Miss. Valley* II 93; *Acts P.C.* VI 458; *Journal B. of T.* for 1768-1775 pp. 90-91, 163; and Sosin *Whitehall* 189.

44. W charged off his £27.13.5 investment in the company Jan. 1, 1772, *W Diaries* I 185 n. Richard H. Lee to his brother William, April 15, 1774, shows he still then hoped the company might obtain a large grant, Ballagh *Lee* I 106.

45. As to W's unsuccessful milling venture with Gilbert Simpson, Freeman III 308-309, 324-325, 343, 450, VI 4, 14, 17-19. Another substantial loss which W sustained in our period was in a project to settle south of his western land in which he lost over £300 when the twenty odd slaves and indentured servants he sent out in March 1774 decamped, with tools and supplies, before they even reached his land, W to Thomas Everard Sept. 17, 1775, *W* III 498.

46. In W's appraisal of his estate other than at Mount Vernon as of July 9, 1799, totaling $530,000, his Great Kanawha River lands (obtained under the Proclamation of 1754) are valued at about $200,000, Ford *Washington Wills* 128.

CHAPTER FOURTEEN

1. Gov. Robert Dinwiddie's "A Proclamation for Encouraging Men to Enlist" Feb. 19, 1754, C.O. 5:1330:Virginia, fol. 324 no. 66, Pub. Rec. Office; also in *Mercer Papers* 77; Fernow *Ohio Valley* 97-99; Hening *Va. Statutes* VII 661-662. A copy in the Appendix to *Va. Exec. Council Journals* V 499 omits the heading. The minutes of the Governor and Council of Va. Feb. 18, 1754, relating to the Proclamation, unlike the terms of the Proclamation itself, are compatible with the officers' sharing in the land, same 461-462.

2. In "The Case of the Ohio Company" submitted by George Mercer, one of the officers in the Virginia regiment, to John Pownall, Secretary to the British Board of Trade, in 1770, the Proclamation was altered from "Men to enlist" to "persons to enter" and "their officers" to "their superior officers," *Mercer Papers* Part II 17 and Part III 398—thus recognizing the incompatibility of the terms of the Proclamation as issued with the officers' claim to share in the proclamation land.

3. W to Dinwiddie May 29, 1754, apparently assuming that the officers were not to share in the proclamation land, *W* I 60-61.

4. Royal Proclamation of Oct. 7, 1763, *S. & D. Doc.* I 167. Even before this, the British Board of Trade had instructed Gov. Francis Fauquier of Va. not to make any grants of land in the Ohio valley, Board to Fauquier June 13, 1760, C.O. 5:1367, Pub. Rec. Office.

5. Treaty of Hard Labour, Oct. 14, 1768, *Va. House Journals* for 1766-1769 pp. xxvi-xxvii, clarified in Board of Trade to the King April 25, 1769, *N.Y. Col. Doc.* VIII 161, approved, Hillsborough to Gage March 24, 1769, *Gage* II 86. Treaty of Fort Stanwix Nov. 5, 1768, *N. Y. Col. Doc.* VIII 135-137, confirmed July 21, 1770, same 237. In the latter treaty, the grant by the Six Nations extended as far west as the Tennessee ("Cherokee") River.

6. W to Gov. Lord Botetourt Dec. 8, 1769, speaking of having mentioned the proclamation land to Botetourt the preceding May, *W* II 528-529. (Some officers, including W, had earlier sought a share in this land, George Mercer to W Sept. 16, 1759, *Letters to W* III 159-160; undated memorial to the King C.O. 5:1330 Pub. Rec. Office, considered March 2, 1763, *Journal B. of T.* for 1759-1763 p. 339, but evidently without success.)

7. W's petition on behalf of himself and others, undated but marked "consider'd 15th Dec. 1769," Washington Papers 11:106, L.C. All the rivers mentioned were southern tributaries of the Ohio.

8. Resolution of Governor and Council of Va. Dec. 15, 1769, including officers in the proposed allotment of the 200,000 acres of bounty land, Va. Executive Council Journal for 1769 pp. 19-20, Va. State Lib. I have found no explanation of this decision. Possibly the Governor and Council had no copy of the Proclamation before it, and, on referring to the minutes of Feb. 18, 1754, relating to the Proclamation (*Va. Exec. Council Journals* V 461-462) found them compatible with the officers' claim to share.

9. W's undated notices to claimants of proclamation land, published in *Virginia Gazette* (Purdie & Dixon) Dec. 21, 1769, *W* XXXVII 489-490 and of claims filed to Oct. 31, 1771, *Virginia Gazette* (Rind's) Jan. 14, 1773.

10. W's application for William Crawford's appointment and the record of appointment are missing, but we know he did apply from the favorable replies concerning the appointment sent him by two of the masters of William and Mary Dec. 20, and 21, 1769, *Letters to W* III 366-368. Crawford presumably had been appointed by March 5, 1771, when officers of W's old regiment authorized him to employ Crawford to survey their proclamation land for them, minutes of officers' meeting of March 5, 1771, Washington Papers, L.C.

11. W to Crawford Sept. 21, 1767, concerning project for a surreptitious search for western lands despite the Royal Proclamation of 1763, and offering him a share in the project, *W* II 468-471. Crawford to W Sept. 29, 1767, accepting, *Letters to W* III 299-300.

12. Minutes of the meeting of officers and their agents in Winchester, Va., March 5, 1771, authorizing W to employ Crawford as surveyor, Washington Papers, L.C. The meeting was attended by W and five other officers or their representatives. Notice of the proposed meeting was published by W in the *Virginia Gazette* (Rind's) Feb. 7, 1771.

13. W's "Scheme of Partition" referred to in minutes of the Governor and Council, Nov. 6, 1771, and resolutions of Governor and Council concerning the "Scheme," Minutes of Nov. 6 and Dec. 9, 1771, Va. Executive Council Journal of 1771 pp. 10-12 and 14, Va. State Lib.

14. W eventually got 3,500 acres of the 30,000 reserved acres, W to Gov. Lord Dunmore and Council Nov. 5, 1773, *W* III 160, with *Virginia Gazette* (Rind's) Nov. 25, 1773.

15. W's notice of Dec. 23, 1772, to claimants under Dinwiddie's procla-

mation concerning Crawford's surveys, *Virginia Gazette* (Rind's) Jan. 14, 1773.

16. W goes over Crawford's surveys with him, W's diary entries Oct. 25 to 30, 1772, *W Diaries* II 84-85.

17. Minutes of the Governor and Council of Va. Nov. 6, 1772, allotting surveys according to plan submitted by W, Va. State Lib.

18. The 5,147 acres in addition to W's allotment of 15,000 acres, represented interests purchased by W from Maj. George Muse and Sergeant Rudolf Brickner, W's notice to claimants under Dinwiddie's proclamation Dec. 23, 1772, *Virginia Gazette* (Rind's) Jan. 14, 1773.

19. Governor and Council's allotment order of Nov. 6, 1772, Va. State Lib.

20. Governor and Council's supplemental order of Dec. 9, 1772, same.

22. W's notice of Dec. 23, 1772, concerning allotments, published in *Virginia Gazette* (Rind's) Jan. 24, 1773.

22. W took out patents for his four surveys totaling 20,147 acres, Dec. 15, 1772, Va. Land Patent Rolls for 1771-1773, pp. 66-75, Va. State Lib.

23. Crawford to W Nov. 12, 1773, as to the superior quality of W's and Craik's land and their fellow officers' chagrin, *Letters to W* IV 275.

24. W's description of his land as "the cream of the Country," W to Presley Neville June 16, 1794, same XXXIII 407.

25. W to Muse Jan. 29, 1774, concerning the latter's complaint, *W* III 179-180. I have not found Muse's letter of Dec. 24, 1773, to W, but judging from W's letter, Muse's complaint was over a supposed deficiency in the quantity of land surveyed for him rather than over its quality.

26. Dunmore to W April 18, 1775, stating that Crawford was reported not to have taken the required oaths of office when his surveys of W's proclamation land were made, *Letters to W* V 158. There is no evidence that W denied the truth of this report. Valentine Crawford wrote W April 27, 1774, that his brother, had recently been "Swore in to his Comitian," same IV 378; but this, of course, was long after William Crawford had made the surveys in question.

27. The oaths for official surveyors were required and stated by ch. 3 sec. 2 of Va. Laws of Oct., 1712, session, reaffirmed in ch. 19 sec. 1 of Va. Laws of Oct., 1748, session, Hening *Va. Statutes* IV 38 and VI 33.

28. Freeman's statement that Crawford's omission to take the required oaths at the time he made his proclamation land surveys was unknown to W, Freeman III 409.

29. W to Dunmore April 3, 1775, as to the report of the alleged nullity of his land patents based on Crawford's surveys, *W* III 280-283. That others besides Dunmore thought there was something "fishy" about Crawford's surveys for W seems to be indicated by Thomas Lewis, Surveyor of Augusta county, to Col. William Preston, Surveyor of Fincastle county, March 15, 1774, stating that "Colo Washington sent two surveys by one Crawford to be signed by me, but this I refuse. These are Strange Sort of requests and I think ought not to be complyed with," Quaife *Preston and Va. Papers* 102.

30. Va. act requiring that in surveys of Crown land, "the breadth of the tract . . . shall be at least the proportion of one third part of the length except when the courses thereof shall be interrupted by rivers, creeks or impassable swamps," ch. 3 sec. 2 of Va. Laws of Oct., 1712,

session, Hening *Va. Statutes* IV 38– an act designed "to prevent the practice of *Garbling*, as it is called, that is, that the Patentees shall be obliged to take some indifferent land with the good," *Va. House Journals* for 1770 to 1772, p. xxiv.

31. W's 20,147 acres stretched along bottoms of the Ohio and Great Kanawha rivers for 5¼, 3, 5, and 17 miles respectively, or a total of 30¼ miles, W to Neville June 16, 1794, *W* XXXIII 408, whereas, under the anti-garbling law of 1712 the total length of these tracts should not have exceeded about 18 miles. Cook *Washington's Western Lands* 53 has a map of the tracts.

32. Dunmore to W April 18, 1775, concerning the apparent nullity of Crawford's surveys, *Letters to W* V 158. Freeman III 408 is critical of Dunmore because he wrote "as if he never had entertained Colonel Washington and did not distinguish the Fairfax Burgess and the former commander of the Virginia troops, from any adventurer who might be attempting to defraud the Colony." Dunmore's letter seems to me to have been quite correct.

33. Validation of Crawford's surveys of land allotted under Dinwiddie's proclamation of 1754, Virginia laws of May, 1779, session, ch. 12 sec. 1, Hening *Va. Statutes* X 36. W to Benjamin Harrison, Speaker of the Va. House, Dec. 18, 1778, indicates that W had suggested such an act, *W* XIII 463.

34. Provision of the Royal Proclamation of 1763 relating to bonus land *S & D Doc.* I 166. There was question whether any provincial officers were entitled to land under the proclamation, W to Thomas Lewis, Feb. 17, 1774, *W* III 184, but Dunmore evidently decided that the allowance was not confined to regular officers, W to James Wood March 13, 1773, same 124-125.

35. As to meaning of "reduced" officer, *Oxford English Dictionary* VIII 316, under "Reduced" 2a. See also *Va. House Journals* for 1761-1765, p. 124.

36. Message of Gov. Fauquier to the Va. Council and House March 30, 1762, stating he had recently disbanded the first Virginia regiment on receipt of official word of the conclusion of peace with the Cherokees, same for 1761 to 1765, p. 47.

37. W to Charles W Jan. 31, 1770, as to buying rights of officers who had continued in service until after the Cherokee Expedition, *W* III 2.

38. Dunmore issued a certificate to W for 5,000 acres under the Proclamation of 1763 on or before March 13, 1773, W to James Wood March 13, and to the Governor of West Florida, March 25, *W* III 124-127. I have not found whether Dunmore, who came to Virginia long after W's resignation in 1758, did not know that W was not a "reduced" officer or intentionally ignored the limitation in the Proclamation.

39. The Proclamation of 1763 specified that reduced colonels were to receive 5,000 acres each, *S. & D. Doc.* I 166.

40. By 1778, W had patented only "a small part" of the land covered by Dunmore's certificate under the Proclamation of 1763, W to Benjamin Harrison Dec. 18, 1778, *W* XIII 463. W to William Preston Feb. 28, 1774, and March 27, 1775, indicates that some of this was on the Cole river in present West Virginia, *W* III 191 and 278-279. A particularly valuable tract, the Burning Spring tract, also apparently was obtained

under the Proclamation of 1763. As to this latter tract, Prussing *Estate of Washington* 337.

41. W's "Schedule of property" attached to his will dated July 9, 1799 [misdated 1790], includes his appraisal of the property willed by him, *W* XXXVII 297-298.

42. Minutes of officers at Winchester, Va., meeting March 5, 1771, authorizing W to employ Crawford on their joint behalf, Washington Papers, L.C.

43. Statements by W and his biographers concerning his acquisition of bounty land are discussed in an appendix to this chapter.

44. Sketch published in London in 1779, saying W was "avaritious under the specious appearance of disinterestedness," particularly concerning land, Baker *Early Sketches of Washington* 32.

CHAPTER FIFTEEN

1. W to Jack (John Augustine) W, May 28, 1755, as to running for burgess, *W* I 130-131.

2. W's unsuccessful candidacy in 1755 for burgess from Frederick county in which he received 40 votes, the two successful candidates, Hugh West and Thomas Swearingen 271 and 270, respectively, Freeman II 147. I have found no explanation of the "tender part" which is mentioned in Adam Stephen to W Dec. 23, 1755, as responsible for his defeat, *Letters to W* I 158.

3. W's election as burgess for Frederick county in 1758, John McNeill, Charles Smith, Robert Stewart, and others to W July 24 and 25, 1758, *Letters to W* II 381-389. Thomas Bryan Martin, a nephew of Lord Fairfax, was elected as W's fellow burgess from Frederick, same 385.

4. Bills dated July 24, 1758, for drinks in connection with W's election, same 398-400.

5. W's re-election as burgess for Frederick county in May, 1761, by 505 votes to 399 for George Mercer, the next highest candidate, *W* II 359 n. As to the third principal candidate, Adam Stephen, and his campaign, Robert Stewart to W Feb. 13, 1761, *Letters to W* III 201-203, and W to Van Swearingen May 15, *W* II 358-359.

6. W's election as burgess for Fairfax county in July 1765, with 201 votes to 148 for John West, the next highest candidate, *W* II 424 n. Also W to Burwell Bassett, Aug. 2, 1765, same 424.

7. W's re-election and continuous service as burgess for Fairfax county until the Revolution, *Va. House Journals* for 1766-1769 p. 3, for 1770-1772 pp. 3, 113, 143, and for 1773-1776 pp. 3, 67, and 163.

8. Representation in the Va. House of Burgesses in 1758 and in 1775, *Va. House Journals* for 1758-1761 pp. vii-viii and for 1773-1776 pp. 163-164.

9. W's appointment to and work on the Committee of Propositions and Grievances at his first (Feb.-April, 1759) session, same for 1758-1761 pp. 57-113 *passim*. W was excused April 2, 1759, from attendance for the remainder of the session, same 113. As to the process of legislation in Va. at this period, Knollenberg *Origin* 45-46.

10. W's reappointment to and work of the Committee of Propositions and Grievances at the Nov.-Dec., 1762, session, *Va. House Journals* for 1761-1765 pp. 97-166 *passim*.

11. W's appointment to the Committee of Privileges and Elections at the Nov.-Dec., 1766, session, same for 1766-1769 p. 14. As to the functions of this Committee, same 15-54 *passim.*

12. William Fitzhugh's contest of seating of Thompson Mason same 17, 20, 39, 54.

13. John Robinson's huge embezzlement and loans to friends and members of the Va. House of Burgesses, Mays *Pendleton* I 174-186.

14. The British measures from 1759 to 1764 restricting colonial self government, and colonial opposition to these measures are discussed in Knollenberg *Origin* 57-74, 150-156, and 176-220.

15. W to Francis Dandridge, an English relative of Martha W, Sept. 20, 1765, concerning the Stamp Act, *W* II 425-426. A letter of this same date from W to his principal British agent, Robert Cary & Co., contains a similar passage concerning the Stamp Act which is omitted from the letter as published in *W* II 431.

16. The Townshend Act of 1767 levying duties on colonial imports of tea, paper, glass, and paint, 7 George III ch. 46, Knollenberg *Origin,* 240-241.

17. Address of the House of Lords to the King as to trial in England of persons charged with treason in the colonies, Dec. 15, 1768, and concurrence of the House of Commons, Feb. 8, 1769, *Parliamentary History* XVI 475-480, 494-511. The treason act referred to in the Address was 35 Henry VIII ch. 2 (1543).

18. As to the non-importation agreements in 1768 and 1769 of merchants and traders in the chief northern ports, Schlesinger *Col. Merchants* 113-130.

19. W to George Mason April 5, 1769, as to a proposed non-importation agreement, *W* II 500-504. W's letter was prompted by a letter from Dr. David Ross of Md. enclosing a copy of the Philadelphia non-importation agreement of March 10, 1769, Mason to W April 5, *Letters to W* III 342. A copy of the Philadelphia agreement is in same 351.

20. Mason to W April 5 and 23, 1769, concerning a non-importation agreement for Va., same 342-346. In the first letter Mason said he, too, had heard from Ross and shared W's views that Va. should join the non-importation movement. In the second he referred to a draft of an agreement he had previously sent W, and enclosed a memorandum of some desired changes in the agreement.

21. Resolutions of the House of Burgesses May 16, 1769, denying the right of Parliament to tax the inhabitants of Virginia or to send any of them to England for trial for any crime committed in the colony, *Va. House Journals* for 1766-1769 p. 214. Gov. Lord Botetourt, saying "I have heard of your Resolves," dissolved the House the next day, same 218.

22. The Va. non-importation agreement adopted May 18, 1769, and signed by W, Peyton Randolph, Richard Henry Lee, Patrick Henry, Thomas Jefferson, and nearly forty other members of the recently dissolved House of Burgesses is in Boyd *Jefferson* I 28-31. As to the drafting committee and W's service on it, account of proceeding on May 17, same 27-28 with W's diary for May 17, stating "was upon a Committee at Hay's [Anthony Hay's Raleigh Tavern] till 10 oclock," *W Diaries* I 325.

23. Comparison of the undated draft of a proposed non-importation agreement for Va. in *Letters to W* III 346-349, with Mason's letter and enclosed memorandum of April 23, 1769, same 345-346, discloses that the draft

agreement is Mason's. It differs from the agreement adopted at Williamsburg on May 18 in the following particulars: the latter included engage-
ments not to import any wine after Sept. 1, 1769, and to stop killing
lambs (presumably to encourage the production of more wool in Va.),
neither of which was in Mason's draft, and dropped a provision in his
draft for a later non-exportation agreement if the non-importation agreement alone proved ineffectual.

24. W again chosen member for Fairfax county in 1769, W's diary for
Sept. 14, 1769, stating "Went to Alexandria, to the Election of Burgesses
for Fairfax and was chosen, together with Colo. [John] West, without a
Pole, there being no opposition," *W Diaries* I 344.

25. W's appointment to the Committee for Religion at the Nov.-Dec.
session and reappointment as a member of the Committee of Privileges
and Elections, *Va. House Journals* for 1766-1769 p. 228. Activities of the
Committee for Religion, same 238, 247, 252, 260, 270, and 327.

26. W's service in the Va. House of Burgesses from 1770 to 1774 can
be followed by turning to his name in the indexes to the *Va. House
Journals* for 1770-1772 and 1773-1776.

27. The June 1775 session from June 1 to June 24. W had left Virginia May 4, 1775, *W Diaries* II 194, to attend the Second Continental
Congress at Philadelphia, and many years passed before he returned.

28. Bill in 1769 for making the upper Potomac navigable, *Va. House
Journals* for 1766-1769, p. 314. W was also active in connection with a
supplementary bill introduced in 1772, same for 1770-1772 p. 292. As to
W's earlier interest in such a project, W to Thomas Lee in 1754 and to
Thomas Johnson in 1762, *W* I 100-101, II 391. See also Nute "Washington
and the Potomac" 497-518.

29. Collaboration of Johnson and George Mason with W on the
Potomac project, W to Johnson July 20, 1770, May 5, 1772, *W* III 17-21,
82-83; Johnson to W May 10, 1772, Jan. 24, 1775, *Letters to W* IV 122-123,
V 84-86; and Mason to W Feb. 17, 1775, Rowland *Mason* I 187. W's leadership in the project after the Revolution, Freeman VI 28-31, 65, 75, 150, 283
and index under "Potomac Company" in Carroll and Ashworth *Washington*.

30. As to the responsibilities of the parish vestry in colonial Va., Sydnor
Gentlemen Freeholders 90-91.

31. As to W's election to the Truro vestry in Oct., 1762, and his
service as vestryman, and, for a time, as church-warden, too, Freeman
III 87, 126-128, 142, 178. For a brief period in 1764-1765, a separate
parish, Fairfax parish, was set off from Truro, to which W was chosen
a member, same 126-128. Of thirty-one meetings of the Truro parish
vestry from 1763 to 1774, W attended nineteen, Truro Vestry Book, L.C.

32. W was included in a Commission of the Peace, issued by the
Governor July 29, 1768, naming twenty-three justices for Fairfax county,
and he took the oath of office on Sept. 21, Fairfax County Order Book
for 1768-1770, 36-37 and 53, Va. State Library. For his attendance at meetings from 1768 to 1774 and proceedings of the court at these meetings,
W Diaries I 291-397 and II 5-139 *passim*, and Fairfax County Order
Books for 1768-1770, 1770-1772, and 1772-1774 *passim*.

33. As to the powers and duties of the Virginia county courts, Flippin
Royal Government in Va. 317-318; Sydnor *Gentlemen Freeholders* 80-90;
Fairfax County Order Books from 1768 to 1774, Va. State Library; Porter

County Government in Va. 9-99. Minutes of a typical meeting of a Va. county court (Botetourt county, March 10, 1770) are in Jensen *Eng. Hist. Doc.* IX 309-311.

CHAPTER SIXTEEN

1. 10 Geo. III ch. 17 (1770) repealed the duties levied by the Town-shend Act except those on tea and paper, glass, and paint not manu-factured in Great Britain.

2. Va. agreement or "Association" of June 22, 1770, relaxing the earlier agreement, Boyd *Jefferson* I 43-47. There was a further relaxation a year later, Thomas Jefferson to Thomas Adams June 1, 1771, same 71-72, and W to Robert Cary & Co. July 20, *W* III 60.

3. Act of 13 Geo. III ch. 44 (1773) reducing the duty in England on tea and permitting the British East India Company to export tea on its own account. As to the amount of duty previously payable and other aspects of the act, Farrand "Taxation of Tea" 266-269. Previously the Company could sell tea only at auction sales held in England.

4. Boston Port Act and other British retaliatory acts of 1774, known as the Intolerable Acts, Knollenberg *Origin* 246-247 and 384.

5. Resolution of Va. House of Burgesses May 24, 1774, *Va. House Journals* for 1773-1776 p. 124.

6. Lord Dunmore's dissolution of the House of Burgesses May 26, 1774, same 132.

7. Resolutions of the late members of the dissolved House of Bur-gesses, May 27, 1774, Boyd *Jefferson* I 107-109.

8. W to George William Fairfax June 10, 1774, expressing disapproval of "destroying the tea" at Boston, *W* III 224.

9. W to Bryan Fairfax July 4, 1774, denouncing recent British meas-ures, *W* III 228-229.

10. Resolves at a meeting of the inhabitants of Fairfax county, W pre-siding, July 18, 1774, 4 Force I 597-602.

11. Calls for an inter-colonial congress in 1774, Knollenberg *Origin* 248. The time and place was proposed in a circular letter June 17, 1774, sent out by the Speaker of the Mass. House of Representatives suggest-ing a meeting of "Committees from the several Colonies on this Conti-nent" in Philadelphia on Sept. 1, *Va. House Journals* for 1773-1776 p. 156. A similar convention, the so-called Stamp Act Congress, had met in New York City in 1765, but Va. was not represented there, Knollenberg *Origin* 228-229.

12. Election of delegates, including W, to the proposed inter-colonial congress, proceedings of Williamsburg convention Aug. 1-6, 1774, 4 Force I 686-690. All the old British continental colonies except Georgia and Nova Scotia sent delegates and, in general, excellent ones, but the Va. delegation was particularly strong. Quebec, East Fla., and West Fla., formed from territory added to Great Britain in 1763, were apparently not invited to send delegates.

13. In giving a pen picture of the Va. delegates to the Congress to his brother-in-law, James Pleasants in Philadelphia, Roger Atkinson of Va. wrote, Oct. 1, 1774, that W "speaks little" but was, he added, "in action cool, like a Bishop at his prayers," *Va. Mag.* XV (1908) 356.

14. W and the First Continental Congress, Sept. 5 to Oct. 26, 1774, *Cont. Congress Journals* I 13-114 *passim.* W's diary for Sept. 5 to Oct. 26 records the names of the many prominent Philadelphians with whom he dined; but, as usual, he makes no comments on them, *W Diaries* II 163-168. He played cards a good deal during his stay in Philadelphia, and came out well, netting about £7, W's Ledger B fol. 125, but what game or games of cards were played we do not know.

15. John Adams' diary Aug. 31, 1774, as to Lynch's story of W's offering to furnish a regiment, *Adams Papers* II 117. Silas Deane of Conn. to his wife Sept. 10, 1774, as to W's saving the remains of Gen. Braddock's defeated army, Burnett *Letters* I 28. In this letter Deane, too, gives Lynch's story concerning W's offering a regiment.

16. As to the lack of evidence and improbability of the story concerning W's offer to raise and subsist a regiment, Freeman III 377 n. As brought out in Chapter 6, W behaved gallantly at the time of Braddock's defeat; but there is no evidence of his having been particularly instrumental in saving the survivors.

17. Deane to his wife Sept. 10, 1774, describing Washington, Burnett *Letters* I 28. I have found no portrait or description of "Col. Fitch," who, I assume, was Col. Thomas Fitch of Norwalk, Conn. "Hard" was probably used by Deane in its 18th-century sense of "firm." Some months later (May 9, 1775), Samuel Curwen of Mass. wrote of W as a "fine figure and of a most agreeable and easy address," *Curwen's Journal* 28.

18. Conditional resolution Oct. 22, 1774, for a second Congress on May 10, 1775, and self-dissolution of the first Congress Oct. 26, 1774, *Cont. Congress Journals* I 102 and 114.

19. W leaves Philadelphia Oct. 27, 1775, and arrives home Oct. 30, *W Diaries* II 169.

20. W's public activities Dec. 14, 1774, to March 16, 1775, *W Col. Traveller* 371-375 *passim.*

21. Resolutions of Fairfax county committee, W presiding, Jan. 17, 1775, 4 Force I 1145. The Massachusetts provincial congress sitting from Oct. 7 to Oct. 29, 1774, had taken many steps to prepare for defense of the province in case of war, including the adoption of the recommendation of the British "Military Exercise" referred to in the Fairfax county resolutions, *Mass. Prov. Congress Journals* 7-48 at p. 41.

22. Further evidence of W's military activities in the winter of 1774-1775, W's diary entries of Jan. 16 and 17 and Feb. 18, 1775, *W Diaries* II 182 and 185; W to William Minor, John Augustine W, and George Mercer Jan. 23, March 25, and April 5, 1775, *W* III 265, 276, and 288; and nineteen letters to W from Oct. 19, 1774, to April 30, 1775, same 276 n. and *Letters to W* V 56 to 166 *passim.* Several of the letters relate to a proposal to retake the provincial powder seized by Gov. Lord Dunmore in April 1775, as to which see Freeman III 410-412 and 414-415.

23. Minutes of the Richmond convention, March 20 to 27, 1775, 4 Force II 165-172.

CHAPTER SEVENTEEN

1. News of bloodshed in Mass. April 19, 1775, reaches Va. April 28 same II 366.

2. W leaves for Philadelphia May 4, 1775, via Baltimore, Md., and Wilmington, Del., and arrives May 9, *W Diaries* II 194-195.

3. Second Continental Congress convenes, with Peyton Randolph and Charles Thomson of Pa. elected President and Secretary respectively, minutes of May 10, 1775, *Cont. Congress Journals* II 11-12.

4. Resolutions of Congress May 15, 1775, for recommendation to the people of New York that they prevent the expected British troops from erecting fortifications or cutting off communication between the town and country and for appointment of a committee "to consider which posts are necessary" and "by what number of troops it will be necessary they should be guarded," same 52.

5. W chosen head of the committee on the defense of New York and of other committees on military affairs, May 15 and 27, and June 3 and 14, 1775, same 53, 67, 79-80, 90. (John Adams wrote Abigail Adams, May 29, that W "appears at Congress in his uniform, and by his great experience and abilities in military matters, is of much service to us . . . ," Burnett *Letters* I 102).

6. Resolution of Congress June 14, 1775, for the enlistment and pay of ten companies of riflemen to serve "in the American continental army, for one year, unless sooner discharged," *Cont. Congress Journals* II 89-90.

7. Resolution of Congress June 15, 1775, that "a General be appointed to command all the continental forces, raised, or to be raised, for the defence of American liberty," with provision for pay of $500 a month, same 91.

8. John Adams' account in his autobiography of W's election as Commander-in-Chief, *Adams Papers* III (1961) 322-323. Adams wrote his autobiography between 1802 and 1805, editorial Introduction same I lxviii-lxix. Adams wrote James Lloyd April 24, 1815, that at the time he made his speech proposing W as Commander-in-Chief, "a number were for Washington. But the greatest number were for Ward," Adams *Works* X 164.

9. The editorial notes in the new edition of Adams' autobiography in the *Adams Papers* correct numerous misstatements in the autobiography. It would have been useful also to point out the many statements in the autobiography, including those relating to W's election, which, though not demonstrably untrue, are highly dubious. Many of Adams' letters written long after the events described, likewise contain statements which are demonstrably untrue or very dubious.

10. Eliphalet Dyer to Joseph Trumbull June 17, 1775, concerning Washington's personality, Burnett *Letters* I 128.

11. Ward's election May 19, 1775, as "general and commander in chief of all the forces" raised by the Congress of the Colony of Massachusetts Bay, *Mass. Prov. Congress Journals* 239, 243.

12. Ward served creditably at the front as major and later lieut. colonel in a Mass. regiment during the campaign of 1758, Martyn *Ward* 15-27, but I have found no evidence of his having particularly distinguished himself. As to Ward on the day of Lexington and Concord, same 89. My impression is that Ward was a competent, though obviously not brilliant commander, and that the defense of him in same 89-240 *passim* and Shipton *Harvard Graduates* XII 332-339 against the aspersions of James Warren, Washington, and others is well founded.

13. Elbridge Gerry to the Mass. delegates in Congress, June 4, 1775,

commenting on the need for better discipline in the army and adding "I should heartily rejoice to see this way the beloved colonel Washington, and do not doubt the New-England generals would acquiesce in showing to our sister colony Virginia, the respect, which she has before experienced from the continent, in making him generalissimo. This is a matter in which Dr. [Joseph] Warren agrees with me, and we had intended to write you jointly on the affair," Austin *Gerry* I 79.

14. Dyer to Joseph Trumbull June 17, 1775, as to fear of having a New Englander for Commander-in-Chief, Burnett *Letters* I 128.

15. The charters of Conn., Mass., N.H., N.Y., and Pa., with their overlapping boundary lines defined, are in Thorpe *Charters* I, III, IV, and V *passim*.

16. As to the boundary disputes between N.H. and N.Y., Hall *Vermont* 127-193; between Conn. and Pa., Boyd *Susquehannah Company* 1-42 and Boyd *Susquehannah Co. Papers* I-IV *passim*; between Mass. and N.Y. Mark *Conflicts* 116-162. The dispute between Mass. and N.Y. over territory east of the Hudson had quieted down after 1766; but there was a latent source of dispute between them because the charter of Mass. gave it a claim to land west of N.Y., and the disputed boundary between this western Mass. territory and N.Y. was not settled until 1786, Dangerfield *Livingston* 204-206, 486.

17. Jared Ingersoll to his nephew Jonathan Ingersoll March 12, 1774, concerning the New Englanders "as a set of Goths & Vandals," "Ingersoll Letters" 446.

18. As to recent renewed outbreaks in the border disputes between New Englanders, largely from Conn., and the N.Y. and Pa. authorities, Hall *Vermont* 188-193; Boyd *Susquehannah Co. Papers* IV *passim*. The Conn. legislature had given fresh cause for fear and indignation by passing an act in May, 1775, formally incorporating as part of Conn. a large new area within the boundaries of Pa., *Conn. Col. Rec.* XV 11-13.

19. Gen. Nathanael Greene of R.I. to Samuel Ward, one of the R.I. delegates in Congress, as to the New Englanders not wishing to dominate, Oct. 16, 1775, Knollenberg *Ward* 104.

20. The desire to allay fear in other colonies of a victorious army led by a general from the New England colonies was probably the "political motive" referred to by W to John Augustine W June 20, 1775, stating "the partiallity of the Congress, joined to a political motive, really left me without a choice" over acceptance of the chief command, *W* III 299.

21. Minute of June 15, 1775, "The Congress then proceeded to the choice of a general, by ballot, when George Washington, Esq. was unanimously elected," *Cont. Congress Journals* II 91. I have found no contemporary evidence supporting statements made long after the event that Thomas Johnson of Md. nominated W; but I have no reason to suppose he did not.

22. W's acceptance of command in a brief, modest letter June 16, 1775, waiving any pay other than reimbursement of his expenses, *W* III 292-293. (The draft of the letter, except for one brief phrase in W's hand, is in the hand of his friend, lawyer and fellow Va. delegate Edmund Pendleton, same 293 n.).

23. John Adams wrote his wife Abigail June 23, 1775, "I have this morning been out of town to accompany our generals, Washington, Lee and Schuyler, a little way of their journey to the American camp before

Boston. The three generals were all mounted on horse-back, . . . [attended by] delegates from the Congress; a large troop of light horse in their uniforms; . . . music playing, etc. etc.," Adams *Familiar Letters* 70. Congress had chosen Charles Lee, a British officer on half pay, and Philip Schuyler of N.Y. major generals on June 17 and 19, *Cont. Congress Journals* II 97, 99. Schuyler left the party at New York City, *W* III 302.

24. W's tender, farewell letter to Martha June 23, 1775, Freeman III 459. The signature is missing. Another copy of the letter, in *W* III 300-301 has "would" for "could" in the first sentence and "return" for "retain" in the next to the last. There is another fine letter of W to Martha dated June 18, in *W* III 293-295, with a P.S. in Freeman III 454.

25. In a letter dated June 24, 1775, W wrote the President of Congress (John Hancock) from New York City stating that he had arrived "the Afternoon of this day," *W* III 301. But a reference in this very letter to the previous day as Saturday, which was June 24, the notice of W's arrival and reception in *Rivington's New-York Gazetteer* June 29, and the minutes of the N.Y. Provincial Congress of June 25, 4 Force II 1318, show that the correct date was June 25. (Hancock had recently succeeded Randolph as President.)

26. As to W's activities in N.Y. City during his stay there, W to Gen. Schuyler June 25, 1775, and to the N.Y. Provincial Congress June 26, *W* III 302-305; also Freeman III 464-470.

27. As to W's journey from N.Y. to Cambridge June 26 to July 2, Baker *Itinerary of W* 7-8; Freeman III 471-477; and *Mass. Prov. Council Journals* 398 outlining W's itinerary through Mass. Part of the itinerary as given by Baker and Freeman is based on inference; but the inferences seem well justified except Freeman's conjecture (p. 474) that W traveled from New Haven to Wethersfield, Conn., by way of New London. There is no evidence that W took this roundabout way, and, since he was in a hurry, he almost certainly took the direct road from New Haven to Wethersfield by way of Wallingford.

28. W wrote the President of Congress July 10, 1775, that he had arrived at Cambridge on "the 3d instant," *W* III 320; but a dispatch from Watertown to the *Pennsylvania Gazette* dated July 3 said that W "passed through this town [only a few miles from Cambridge] yesterday," *Pennsylvania Gazette* July 12, 1775; Gen. Lee wrote Robert Morris from Cambridge July 4, "We arrived here on Sunday [July 2] before dinner," *Lee Papers* I 188; and a Committee of the Mass. Provincial Congress wrote Gov. Jonathan Trumbull of Conn. July 4, "Generals Washington and Lee . . . arrived at Cambridge last Sabbath . . . a little after 12 o'clock, at noon . . . ," *Mass. Prov. Council Journals* 447.

29. W's General Orders on taking command, Headquarters, Cambridge, July 3, 1775, *W* III 305. The statements in Lodge *Washington* I 137 and elsewhere as to W's taking command, with a flourish of his sword, before a "great multitude" is utterly unsupported by any contemporary evidence. On June 26, the Mass. Provincial Congress had ordered Ward to give W and Lee an "honorable reception," but without "any expense of powder, and without taking the troops off from the necessary attention to their duty, at this crisis of our affairs," *Mass. Prov. Congress Journals* 398, and the transfer of command took place so far as we know in the simple manner thus indicated.

30. When Washington took command at Cambridge, the troops there were exclusively from the four New England colonies. The companies of

riflemen from Virginia, Pennsylvania, and Maryland did not begin to arrive until the latter part of July, 1775, French *First Year* 466 n. Curiously there is no recorded vote of Congress formally adopting the New England troops investing Boston as the nucleus of the Continental Army; but there is evidence that this had been done by June 14, and perhaps as early as June 3, same 750-752.

APPENDIX TO CHAPTER TWELVE

1. Freeman's reasons for regarding letter of W to Burwell Bassett Aug. 28, 1762 (*W* XXXVII 484-485), as probably spurious, at least in part, Freeman III 82 n.

2. Facetious letter of W to Bassett Feb. 15, 1773, concerning the Misses French and More, *W* III 114-115.

3. W to the Rev. William Gordon Dec. 20, 1784, concerning the vigorous passions of his former aide, Col. Joseph Ward, same XXVIII 15.

4. W to Lafayette May 10, 1786, concerning the young jackass, Royal Gift, same 423.

5. W to various other correspondents concerning Royal Gift's lack of ardor, same 409, 426, 454, 478. A jenny presented by Lafayette to W behaved more commendably; when bred to a stallion of W's friend Richard Sprigg, "like a true female . . . not to be terrified at the disproportionate size of her paramour . . . [she] renewed the conflict twice or thrice," W to Sprigg June 28, 1786, same 471.

APPENDIX TO CHAPTER FOURTEEN

1. For examples of W's biographers apparently being misled by his statements as to his acquisition of land under Governor Dinwiddie's proclamation of 1754, Woodward *Washington* 217-218; Freeman III 335; Toner "List of Early Land Grants" 177.

2. W to Charles Mynn Thruston March 12, 1773, as to Andrew Waggener's allotment of proclamation of 1754 land and W's statements as to the surveys allotted to himself, *W* III 124.

3. W to Edward Graham April 25, 1798, concerning proclamation of 1754 land, same XXXVI 251-252.

4. Minutes of a meeting of the Governor and Council of Va. Nov. 6, 1771, giving the respective contributions of claimants to proclamation of 1754 land, Va. Exec. Council Journal for 1771, pp. 14-15, Va. State Lib.

5. W to the Governor and Council of Va. Nov. 5, 1773, as to supplemental distribution of proclamation of 1754 land on the basis of the claimants' cash contributions, *W* III 159-160.

6. Minutes of the Governor and Council of Va. Nov. 6, 1772, allotting proclamation of 1754 land to W and others, Va. State Lib.

7. W to the Governor and Council of Va. Nov. 5, 1773, proposing method of supplemental distribution of proclamation of 1754 land to W and others, *W* III 160 and *Virginia Gazette* (Rind's) Nov. 25, confirming the distribution as proposed. (Allotments purchased by W from others in the regiment may well have been "jumbled together" with those of many others; but that, of course, is another story.)

8. W to Presley Neville June 16, 1794, as to his Ohio lands being "the cream of the Country," *W* XXXIII 407. To similar effect W's advertisement of his proclamation land in *The Maryland Journal, and the Baltimore Advertiser* Aug. 20, 1773. The truth of W's glowing description of his land is indicated by the assurance given him by William Crawford, the surveyor who made the surveys for him, in a letter of Nov. 12, 1773, that "none in that Country is so good as your Land and his [Dr. Craik's] land," *Letters to W* IV 275.

LIST OF PUBLICATIONS AND DOCUMENTS CITED

A.H.R.—*American Historical Review.*

Acts P.C.—William L. Grant and James Munro (eds.) *Acts of the Privy Council of England, Colonial Series* 6 vols. (1908-1912).

Adams *Familiar Letters*—Charles Francis Adams *Familiar Letters of John Adams and His Wife Abigail . . .* (1876).

Adams Papers—Lyman H. Butterfield (ed.) *The Adams Papers* 4 vols. (1961).

Adams *Works*—Charles Francis Adams (ed.) *The Works of John Adams* 10 vols. (1850-1856).

Alden *Lee*—John R. Alden *General Charles Lee: Traitor or Patriot?* (1951).

Alden *Stuart*—John R. Alden *John Stuart and the Southern Colonial Frontier . . .* (1944).

Alvord *Miss. Valley*—Clarence W. Alvord *The Mississippi Valley in British Politics . . .* 2 vols. (1917).

Ambler *Washington*—Charles H. Ambler *George Washington and the West* (1936).

Am. Hist. Assoc. Rep.—*Annual Report of the American Historical Association.*

Andrews "Commissions"—Charles M. Andrews "List of the Commissions and Instructions issued to the Governors . . . 1609 to 1784" *Am. Hist. Assoc. Rep.* for 1911, I 393-528.

Appletons' Cyclopaedia of American Biography (1887-1889).

Austin *Gerry*—James T. Austin *The Life of Elbridge Gerry . . .* 2 vols. (1828).

Bailey *Ohio Company*—Kenneth P. Bailey *The Ohio Company of Virginia . . . 1748-1792* (1939).

Baker *Early Sketches of Washington*—William S. Baker (ed.) *Early Sketches of George Washington . . .* (1894).

Baker *Itinerary of W*—William S. Baker *Itinerary of General Washington . . .* [1775-1783] (1892).

Baker-Crothers *Virginia and the French War*—Hayes Baker-Crothers *Virginia and the French and Indian War* (1928).

Ballagh *Lee*—James C. Ballagh (ed.) *The Letters of Richard Henry Lee* 2 vols. (1911).

Bancroft *History*—George Bancroft *History of the United States* . . . 10 vols. (1857-1874).

Bassett *Byrd*—John S. Bassett (ed.) *The Writings of Colonel William Byrd* . . . (1901).

Bining *Col. Iron Industry*—Arthur C. Bining *British Regulation of the Colonial Iron Industry* (1933).

Bouquet—Sylvester K. Stevens *et al.* (eds.) *The Papers of Henry Bouquet* Vol. II (1951).

Bouquet Papers—Sylvester K. Stevens and Donald H. Kent (eds.) *The Papers of Col. Henry Bouquet* Series 21643 (1941) sometimes numbered Vol. IV.

Boyd *Jefferson*—Julian P. Boyd *et al.* (eds.) *The Papers of Thomas Jefferson* I (1760-1776) (1950).

Boyd *Susquehannah Co.*—Julian P. Boyd *The Susquehannah Company: Connecticut's Experiment in Expansion* (1935).

Boyd *Susquehannah Co. Papers*—Julian P. Boyd (ed.) *The Susquehannah Company Papers* 4 vols. (1930-1933).

Burnett *Letters*—Edmund C. Burnett (ed.) *Letters of Members of the Continental Congress* Vol. I (1921).

Campbell *Virginia*—Charles Campbell *History of the Colony and Ancient Dominion of Virginia* (1860).

Carroll and Ashworth *Washington*—John A. Carroll and Mary Wells Ashworth *George Washington* (Douglas S. Freeman's projected Vol. VII) (1957).

Carter "Documents"—Clarence E. Carter "Documents relating to the Mississippi Land Company, 1763-1769" *A.H.R.* XVI (1911) 311-319.

Cary *Sally Cary*—Wilson M. Cary *Sally Cary, a Long Hidden Romance* (1916).

Columbia Register—Columbia University *Alumni Register 1754-1931* (1932).

Conn. Col. Rec.—Charles J. Hoadley (ed.) *The Public Records of the Colony of Connecticut* Vol. XV (1890).

Cont. Congress Journals—Worthington C. Ford (ed.) *Journals of the Continental Congress* . . . Vol. I, II and III (1904-1905).

Conway *Barons*—Moncure D. Conway *Barons of the Potomac and the Rappahannock* (1892).

Conway *Washington*—Moncure D. Conway *George Washington and Mount Vernon* (1889).

Cook, Roy, *Washington's Western Lands* (1930).

Creswell's Journal—*The Journal of Nicholas Creswell 1774-1777* (1928).

Critical Period—Clarence W. Alvord and Clarence E. Carter (eds.) *The Critical Period, 1763-1765, Collections of the Illinois State Historical Library* Vol. X.

Curwen's Journal—George A. Ward (ed.) *The Journal and Letters of Samuel Curwen . . . 1775 to 1783* (1864) .

Custis *Recollections*—*Recollections and Private Memoirs of Washington by His Adopted Son, George Washington Parke Custis . . .* (1860).

D. A. B.—*Dictionary of American Biography* (1943).

D.N.B.—*Dictionary of National Biography* (1908-1909).

Dangerfield *Livingston*—George Dangerfield *Chancellor Robert R. Livingston of New York 1746-1813* (1960).

Darlington *Gist*—William M. Darlington (ed.) *Christopher Gist's Journals . . .* (1893).

Decatur *Private Affairs of Washington*—Stephen Decatur *Private Affairs of George Washington from the Records and Accounts of Tobias Lear . . .* (1933).

Dinwiddie—Robert A. Brock (ed.) *The Official Records of Robert Dinwiddie . . . 1751-1758 . . .* 2 vols. (1883-1884).

Draper "Expedition"—Lyman Draper "The Expedition Against the Shawanoe Indians in 1756" *Va. Hist. Reg.* V 61-76.

Duane *Letters to Benjamin Franklin*—William Duane (ed.) *Letters to Benjamin Franklin from His Family and Friends 1751-1790* (1859).

Dunbar "Royal Governors"—Louise B. Dunbar "The Royal Governors in the Middle and Southern Colonies on the Eve of the Revolution" in Morris *Era of the American Revolution* (1939) 214-268.

Evans *Am. Bibliography*—Charles Evans *American Bibliography . . . 1639-1820* 12 vols. (1941).

Farrand "Taxation of Tea"—Max Farrand "The Taxation of Tea, 1767-1773" *A.H.R.* III (1898) 266-269.

Fernow *Ohio Valley*—Berthold Fernow *The Ohio Valley in Colonial Days* (1890).

Fitzpatrick *Washington*—John C. Fitzpatrick *George Wash-*

ington Himself: A Common-Sense Biography Written from His Manuscripts (1933).

Fitzpatrick, John C., *The George Washington Scandals* (1929). Fitzpatrick's other works, see *W.*

Fleming *Kenmore*—Virginia M. Fleming *The Story of Kenmore* (Lewis home) (1924).

Flippin *Royal Government in Va.*—Percy S. Flippin *The Royal Government in Virginia 1624-1775* (1919).

Forbes—Alfred Procter James (ed.) *Writings of General John Forbes . . .* (1938).

Force—Peter Force (ed.) *American Archives . . .* Fourth Series 6 vols. (1837-1846).

Ford—Worthington Chauncey Ford (ed.) *The Writings of George Washington* 14 vols. (1889-1893).

Ford "Beverly Letters"—Worthington Chauncey Ford "Some Letters of William Beverly" 1 *W.M.Q.* III (1895) 223-239.

Ford *British Officers*—Worthington Chauncey Ford *British Officers Serving in America 1754-1773* (1894).

Ford *True Washington*—Paul Leicester Ford *The True George Washington* (1897).

Ford *Washington as an Employer*—Worthington Chauncey Ford *Washington as an Employer and Importer of Labor* (1889).

Ford *Washington Family*—Worthington Chauncey Ford *The Washington Family* (1893).

Ford *Washington Wills*—Worthington Chauncey Ford *Wills of George Washington and His Immediate Ancestors* (1891).

Ford, Worthington Chauncey, *Washington and "Centinel X"* (1899), reprint from *Pa. Mag. Hist.* of Jan. 1899.

Ford, Worthington Chauncey, "Washington's Map of the Ohio" *Mass. Hist. Soc. Proc.* LXI (1928) 71-79.

Freeman—Douglas Southall Freeman *George Washington: A Biography* 6 vols. (1948-1954).

French, Allen, "The First George Washington Scandal" *Mass. Hist. Soc. Proc.* LXV (1940) 460-474.

French *First Year*—Allen French *The First Year of the American Revolution* (1934).

Frothingham *Warren*—Richard Frothingham *Life and Times of Joseph Warren* (1865).

Gage—Clarence E. Carter (ed.) *The Correspondence of General Thomas Gage . . . 1763-1775* 2 vols. (1931-1933).

Gipson *Brit. Empire*—Lawrence Henry Gipson *The British Empire before the American Revolution* Vols. IV-VIII (1939-1954).

Goodman *Trent*—Alfred T. Goodman *Journal of Captain William Trent . . . 1752* (1871).

Hall *Vermont*—Hiland Hall *The History of Vermont . . .* (1868).

Hamilton *Braddock's Defeat*—Charles Hamilton *Braddock's Defeat* (1959).

Harrison *Landmarks*—Fairfax Harrison *Landmarks of Old Prince William* 2 vols. (1924).

Harrison *Proprietors of the Northern Neck*—Fairfax Harrison *The Poprietors of the Northern Neck* (1926).

Haworth *Washington Country Gentleman*—Paul L. Haworth *George Washington, Country Gentleman . . .* (1925).

Hayden *Washington and His Masonic Compeers*—Sidney Hayden *Washington and His Masonic Compeers* (1866).

Hening *Va. Statutes*—William W. Hening (ed.) *The Statutes at Large . . . of Virginia from . . . 1619* 13 vols. (1809-1823).

Hoppin—Charles A. Hoppin *The Washington Ancestry . . .* 3 vols. (1932).

Hoppin "House"—Charles A. Hoppin "The House in Which George Washington Was Born" *Tyler's Quart.* VIII (1927) 73-103.

Howe *Hist. Coll. of Va.*—Henry Howe *Historical Collections of Virginia . . .* (1856).

Hughes *Washington*—Rupert Hughes *George Washington . . .* 3 vols. (1926-1930).

Hulbert, Archer B., *The Old Glade (Forbes) Road* (1903).

Hulbert "Washington's Tour"—Archer B. Hulbert "Washington's Tour to the Ohio and Articles of the Mississippi Company" *Ohio Archaeological and Historical Society Publications* XVII (1908) 431-488.

"Ingersoll Letters"—Franklin B. Dexter (ed.) "A Selection from the Correspondence and Miscellaneous Papers of Jared Ingersoll" *New Haven Historical Society Papers* IX 201-472.

Irving *Washington*—Washington Irving *Life of George Washington* 5 vols. (1855-1859).

James *Ohio Company*—Alfred P. James *The Ohio Company: Its Inner History* (1959).

Jensen *Eng. Hist. Doc.*—Merrill Jensen (ed.) Vol. IX of *English Historical Documents* (1955).

Jones "American Regiment"—E. Alfred Jones "The American Regiment in the Carthagena Expedition" *Va. Mag.* XXX (1922) 1-20.

Journal B. of T.—*Journal of the Commissioners for Trade and Plantations* . . . [Board of Trade] 14 vols. (1920-1932).

Keppel *Keppel*—Thomas Keppel *The Life of Augustus Viscount Keppel* . . . 2 vols. (1842).

Kimball *Pitt Corresp.*—Gertrude Selwyn Kimball (ed.) *Correspondence of William Pitt . . . with Colonial Governors . . . in America* 2 vols. (1906).

Knollenberg *Origin*—Bernhard Knollenberg *Origin of the American Revolution: 1759-1766* (1960).

Knollenberg *Ward*—Bernhard Knollenberg (ed.) *Correspondence of Governor Samuel Ward . . . 1725-1776* (1952).

Knollenberg *Washington and the Revolution*—Bernhard Knollenberg *Washington and the Revolution: A Reappraisal, Gates, Conway, and the Continental Congress* (1940).

Koontz *Dinwiddie*—Louis K. Koontz *Robert Dinwiddie: His Career in American Colonial Government and Westward Expansion* (1941).

Koontz *Virginia Frontier*—Louis K. Koontz *The Virginia Frontier 1754-1763* (1925).

Labaree *Royal Instructions*—Leonard Labaree (ed.) *Royal Instructions to British Colonial Governors 1670-1776* (1935).

Leduc *Washington*—Gilbert F. Leduc *Washington and "The Murder of Jumonville"* (1943).

Lee *Lee of Virginia*—Edmund J. Lee *Lee [Family] of Virginia 1642-1692* (1895).

Lee Papers—*The [Charles] Lee Papers,* Vol. I (1871).

Letters to W—Stanislaus M. Hamilton *Letters to Washington* . . . 5 vols. (1898-1902).

Lewis *Walpole*—Wilmarth S. Lewis *et al.* (eds.) *The Yale Edition of Horace Walpole's Correspondence* 31 vols. (1917-1961) .

Lodge *Washington*—Henry Cabot Lodge *George Washington* 2 vols. (1898).

London Mag.—*The London Magazine*.

Lossing *Mary and Martha*—Benson J. Lossing *Mary and Martha the Mother and the Wife of George Washington* (1886).

Lowdermilk *History*—Will H. Lowdermilk *History of Cumberland Maryland . . . with a History of Braddock's Expedition* (1878).

McCardell *Braddock*—Lee McCardell *Ill Starred General: Braddock of the Coldstream Guards* (1958).

Macdonald *Documentary Source Book*—William Macdonald *Documentary Source Book of American History . . .* (1908).

Mag. Am. Hist.—*The Magazine of American History with Notes and Queries*.

Mark *Conflicts*—Irving Mark *Agrarian Conflicts in Colonial New York . . .* (1940).

Martin *Washington Atlas*—Lawrence Martin *The George Washington Atlas* (1932).

Martyn *Ward*—Charles Martyn *The Life of Artemas Ward . . .* (1921).

Mason *Norton*—Frances Norton Mason *John Norton & Sons Merchants of London and Virginia . . . Papers . . . 1750 to 1795* (1937).

Mass. Hist. Soc. Coll.—*Collections of the Massachusetts Historical Society*.

Mass. Hist. Soc. Proc.—*Proceedings of the Massachusetts Historical Society*.

Mass. Prov. Congress Journals—William Lincoln (ed.) *The Journals of the Provincial Congress of Massachusetts in 1774 and 1775* (1838).

May *Principio to Wheeling*—Earl C. May *Principio to Wheeling 1715-1945* (1945).

Mays *Pendleton*—David J. Mays *Edmund Pendleton 1721-1803* 2 vols. (1952).

Md. Arch.—William Hand Brown (ed.) *Archives of Maryland . . .*

Meade *Henry*—Robert D. Meade *Patrick Henry Patriot in the Making* (1957).

Memoire Des Faits—*Memoire contenant le Precis des Faits . . .* (Paris 1756).

Mercer Papers—Lois Mulkearn (ed.) *George Mercer Papers relating to the Ohio Company of Virginia* (1954).

Mitchell *Abigail Adams*—Stewart Mitchell (ed.) *New Letters of Abigail Adams, 1788-1801* (1947).

Moore *George Washington's Rules*—Charles Moore (ed.) *George Washington's Rules of Civility and Behaviour* (1926).

Morison *By Land and By Sea*—Samuel Eliot Morison *By Land and By Sea* (1953).

Morison *Young Washington*—Samuel Eliot Morison *The Young Man Washington* (1932).

Morris *Era of the American Revolution*—Richard B. Morris (ed.) *The Era of the American Revolution . . .* (1939).

Morrison Catalogue—Alfred Morrison *Catalogue of the Collection of Autograph Letters and Historical Documents Formed between 1865 and 1882* 6 vols. (1883-1897.)

Morton *Col. Va.*—Richard L. Morton *Colonial Virginia* 2 vols. (1960).

Mount Vernon a Handbook (1947).

Mount Vernon Report—The Mount Vernon Ladies' Association of the Union, *Annual Report* for 1945 and for 1959.

Mulkearn *Mercer Papers*—Lois Mulkearn (ed.) *George Mercer Papers Relating to the Ohio Company of Virginia* (1954).

N.J. Col. Doc.—Frederick W. Ricord and William Nelson (eds.) *Documents relating to the Colonial History of New Jersey* 10 vols. (1880-1885).

N.Y. Col. Doc.—Edmund B. O'Callaghan (ed.) *Documents Relative to the Colonial History of . . . New York* 15 vols. (1853-1887).

N.Y. Doc. Hist.—Edmund B. O'Callaghan (ed.) *The Documentary History of the State of New York* 4 vols. (1849-1851).

Namier *Structure*—Sir Lewis Namier *The Structure of Politics at the Accession of George III* (1957).

Nat. Geographic—The National Geographic Magazine.

Nettels *Washington*—Curtis P. Nettels *George Washington and American Independence* (1951).

Nichols "Braddock's Army"—Franklin T. Nichols "The Organization of Braddock's Army" 3 *W.&M.Q.* IV 125-147.

Nixon *Burd*—Lily Lee Nixon *James Burd, Frontier Defender 1726-1793* (1941).

Nute "Washington and the Potomac"—Grace L. Nute "Washington and the Potomac" *A.H.R.* XXVIII (1923) 497-519, 705-722.

Olden Time—Neville B. Craig (ed.) *The Olden Time* . . . 2 vols. (1876).

Pa. Arch.—*Pennsylvania Archives,* First Series (1852-1856).

Pa. Col. Records—*Colonial Records of Pennsylvania* 16 vols. (1851-1853).

Pa. Mag. Hist.—*The Pennsylvania Magazine of History and Biography.*

Pargellis "Braddock's Defeat"—Stanley M. Pargellis "Braddock's Defeat" *A.H.R.* XLI (1936) 253-269.

Pargellis *Loudoun*—Stanley M. Pargellis *Lord Loudoun in North America* (1933).

Pargellis *Military Affairs*—Stanley M. Pargellis (ed.) *Military Affairs in North America 1748-1765 . . . the Cumberland Papers* . . . (1936).

Parliamentary History—William Cobbett and Thomas C. Hansard (eds.) *The Parliamentary History of England . . . to 1830* 36 vols. (1806-1820).

Pa. Statutes—Charles R. Hildeburn (ed.) *The Statutes at Large of Pennsylvania 1692 to 1801* Vol. V (1898).

Paullin "Birthplace of George Washington"—Charles L. Paullin "The Birthplace of George Washington" 2 *W. & M. Q.* XIV (1934) 1-8.

Pease *Anglo-French*—Theodore Calvin Pease (ed.) *Anglo-French Boundary Disputes in the West 1749-1763* (1936).

Porter *County Government in Va.*—Albert O. Porter *County Government in Virginia: A Legislative History 1607-1904* (1947).

Prussing *Estate of Washington*—Eugene E. Prussing *The Estate of George Washington Deceased* (1927).

Quaife *Preston and Va. Papers*—Milo M. Quaife (ed.) *The Preston and Virginia Papers of the Draper Collection of Manuscripts* (1915).

R. I. Col. Rec.—John R. Bartlett (ed.) *Records of the Colony of Rhode Island . . .* 9 vols. (1856-1864).

Riker "Politics"—Thad W. Riker "The Politics behind Braddock's Expedition" *A.H.R.* XIII (1908) 742-752.

Roelker *Franklin and Catharine Ray Greene*—William G. Roelker (ed.) *Benjamin Franklin and Catharine Ray Greene, Their Correspondence 1765-1790* (1949).

Rowland *Mason*—Kate Mason Rowland *The Life of George Mason 1725-1792* 2 vols. (1892).

S. & D. Doc.—Adam Shortt and Arthur G. Doughty (eds.) *Documents relating to the Constitutional History of Canada* . . . Vol. I (1918).

Sargent *Braddock Expedition*—Winthrop Sargent *A History of an Expedition . . . under Major-General Edward Braddock* (1855).

Sawyer *Washington*—Joseph D. Sawyer *George Washington* 4 vols. (1927).

Schlesinger *Col. Merchants*—Arthur M. Schlesinger *The Colonial Merchants and the American Revolution 1763-1776* (1939).

Sharpe—William Hand Browne (ed.) *Correspondence of Governor Horatio Sharpe* 3 vols. (1888-1895).

Shepherd *Pennsylvania*—William R. Shepherd *History of Proprietary Government in Pennsylvania* (1896).

Shipton *Harvard Graduates*—Clifford K. Shipton *Sibley's Harvard Graduates Biographical Sketches Of Those Who Attended Harvard College* . . . Vol. XII (1962).

Shirley—Charles Henry Lincoln (ed.) *Correspondence of William Shirley . . . 1731-1760* 2 vols. (1912).

Showalter "Travels of W"—William S. Showalter "The Travels of George Washington . . ." *Nat. Geographic* LXI (1932) 1-63.

Slaughter *Hist. of Truro Parish*—Philip Slaughter *The History of Truro Parish in Virginia* (1908).

So. Lit. Messenger—Southern Literary Messenger; *devoted to every department of literature, and the fine arts* 36 vols. (1834-1864), Richmond, Va.

Soltow "Williamsburg"—James H. Soltow "The Role of Williamsburg in the Virginia Economy, 1750-1775" 3 *W. & M. Q.* XV (1958) 467-482.

Sosin *Whitehall*—Jack M. Sosin *Whitehall and the Wilderness . . . 1760-1775* (1961).

Sparks—Jared Sparks (ed.) *The Writings of George Washington* . . . 11 vols. (1834-1837).

Stephenson, Nathaniel W. "The Romantics and George Washington" *A.H.R.* XXXIX (1934) 274-283.

Stephenson and Dunn *Washington*—Nathaniel W. Stephenson and Waldo H. Dunn *George Washington* 2 vols. (1940).

Sydnor *Gentlemen Freeholders*—Charles S. Sydnor *Gentlemen Freeholders, Political Practices in Washington's Virginia* (1952).

Thorpe *Charters*—Francis N. Thorpe (ed.) *The Federal and State Constitutions, Colonial Charters and Other Organic Laws* . . . 7 vols. (1909).

Toner *Daily Journal of Washington 1751-1752*—Joseph M. Toner *The Daily Journal of Major George Washington in 1751-1752* . . . (1892).

Toner "List of Early Land Grants"—Joseph M. Toner "A List of Early Land Patents and Grants" *Va. Mag.* V (1898) 173-180.

Toner "Washington in the Forbes Expedition"—Joseph M. Toner "Washington in the Forbes Expedition of 1758" *Records of the Columbia Historical Society* I (1897) 185-213.

Toner *W Journal in 1754*—Joseph M. Toner *Journal of Colonel George Washington* . . . *in 1754* . . . (1893).

Trevelyan *American Revolution*—George Otto Trevelyan *The American Revolution* Vol. I (1917).

Tyler's Quart.—*Tyler's Quarterly Historical and Genealogical Magazine*.

Va. Exec. Council Journals—Henry R. McIlwaine (ed.) *Executive Journals of the Council of Colonial Virginia* 5 vols. (1925-1945).

Va. Hist. Reg.—William Maxwell (ed.) *The Virginia Historical Register* 6 vols. (1848-1853).

Va. House Journals—John P. Kennedy and Henry R. McIlwaine (eds.) *Journals of the House of Burgesses of Virginia* 13 vols. (1905-1913).

Va. Legislative Council Journals—Henry R. McIlwaine (ed.) *Legislative Journals of the Council of Colonial Virginia* 3 vols. (1918-1919).

Va. Mag.—*The Virginia Magazine of History and Biography*.

Van Doren *Franklin-Mecom Letters*—Carl Van Doren (ed.) *The Letters of Benjamin Franklin & Jane Mecom* (1950).

Van Doren *Franklin's Writings*—Carl Van Doren (ed.) *Benjamin Franklin's Autobiographical Writings* (1945).

W—John C. Fitzpatrick (ed.) with two index vols. by David M. Matteson *The Writings of George Washington* . . . 39 vols. (1931-1944).

W Atlas—Lawrence Martin *The George Washington Atlas* (1932).

W Col. Traveller—John C. Fitzpatrick *George Washington Colonial Traveller 1732-1775* (1927).

W Diaries—John C. Fitzpatrick (ed.) *The Diaries of George Washington 1748-1799* 4 vols. (1925).

W. & M. Q.—*The William and Mary Quarterly.*

Wallace *Weiser*—Paul A. W. Wallace *Conrad Wieser 1696-1760* . . . (1945).

Walpole *Memoirs of Geo. II*—Horace Walpole *Memoirs of The Reign of King George the Second* . . . 3 vols. (Lord Holland's 1846 ed.).

Ward and Alden *War of the Revolution*—Christopher Ward and John R. Alden *The War of the Revolution* 2 vols. (1952).

Warren-Adams Letters—Worthington Chauncey Ford (ed.) *Warren-Adams Letters* . . . *John Adams, Samuel Adams, and James Warren* 2 vols. (1917-1925).

"Washington and Mount Vernon"—"General Washington and Mount Vernon from the Diary of Robert Hunter, Jr. in 1785" *Mount Vernon Report* for 1945, 21-26.

Washington's Journal—*The Journal of Major George Washington, sent by the Hon. Robert Dinwiddie* . . . *to the Commandant of the French Forces in Ohio* . . . (Williamsburg 1754).

Washington's "Remarks"—George Washington's autobiographical "Remarks" *W* XXIX 36-50.

Waterman *Mercer*—Joseph M. Waterman *With Sword and Lancet: The Life of General Hugh Mercer* (1941).

Weems *Washington*—Mason Locke Weems *A History of the Life and Death, Virtues and Exploits of General George Washington* (Mark Van Doren [ed.] 1947).

Wharton *Martha Washington*—Anne Hollingsworth Wharton *Martha Washington* (1897).

Whitely "Principio Company"—William G. Whitely "The Principio Company" *Pa. Mag. Hist.* XI (1887) 63-68, 190-198, 288-295.

Winsor *History*—Justin Winsor *Narrative and Critical History of America* 8 vols. (1884-1889).

Wisc. Hist. Coll.—*Collections of the State Historical Society of Wisconsin.*

Woodward *Washington*—William E. Woodward *George Washington: The Image and the Man* (1926).
Wright *Am. Negotiator*—John Wright *The American Negotiator . . .* (London, 1765).
Wright *Atlantic Frontier*—Louis B. Wright *The Atlantic Frontier . . .* (1947).
Wroth *Am. Bookshelf*—Lawrence C. Wroth *An American Bookshelf, 1755* (1934).

DEPOSITORIES OF DOCUMENTS CITED

Brit. Museum Lib.—Library of the British Museum, London.
Duke U. Lib.—Duke University Library, Durham, N. C.
Harv. Coll. Lib.—Harvard College Library, Cambridge, Mass.
Hist. Soc. of Pa.—The Historical Society of Pennsylvania, Philadelphia, Pa.
Huntington Lib.—Huntington Library, San Marino, Cal.
Institute—The Institute of Early American History and Culture, Williamsburg, Va.
L.C.—Library of Congress, Washington, D. C.
N.Y. Pub. Lib.—New York Public Library, New York, N. Y.
Princeton U. Lib.—Princeton University Library, Princeton, N. J.
Pub. Rec. Office—Public Record Office, London.
Va. Hist. Soc.—Virginia Historical Society, Richmond, Va.
Va. State Lib.—Virginia State Library, Richmond, Va.
W. and M. Lib.—College of William and Mary Library, Williamsburg, Va.
Yale U. Lib.—Yale University Library, New Haven, Conn.

MIMEOGRAPHS CITED

Va. Col. Rec. Project—Virginia Colonial Records Project, reports of the Virginia Committee on Colonial records, headquarters Virginia State Library.

NEWSPAPERS CITED

Boston Gazette, Boston, 1719-1775.
Maryland Gazette Annapolis, 1745-1775.
Maryland Journal, and the Baltimore Advertiser Baltimore, 1773-1775.

Pennsylvania Gazette Philadelphia, 1753-1775.
Rivington's New-York Gazetteer New York City, 1773-1775.
Virginia Gazette (Purdy & Dixon) Williamsburg, 1751-1775.
Virginia Gazette (Rind's) Williamsburg, 1766-1775.

INDEX

In this index, W stands for Washington, or when no additional initial or name is given, for George Washington.

Lewis, Fielding (of Fredericksburg, Va., husband of W's sister Elizabeth): 34, 87
Lewis, Mrs. Fielding (née Elizabeth Washington, sister of W): *see* Washington, Elizabeth
Lewis, Thomas (Surveyor of Augusta county, Va.): 184, 185
Lexington, Massachusetts: 113, 191
Ligonier, Pennsylvania: 68
"Lineage," W's statement of: 139, 140, 142, 143, 173
Liquor: furnished by surveying party, including W, to some Indians, puts them "in the Humour of Dauncing" 7-8; French commander at Fort Le Boeuf supplies W with, for return trip, 14; W provides bountifully for Frederick county election 103
Litigation: over Custis estate and over W's shipment of flour to Barbados 178
Little Hunting Creek plantation (later called Mount Vernon): 3, 6, 140, 142, 143
Littleton's *Dictionary:* purchased for Jack Custis 73
Lloyd, James (Mass.): 191
Lodge's *Washington:* questioned 167, 193
Logstown (Indian village on Ohio River in Pa.): 12, 13, 15, 146
Lomax, Lunsford (Va.): buys Lawrence W's share in the Ohio Company 143
London, England: 61, 81, 89
London Magazine: publishes large part of W's journal of his trip to Fort Le Boeuf, in 1754, 16
Lonem, John: chainman for W as surveyor 144
Loo: W plays 132
Lords, House of: W is surfeited with appealing to 109
Loudoun, Lord (John Campbell, 1705-1782, British general and titular Governor of Va.): 48-51, 156-159, 162, 163, 168, 176
Louisbourg, Nova Scotia: 163
Loyalhanna River (Pa.): 68, 69, 171
Lunenburg county, Va.: 103, 166
Lynch, Thomas (South Carolina delegate to Continental Congress): 110, 190

Macauley, "Mrs." (née Catharine Sawbridge, m. George Macauley): her "histories" ordered for Jack Custis 74
McCarty, Captain Daniel (of Fairfax county, Va.): 101, 134
McDaniel, Mary: steals W's clothes while he is in swimming 144
McHantry, Barnaby: W makes surveys for in Frederick county, Va. 144
Mackay, James (Captain in British army in America): declines to accept W's demand for precedence in command 22, 25, 149; earliest commission as British regular officer issued in 1737, 149; remains at Fort Necessity when W advances 22; joins with W in defense of Fort Necessity and surrender to the French 23; retires with W to Williamsburg 24; mentioned 46, 63
Mackenzie, Robert (British officer in America): 176
McMickan, Robert (Jamaica): 179
McNeill, John (Frederick county, Va.): 186
Maggs Brothers (London book dealers): 61
Magowan, Walter (Md.): tutored Custis children at Mount Vernon 73, 134, 174
Main's *Erasmus:* ordered for Jack Custis 73
Manley, John (Fairfax county, Va.): 134

Marlborough, Massachusetts: 117
Martin, Thomas Bryan (nephew of Lord Fairfax; W's fellow burgess for
Frederick county, Va.): 186
Maryland: 12, 24, 25, 30, 32, 41, 42, 46, 48, 52, 63, 64, 73, 124, 160,
164, 169, 175, 193
Maryland Gazette: 16
Mason: W becomes a 10, 145
Mason, George (neighbor and political adviser of W): mentioned 103,
176; works with W in connection with Virginia non-importation
agreement of 1769 104, 187-188; informs W of Lawrence W's burial
145
Mason, Thomas (of Stafford county, Va.; brother of George Mason):
contest for seat in House of Burgesses 103
Massachusetts: 108-110, 115, 192
Massachusetts delegates in Congress: 191
Massachusetts Provincial Congress: 111, 115, 190, 193
Mathematics: W wishes to have Jack Custis study 74; Jack studies at
King's College 76
Measles: Martha W and later a slave boy (Nat) have measles 124, 129
Mecom, Jane (of Boston, née Jane Franklin, sister of Benjamin Franklin
and wife of Edward Mecom): 141
Mercer, George (Captain in W's regiment, later Lieutenant Colonel in
the Second Virginia regiment): appointed by W as his aide-de-camp
36, 155; accompanies W to Boston in 1756 47; Sally Fairfax sends
regards to 59, 167; supposed description of W by, questioned, 161;
W writes to, concerning Robert Stewart, 176-177; alters wording of
Dinwiddie's Proclamation of 1754, in memorandum to the Board of
Trade, 182; elected as W's fellow burgess from Frederick county 186;
W writes to, concerning military company, in 1775 190
Mercer, Hugh (Colonel in Pa. regiment; later moved to Va. and became
a Brigadier General in the Revolution): 69, 172
Mercer, James (of Va., appointed captain in Cartagena expedition): 142
Midshipman: supposed offer to appoint W midshipman questioned 141,
142
"Military Exercize": adopted by Massachusetts Provincial Congress rec-
ommended by W in 1775 111, 190
Militia of Virginia: unreliability of 40; help build frontier forts 40, 158;
act regulating 102; justices of peace exempt from serving in 103
Mill, flour: mill at Mount Vernon 82, 83, 84, 127, 132-134, 178; mill in
partnership with Gilbert Simpson in Pa. 90, 182
"Mill people": probably slaves, employed at W's Mount Vernon flour
mill 131
Milton's complete works: ordered for Jack Custis 74
Minor, William (Va.): 190
Minorca island: 162
Mississippi Company: 88, 90, 181, 182
Mississippi River: 88, 89
Mitchell, Burgess: W's contract with, to act as an overseer, 179
Monacatoocha: Indian chief who accompanied W in attack on Jumon-
ville's party 19
Monongahela River: 15, 18, 19, 33, 92
Montreal: 13, 70, 172
Montreal, capitulation of: 172
Moral philosophy: W wishes Jack Custis to study 74; Jack studies this
at King's College 76

INDEX

[231]

INDEX [233]

Washington, George: birth, Feb. 22, 1732, ancestry, parents, brothers and
sisters and changes of residence in youth 3-4, 139-140; father's death
in 1743 3, 140; schooling 5, 141-142; plan to send to sea in 1746
successfully opposed by his mother 5-6, 141; resides with his mother
until 1755 4, 141; surveyor 1747-1752 7-9, 144-145; trip to Valley of Virginia west of Blue Ridge mountains in 1748 7-8, 144; trip to Barbados
with Lawrence W in 1751-1752 during which W had the smallpox
8-9, 144; dines with Gov. Dinwiddie on his return 9, 144; unsuccessful proposal of marriage to Betsy Fauntleroy 9, 145; has severe attack
of pleurisy 9; Dinwiddie appoints him Adjutant of the Southern
District of Va. militia with rank of major in Dec. 1752 9-10, 145; W
joins Masonic lodge 10, 145; Dinwiddie and the Virginia Council,
including W's benefactor William Fairfax, send W on important mission to the French commander at Fort Le Boeuf in 1753 11-12, 145-
146; his highly successful accomplishment of his mission, including
gathering of important intelligence concerning French positions, 12-
15, 146; Dinwiddie makes W's name widely and favorably known by
printing and distributing W's journal covering his mission 15-16,
146-147
—— military career 1754-1755: in January 1754, Gov. Dinwiddie commissions him captain in a Va. company established to protect workmen constructing a fort at the Forks of the Ohio (present Pittsburg)
and in March, Lieutenant-Colonel of a Va. regiment under Col.
Joshua Fry for protection of Va. settlers in the Ohio valley 17, 147;
in May he attacks a party of French under Jumonville and kills
him and nine of his men 19-20, 148; W's letter to Dinwiddie describing the attack quoted 19-20, 148; in June, Dinwiddie, on death of
Fry, appoints W colonel of the regiment 21, 148; has dispute with
Mackay, captain of a British independent (non-regimented) company,
over precedence in command 22, 149; large party sent out from Fort
Duquesne, which the French had recently established at the Forks
of the Ohio, force W and Mackay to surrender at Fort Necessity under
Articles of Capitulation admitting the murder, "l'assassinat," of
Jumonville 22-23, 149-150; W's charge that he had signed the Articles
because of mistranslation by his interpreter, Capt. Van Braam, questioned 23-24, 150; Va. regiment being broken up into independent
companies, W retires from the army in Nov. 1754, 25, 151; in April
or May 1755, W accompanies Gen. Braddock as volunteer aide on
expedition against French at Fort Duquesne 30-31, 153; W's letter
to his mother describing Braddock's disastrous defeat in July quoted
33-34, 154, W behaves with great gallantry in the battle 35, 154
—— military career, 1755-1757: in Aug. 1755, Va. regiment is re-established, and Dinwiddie commissions W Colonel of it and commander-
in-chief of all forces to be raised by Va. 35-36, 154-155; W assembles
forces and makes tour of the northern frontier of Va. 37, 155-156;
Indians under French influence begin frontier raids in fall of 1755
37, 156; efforts in 1756 to protect settlers on Va. frontier from Indian
raids, establishment of chain of small frontier forts with a larger
fort at Winchester and W's letters describing terrible plight of the
frontier settlers 38-40, 156-158; in Oct. and Nov. 1756, W makes tour
of frontier forts in southern Va. 40, 158; difference of opinion with
Dinwiddie over evacuation of Fort Cumberland in Md. 41-42, 159-
160; criticism of officers of Va. troops, including W, who contemplates
but is dissuaded from resigning in Oct. 1756 42-43, 160; in 1757, W
continues to try to protect Va. frontier settlers from recurrent Indian

Washington, George, military career (continued)
raids but is handicapped by scarcity of recruits and desertion and by difficulties with Southern Indian allies 51-52, 163-164; renewed criticism of W greatly disturbs him 52-53, 164-165; compelled to retire from active service to Mount Vernon in Oct. 1757, by severe dysentery and pleurisy 55-56, 166
—— military career 1758: William Pitt, great British war minister, prepares for expedition against Fort Duquesne with combined British and British colonial troops under Gen. Forbes 63, 168-169; order as to precedence in rank favorable to colonial officers is issued by the King 63, 168; Va. legislature provides for two regiments for the Forbes Expedition 64, 169; in April 1758, W returns to active duty at Winchester (Fort Loudoun) as colonel of the first Va. regiment and senior Va. officer 63-64, 168-169; difference of opinion between W and Forbes over route to be taken to reach Fort Duquesne 63-66, 169-170; W's letter to Speaker Robinson denouncing Forbes' alleged favoritism to Pennsylvania, quoted 66-67, 170; slowness in building new road along the route chosen by Forbes and W's letters to Va. correspondents despairing of success of the Expedition 66-67, 170; W leads a foray in which prisoners are taken who give highly valuable intelligence as to weakness of French at Fort Duquesne 69, 171; W commands one of the three brigades formed by Forbes in final approach to Fort Duquesne 69, 171-172; French burn and abandon and British enter Fort Duquesne Nov. 25, 1758, 69, 172; W, ill with "an inveterate disorder in his Bowels," returns to Va. and resigns his commission, 69-70, 172
—— miscellaneous developments 1754-1758: in December 1754, W leases Mount Vernon from Lawrence W's widow for the entire period of her life 27, 152; W takes up residence at Mount Vernon by March 1755 26, 151; statement of facts concerning W's "ownership" of Mount Vernon 26-28, 151-152; dispute over precedence in command with Captain Dagworthy in 1755, similar to dispute with Capt. Mackay in 1754, leads W to seek a royal commission in the British army at least as high as major 41, 46-47, 160-161; in February and March 1756, W goes to Boston to try to secure royal commissions for himself and other Va. field officers from Gen. Shirley, Braddock's successor as Commander-in-Chief of British forces in North America, 47-48, 161-162; similar effort for himself in April 1756, with Lieutenant-Colonel Sharpe, named commander of force for proposed attack on Fort Duquesne, 48, 162; writes letter to Lord Loudoun and goes to Philadelphia to see him in similar effort in 1757 48-50, 162-163; all three efforts fail 50; Dinwiddie becomes aloof in dealing with W after Sept. 1756, and accuses him of "Ingratitude," probably because of a letter from W to Speaker Robinson unjustly condemning Dinwiddie 53-55, 165-166; W's disputed love letter of Sept. 1758 to Sally Cary Fairfax quoted, with comments on its background and authenticity and W's subsequent relations with Sally and her husband, 57-62, 166-168
—— marriage: in Jan. 1759 to Martha Dandridge Custis, mother of two young children, Jack and Patcy Custis, 71, 173; meagerness of surviving letters between W and Martha and supposed explanation of this 71, 73; Martha's affectionate, modest nature 71-72, 173; great attention paid by W to the education of his step-son, including lengthy correspondence with his schoolmaster, Rev. Jonathan Boucher, trip with Jacky to New York in 1773, to get him settled at King's College (forerunner of Columbia University), and negotiation in con-

Washington, George, marriage (continued)
nection with his marriage in 1774 to Nelly Calvert 72-76, 174-175;
Patcy Custis' lingering illness (epilepsy), remedies tried for her relief
and her death in 1773, 77, 176; W's friendship with George William
Fairfax, husband of Sally Fairfax, and Robert Stewart, to whom W
lent a large sum without interest 77-78, 176-177; W's friendship with
Burwell Bassett, husband of Martha W's sister, with quotations from
W's letters to him 78-80, 121, 178, 194; social life after his marriage,
chiefly at Mount Vernon 123-134 *passim*
—— business affairs 1759-1774: acquires large estate by marriage to
Martha Custis in 1759 81-82, 178; becomes owner for life of Mount
Vernon on death of Lawrence W's widow in 1761 27, 152; further
increase in wealth through death of his step-daughter Patcy Custis in
1773; details of management of Mount Vernon and other plantations, including dealings with Robert Cary & Co. of London, his
principal British factor, and sales of flour from his mill on or near
Mount Vernon to Barbados and Jamaica 82-86, 178-179; wheat re-
places tobacco as chief cash crop at Mount Vernon by 1766 82, 178;
participation in 1763 in the Dismal Swamp Company organized to
acquire and develop 148,000 acres in the Great Dismal Swamp of
Va. and in the Mississippi Company organized to acquire and settle
2,500,000 acres on and eastward of the Mississippi river 87-90, 180-182;
ill-fortuned investment in a Pa. flour mill in 1773 90, 182; successful
maneuvers from 1769 to 1772 to secure a large share of the bounty
lands promised in a proclamation issued by Gov. Dinwiddie in 1754
to induce "Men to enlist" in the Va. regiment organized in that year,
including a land inspection trip to the Great Kanawha river in 1770,
86-87, 91-100, 135-137, 179-180, 182-186, 194-195; W's acquisition of
land under Royal Proclamation of 1763 98-99, 185-186
—— public service in civil affairs in Virginia 1758-1774: runs unsuccess-
fully in 1755 for representative of frontier county of Frederick in
Va. House of Burgesses, but is elected burgess for Frederick county
in 1758 and 1761 and for Fairfax county in 1765 and subsequent
elections to 1774, 101-102, 186; committee and other services in the
House of Burgesses 1759 to 1774 102-103, 105-106, 186-188; election
to vestry of Truro parish, whose responsibilities were largely non-
ecclesiastical, in 1762 and service as vestryman from 1762 to 1774 106,
188; appointed by Acting Governor John Blair as a justice of the
peace for Fairfax County Court and service from 1768 to 1774 106, 188
—— activities in events leading to the American Revolution: takes
prominent part in securing adoption of the Va. non-importation
agreement of 1769 designed to secure repeal of the obnoxious Townshend Act 104-105, 187-188; W's powerful letter to George Mason
denouncing "our lordly masters in Great Britain" quoted 104-105,
187; W participates in resolution of Va. House of Burgesses in May
1774 denouncing the Boston Port Act of 1774 and calling for an
inter-colonial congress to protect the united interests of America
108, 189; powerful letter to Bryan Fairfax, denouncing the "system-
atic plan" of the British Parliament "as clear as the sun in its
meridian brightness" to subject the colonists to British taxation,
quoted 109, 189; presides at the Fairfax county meeting in July
which adopted the fiery Fairfax Resolves 109, 189; present at Williamsburg Convention in Aug. and is elected a delegate for Va. to
the first Continental Congress in Philadelphia which he attends 110-
111, 189-190; active in organizing and drilling Va. volunteer companies in 1774-1775 111, 190; attends Richmond Convention of March